W9-DEU-191

THE

UNOFFICIAL®

MINI-MICKEY

Also available from Macmillan Travel:

The Unofficial Disney Companion: The Inside Story of Walt Disney World and the Man Behind the Mouse, by Eve Zibart

The Unofficial Guide to Atlanta, by Bob Sehlinger and Fred Brown

The Unofficial Guide to Branson, Missouri, by Bob Sehlinger and Eve Zibart

The Unofficial Guide to Chicago, by Bob Sehlinger and Joe Surkiewicz

The Unofficial Guide to Cruises, by Kay Showker and Bob Sehlinger

The Unofficial Guide to Disneyland, by Bob Sehlinger

The Unofficial Guide to Ethnic Cuisine and Dining in America, by Eve Zibart, Muriel Stevens, and Terrell Vermont

The Unofficial Guide to Euro Disneyland, by Bob Sehlinger

The Unofficial Guide to the Great Smoky and Blue Ridge Mountains, by Bob Sehlinger and Joe Surkiewicz

The Unofficial Guide to Las Vegas, by Bob Sehlinger

The Unofficial Guide to Miami and the Keys, by Bob Sehlinger and Joe Surkiewicz

The Unofficial Guide to Skiing in the West, by Lito Tejada-Flores, Peter Shelton, Seth Masia, and Bob Sehlinger

The Unofficial Guide to Walt Disney World, by Bob Sehlinger

The Unofficial Guide to Washington, D.C., by Bob Sehlinger and Joe Surkiewicz

THE

UNOFFICIAL®

MINI-MICKEY

THE POCKET-SIZED GUIDE TO

Walt Disney World®

Bob Sehlinger

1997 Edition

Macmillan • USA

Dedicated to the Dirty Dozen:

Mike Jones   Holly Brown   Grant Tatum
Molly Burns   Patt Palmer   Budd Zehmer
Brenda Robbins   Marie Hillin   Katie Woychak
Clay White   Scott Gardner   Joan Burns

Macmillan Travel
A Simon & Schuster Macmillan Company
1633 Broadway
New York, New York 10019

Copyright © 1997
by Robert W. Sehlinger
First edition

All rights reserved, including the right of reproduction
in whole or in part in any form

Produced by Menasha Ridge Press
Design by Barbara E. Williams

Macmillan is a registered trademark of Macmillan, Inc.
The Unofficial Guide is a registered trademark
of Robert W. Sehlinger.

ISBN 0-02-861558-1

ISSN 1089-8042

Manufactured in the United States of America

10 9 8 7 6 5 4 3 2 1

CONTENTS

List of Maps

ACKNOWLEDGMENTS

Mary Ellen Botter edited this guide. Starting with a tome delivered by forklift and as big as a bale of hay, she chopped, slashed, burned, and purged every non-essential word. The final product is so portable that a Southern lady can tote it all day without a hint of perspiration.

Thanks also to Molly Burns, Holly Brown, and Clay White, who turned what Mary Ellen left into a book.

INTRODUCTION

Why This Pocket Guide?

The optimum stay at Walt Disney World is five days, but many visitors don't have that long to devote to Disney attractions. Some are on business with only a day or two available for Disney's enticements. Others are en route elsewhere or want to sample additional attractions of Orlando and central Florida. For these visitors, efficient, time-effective touring is a must. They can't afford long waits in line for rides, shows, or meals. They must determine as far in advance as possible what they really want to see.

This guide distills information from the comprehensive *Unofficial Guide to Walt Disney World* to help short-stay or last-minute visitors decide quickly how best to spend their limited hours. It will help these guests answer questions vital to their enjoyment: What are the rides and attractions that appeal to me most? Which additional rides and attractions would I like to experience if I have any time left? What am I willing to forgo?

• Declaration of Independence •

The author and researchers of this guide are totally independent of Walt Disney Co. Inc., Disneyland Inc., Walt Disney World Inc., and all other members of the Disney corporate family. We represent and serve the consumer.

The material in this guide originated with the author and researchers and hasn't been reviewed or edited by the Walt Disney Co., Disneyland, or Walt Disney World.

Ours is the first comprehensive *critical* appraisal of Walt Disney World. It aims to provide the information necessary to tour Walt Disney World with the greatest efficiency and economy. The authors believe in the wondrous excitement of the Disney attractions, but we recognize that Walt Disney World is a business.

• The Death of Spontaneity •

When it comes to touring Walt Disney World, we researchers agree that you absolutely must have a plan. We aren't saying you can't have a great time without one. We're saying you need one.

• How This Guide Was •
Researched and Written

Very little written about Disney World has been comparative or evaluative. Most guides parrot Disney's promotional material. In preparing this guide, however, we took nothing for granted. Each theme park was visited at different times throughout the year by a team of trained observers. They conducted detailed evaluations and rated each park, with all its component rides, shows, exhibits, services, and concessions, according to a formal, pretested rating method. Interviews with patrons were conducted to determine what tourists—of all ages—enjoyed most and least during their Disney World visit.

The essence of this guide consists of individual critiques and descriptions of each feature of the Magic Kingdom, EPCOT, and Disney-MGM Studios, along with detailed touring plans to help you avoid bottlenecks and crowds. Also included are descriptions for Typhoon Lagoon, Blizzard Beach, Pleasure Island, and **nearby Universal Studios Florida.**

Walt Disney World: An Overview

There's nothing on earth like Walt Disney World. Incredible in its scope, genius, beauty, and imagination, it's a joy and wonder for all ages. Disney attractions are a quantum leap beyond any man-made entertainment we know. We can't understand how anyone could visit Florida and bypass Walt Disney World.

• What Walt Disney World Encompasses •

Walt Disney World encompasses 43 square miles, an area twice as large as Manhattan Island. In this expanse are the Magic Kingdom, EPCOT, and Disney-MGM Studios theme parks, three swimming parks, a botanical and zoological park, a night-life area, a sports complex, golf courses, hotels and campgrounds, almost 100 restaurants, four interconnected lakes, a shopping complex, a convention center, a nature preserve, and a transportation system consisting of four-lane highways, elevated monorails, and a system of canals.

The formal name is Walt Disney World, but most tourists refer to the entire Florida Disney facility simply as Disney World. The Magic Kingdom, EPCOT, and Disney-MGM Studios are thought of as being "in" Disney World.

• The Major Theme Parks •

The Magic Kingdom

The Magic Kingdom is the heart of Disney World. It's the collection of adventures, rides, and shows symbolized by the Disney cartoon characters and Cinderella Castle. The Magic Kingdom is divided into seven subareas or "lands," six of which

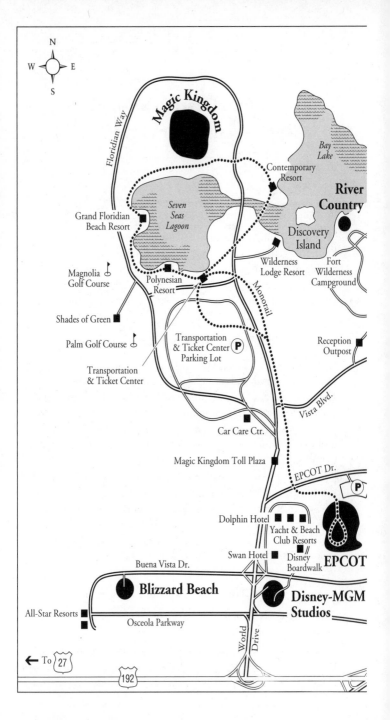

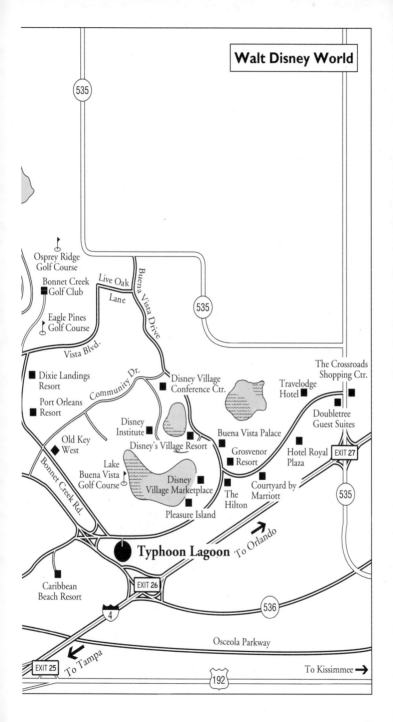

Walt Disney World

Osprey Ridge
Golf Course

Bonnet Creek
Golf Club

Eagle Pines
Golf Course

Vista Blvd.

Live Oak
Lane

Buena Vista Drive

535

The Crossroads
Shopping Ctr.

Dixie Landings
Resort

Community Dr.

Disney Village
Conference Ctr.

Travelodge
Hotel

Port Orleans
Resort

Doubletree
Guest Suites

Disney
Institute

Buena Vista Palace

Old Key
West

Disney's Village Resort

Grosvenor
Resort

Hotel Royal
Plaza

EXIT 27

Lake
Buena Vista
Golf Course

Disney
Village
Marketplace

Courtyard by
Marriott

535

Bonnet Creek Rd.

The
Hilton

Pleasure Island

Typhoon Lagoon

To Orlando

Caribbean
Beach Resort

EXIT 26

4

EXIT 25

To Tampa

536

Osceola Parkway

To Kissimmee →

192

are arranged around a central hub. First encountered is Main Street, U.S.A. Moving clockwise around the hub, other lands are Adventureland, Frontierland, Liberty Square, Fantasyland, and Tomorrowland. Mickey's Starland, the first new land in the Magic Kingdom since the park opened, is along the Walt Disney Railroad on three acres between Fantasyland and Tomorrowland. Access is through Fantasyland or via the railroad. Three hotel complexes (Contemporary Resort, Polynesian Resort, and Grand Floridian Beach Resort) are close to the Magic Kingdom and connected to it by monorail and boat. Two additional hotels, Shades of Green (formerly the Disney Inn) and Disney's Wilderness Lodge Resort, are nearby but aren't served by the monorail.

EPCOT

EPCOT (Experimental Prototype Community of Tomorrow) Center opened in October 1982. Divided into two major areas, Future World and World Showcase, it's twice as big as the Magic Kingdom. Future World consists of futuristic pavilions, each with a different theme relating to man's creativity and technological advancement. World Showcase, arranged around a 41-acre lagoon, presents the architectural, social, and cultural heritages of 11 nations, each represented by famous landmarks and local settings. EPCOT is more educational than the Magic Kingdom and has been characterized as a permanent world's fair entity.

EPCOT has five hotels: Beach Club, Yacht Club, Boardwalk Resort, Swan, and Dolphin. All are within a 5- to 15-minute walk of the International Gateway entrance to EPCOT. The hotels are also linked by canal and tram. The monorail links EPCOT to the Magic Kingdom and its hotels.

Disney-MGM Studios

This $300 million, 100-plus-acre attraction opened in 1989 and has two areas. The first is a theme park relating to the past, present, and future of the movie and television industries. It contains movie-theme rides and shows and covers about half the complex. The remaining half is a working motion picture and television production facility comprising three sound stages, a back lot of streets and sets, and creative support services.

Disney-MGM is connected to other Disney World areas by highway and canal but not by monorail. Guests can park in the Studios' lot or commute by bus from EPCOT, the Transportation and Ticket Center, or any Disney World lodging. Lodgers in EPCOT hotels can also arrive by boat.

• Water Theme Parks •

Disney World has three swimming theme parks: Typhoon Lagoon, River Country, and Blizzard Beach. Typhoon Lagoon, the world's largest of its kind, has a wave pool capable of producing six-foot waves. The much smaller River Country is a pioneer among water theme parks. Blizzard Beach, the trio's newest, features more slides than the other two swimming parks combined. Typhoon Lagoon and Blizzard Beach have their own parking lots. River Country can be reached on foot by campground guests or by boat or bus for others.

• Minor Theme Parks •

Pleasure Island

Part of Walt Disney World Village, Pleasure Island is a six-acre nighttime entertainment center where one cover charge will get a visitor into any of seven nightclubs, each having a different theme. A ten-screen movie complex, shops, and restaurants complete the scene.

Discovery Island

Discovery Island is a small zoological park on an island in Bay Lake. Featuring birdlife and tropical plants, it can be reached by boat from the Magic Kingdom or Fort Wilderness docks. Low-key and quite scenic, the tiny park offers several short, circular trails and three educational shows with resident wildlife.

Planning Before You Leave Home

Gathering Information

In addition to this guide, if you have time, obtain copies of:

1. The Disney Travel Co. Florida Brochure Describes Walt Disney World and vacation packages and lists rates for all Disney resort hotels and campgrounds. Call your travel agent or Walt Disney Travel Co. (phone (800) 327-2996 or (407) 828-3232).

2. The Official Map of the Walt Disney World Resort Also called the Disney Transportation Guide, this folding map contains Disney transportation system route information on one side and a road map of Disney World on the other. Call Walt Disney World Information at (407) 824-4321.

3. Walt Disney World Guidebook for Guests with Disabilities For sight- or hearing-impaired or partially or wholly non-ambulatory guests. Call (407) 824-4321.

4. Orlando MagiCard Makes you eligible for discounts at hotels, restaurants, and attractions outside Disney World. Get a card, Vacation Planner, and Orlando Official Accommodations Guide from the Orlando/Orange County Convention & Visitors Bureau (phone (800) 255-5786 or (407) 363-5874).

5. Florida Traveler Discount Guide Good source of lodging, restaurant, and attraction discounts throughout Florida. Call (904) 371-3948, 8 a.m. to 5 p.m. EST, Monday–Friday. Cost is $3 ($5 USD if mailed to Canada).

Important Walt Disney World Addresses

Walt Disney World Information/Guest Letters
P.O. Box 10040
Lake Buena Vista, FL 32830-0040

Walt Disney World Central Reservations
P.O. Box 10100
Lake Buena Vista, FL 32830-0100

Walt Disney World Educational Programs
Wonders of Walt Disney World (ages 10–15)
The Disney Learning Adventure (adults)
P.O. Box 10000
Lake Buena Vista, FL 32830-1000

Merchandise Mail Order (Guest Service Mail Order)
P.O. Box 10070
Lake Buena Vista, FL 32830-0070

6. Kissimmee–St. Cloud Tour & Travel Sales Guide Directory of hotels and attractions; one of the most complete available. Call Kissimmee–St. Cloud Convention and Visitors Bureau (phone (800) 327-9159).

Request information far in advance, if possible. Allow four weeks for delivery.

Facts On-Line

Recent Disney World vacationers and employees supply late-breaking news on-line through Prodigy, CompuServe, America Online, and other user services, including the Internet. A newsgroup on usenet called rec.arts.disney provides current information and answers questions about the complex. Find official information on the Disney World home page on the World-Wide Web at http://disneyworld.com. Universal Studios Florida also offers a home page, at http://www.usf.com.

Important Telephone Numbers

Additional information on Walt Disney World is available at public libraries, travel agencies, or AAA, or by calling Walt Disney World directly.

Important Phone Numbers

General Information	(407) 824-4321
Accommodations/Reservations	(407) 934-7639
	or (407) 824-8000
All-Star Resorts	(407) 939-5000
Beach Club Resort	(407) 934-8000
Blizzard Beach	(407) 560-3400
Boardwalk Resort	(407) 939-5100
Caribbean Beach Resort	(407) 934-3400
Contemporary Resort	(407) 824-1000
Dining Reservations for	
Walt Disney World	
Lodging Guests	(407) 939-3463
If calling from:	
Home	(407) 939-3463
WDW guest room	Dial 55 for same-day reservations
	Dial 56 for advance reservations
WDW campground	Dial 44 for same-day reservations
	Dial 45 for advance reservations
Discovery Island	(407) 824-3784
Disney Institute Resort	(800) 827-1100
Dixie Landings Resort	(407) 934-6000
Fishing Reservations	
& Information	(407) 824-2621
Fort Wilderness Campground	(407) 824-2900
Grand Floridian Beach Resort	(407) 824-3000
Guided Tour Information	(407) 824-4321
Guided VIP Solo Tours	(407) 560-6223
Lost and Found for articles lost:	
Yesterday or before (all parks)	(407) 824-4245
Today at Magic Kingdom	(407) 824-4521
Today at EPCOT	(407) 560-6105
Today at Disney-MGM	(407) 560-3764
Medical Care in WDW	(407) 648-9234

Important Phone Numbers

Ocala Information Center	(904) 854-0770
Old Key West Resort	(904) 827-7700
Pleasure Island	(407) 934-6374
Polynesian Resort	(407) 824-2000
Port Orleans Resort	(407) 934-5000
Resort Dining and Recreational Information	(407) 939-3463
River Country	(407) 824-2760
Shades of Green U.S. Armed Forces Hotel	(407) 824-3400
Tee Times and Golf Studio	(407) 824-2270
Telecommunication for the Deaf	(407) 827-5141
Tennis Reservations/Lessons	(407) 824-3578
Typhoon Lagoon	(407) 560-4141
Vacation Club Resort	(407) 827-7700
Village Resort	(407) 827-1100
Walt Disney Travel Co.	(407) 828-3232
Walt Disney World Dolphin	(407) 934-4000
Walt Disney World Swan	(407) 934-3000
Wilderness Lodge Resort	(407) 824-3200
Yacht Club Resort	(407) 934-7000

When to Go to
Walt Disney World

Walt Disney World is busiest Christmas Day through New Year's Day, Thanksgiving weekend, Washington's Birthday week, college spring break, and the two weeks around Easter.

The slowest time is after Thanksgiving weekend until the week before Christmas. Next are November through the weekend before Thanksgiving, January 4 through the first week of February, and the week after Easter through early June. Late February, March, and early April are dicey. Disney promotions boost crowds during September and October, but these months remain good for weekday tours at the Magic Kingdom and Disney-MGM and for weekends at EPCOT. We would never choose to go in summer or during a holiday period.

The Down Side of Off-Season Touring

We strongly recommend visiting Disney World in fall or spring, but there are trade-offs. The parks often open late and close early then. When they open as late as 10 a.m., everyone arrives about the same time; it's hard to beat the crowd. Late opening coupled with early closing drastically reduces touring hours. Even with small crowds, it's difficult to see the Magic Kingdom or EPCOT between 10 a.m. and 6 p.m. Closing before 8 p.m. also eliminates evening parades or fireworks. Also, some attractions may be closed for maintenance or renovation. And temperatures fluctuate wildly during late fall, winter, and early spring; daytime highs in the 40s aren't uncommon.

Avoid the Magic Kingdom on Saturday and EPCOT on weekdays in September and October to bypass crowds of locals. Large groups taper off parkwide by early November.

• Selecting the Day of the Week for Your Visit •

Typical summer vacationers arrive in the Orlando area on Sunday, visit the Magic Kingdom and EPCOT on Monday and Tuesday, Disney-MGM on Wednesday, and Typhoon Lagoon or a non-Disney attraction on Thursday. Friday is often reserved for heading home. If this was all we had to consider, we could recommend Fridays and Sundays as the best days all year long to avoid crowds.

Off-season promotions attract locals on the weekend at the Magic Kingdom and Disney-MGM. Crowds at EPCOT, particularly in September and October, are almost always larger on weekdays. Disney brings thousands of schoolchildren to EPCOT in March, September, and October. In late spring, teenagers fill the parks on "senior days" or prom nights, many on weekdays.

The most significant shift in attendance patterns results from the early-entry program for guests at Disney resort hotels and campgrounds (but not guests at Disney Village hotels). Each day, Disney World lodging guests are invited to enter a designated theme park one hour before the general public. The early-entry park will be more crowded that day, the others less crowded. During holiday periods and summer, when Disney hotels are full, the early-entry park fills by about 10 a.m. and is practically gridlocked by noon. At any season, whether you're eligible or not, avoid the early-entry park. Or exercise your early-entry privilege, enjoy the attractions there, and move to another park when crowds build.

Although the program changes frequently and may be abandoned, here's how it looked at press time:

Monday	Magic Kingdom
Tuesday	EPCOT
Wednesday	Disney-MGM Studios
Thursday	Magic Kingdom
Friday	EPCOT
Saturday	Magic Kingdom
Sunday	Disney-MGM Studios

Call Walt Disney World Information (phone (407) 824-4321) to verify the early-entry schedule before you visit.

Assuming early-entry days don't change:

Least Crowded Days

During summer, Friday, Saturday, and Sunday are least crowded because locals stay home and out-of-staters travel on those days. September through May (excluding holidays and spring break), the opposite's true.

Magic Kingdom In summer, Sunday and Friday are least crowded. Tuesday and Wednesday are least crowded at other times.

Disney-MGM Studios In summer, Friday and Saturday are best. Off-season, it's Monday and Tuesday.

EPCOT Wednesday, Thursday, and Monday are least crowded January through May, November, and December. During summer, crowds are smaller Saturday and Sunday. In September and October, visit on Saturday or Sunday.

2

Making the Most of Your Time and Money

Allocating Money

• Prices Subject to Change without Notice •

Walt Disney World ticket prices change often. Expect, however, to pay about $42 for an adult One-Day/One-Park Ticket. If you have the time, it's about $138 for a Four-Day Value Pass and $154 for a Four-Day Park-Hopper Pass. Estimates include tax. Tickets for children ages three to nine are about 20 percent less. Children younger than three enter free.

• Walt Disney World Admission Options •

There are seven Walt Disney World admission options, but the short-stay parkgoer is most apt to use the:

One-Day/One-Park Ticket. Good for admission and same-day, unlimited use of attractions at your choice of one of the three major theme parks.

Four-Day Value Pass. Provides four days of separate admissions: a one-day/one-park admission each to the Magic Kingdom, EPCOT, and Disney-MGM, plus an additional one-day wild card admission that can be used to revisit one park. Each part of the pass is valid only at the designated park. A guest who visits the Magic Kingdom in the morning and then goes to EPCOT for dinner would use two of the four admissions. You can, however, enter and exit the *same* park as often as you wish on a single day; have your hand stamped for re-entry as you leave.

Four-Day Park-Hopper Pass. Provides same-day admission to the Magic Kingdom, EPCOT, and Disney-MGM. With it, you can tour the Studios in the morning, eat at EPCOT, and see the evening parades at the Magic Kingdom.

Four-Day Value and Park-Hopper passes needn't be used on consecutive days and are good forever.

Length of Stay Pass. For Disney resort and campground guests. It can be purchased for *any* stay two days or longer and includes admission to all major and minor parks. Savings over the four-day pass is about 7 percent, but the pass is good only during your stay.

• Which Admission Should You Buy? •

If you only have one day to spend, select the park that most interests you and buy the One-Day/One-Park ticket. If you have two days and don't plan to return to Florida soon, buy two One-Day Tickets (or a Length of Stay Pass if you're a Disney resort guest). If you think you'll return soon, spring for a four- or five-day pass. Use two days of admission and save the remaining days for another trip.

• Where to Buy Your Admission in Advance •

Tickets are available at a Disney Store before you leave home or, if you're driving, at Disney's Ocala Information Center at exit 68 on I-75. If you fly to Walt Disney World, purchase tickets at the Orlando airport Disney Store. Most Disney World hotels also sell them.

Buy tickets by mail from Walt Disney World Ticket Mail Order Service, P.O. Box 10030, Lake Buena Vista, FL 32830-0030.

Allocating Time

• **Which Park to See First?** •

Children who see the Magic Kingdom first expect more of the same type of entertainment at EPCOT and Disney-MGM. At EPCOT, they're often disappointed by the educational orientation and more serious tone (adults are, too). Disney-MGM offers some wild action but also generally is educational and adult.

First-time visitors and groups with children should see EPCOT first. You'll tour without having been preconditioned to think of Disney entertainment solely as fantasy or adventure. Next, see Disney-MGM. The Studios help young and older make a fluid transition from imposing EPCOT to the fanciful Magic Kingdom. Also, because the Studios are smaller, you won't have to walk as much or stay as long. Save the Magic Kingdom for last.

• **Operating Hours** •

Disney runs a dozen or more schedules during the year; call (407) 824-4321 for the **exact** hours of operation before you arrive. Generally:

From September through mid-February and during May, excluding holiday periods, the Magic Kingdom is open from 9 a.m. to 7 or 8 p.m. and on some weekends until 9, 10, or even 11 p.m. During the same period, EPCOT is open from 9 a.m. to 9 p.m. and Disney-MGM operates 9 a.m. to 7 p.m.

From the Presidents' Day holiday in mid-February through spring break and Easter, all three stay open an hour or two later and sometimes open an hour earlier. During summer, EPCOT and Disney-MGM are open until 9 or 10 p.m., with the Magic Kingdom sometimes open as late as 1 a.m.

At day's end, all attractions shut down near the official closing time. Main Street in the Magic Kingdom remains open a half hour to an hour after the rest of the park closes.

• Official Opening Time vs. Real Opening •

Disney publishes "official" hours. The parks actually open earlier, depending on projected crowds. If the official hours are 9 a.m. to 9 p.m., for example, the Main Street in the Magic Kingdom will open at 8 or 8:30 a.m. and the remainder of the park will open at 8:30 or 9 a.m.

If you don't have early-entry privileges, tour a park where early-entry is not in effect and arrive 50 minutes before official opening regardless of the time of year. If you go on a major holiday, arrive an hour and 20 minutes early.

If you're a Disney resort guest and want to take advantage of early entry, arrive at the early-entry park one hour and 40 minutes before it's scheduled to open. Buses, boats, and monorails to the early-entry park start operating about two hours before the general public is admitted.

• Walt Disney World on a Tight Schedule •

Even the most efficient plan won't allow visitors to tour two or more major theme parks in one day. Allocate at least an entire day to each park (except when the theme parks close at different times, allowing visitors to tour one park until closing and then go to another). If your schedule permits just one day of touring, concentrate on only one theme park.

One-Day Touring

A comprehensive tour of the Magic Kingdom, EPCOT, or Disney-MGM in one day requires knowledge of the park, good planning, and plenty of energy and endurance. One-day touring leaves little time for sit-down meals in restaurants, prolonged shopping, or lengthy rests. Even so, it can be fun and rewarding.

Successful one-day touring of the Magic Kingdom, EPCOT, or Disney-MGM hinges on **three rules:**

1. Determine in Advance What You Really Want to See

This book describes and evaluates the theme parks. Attractions are rated in stars. Five stars is the best rating.

Because attractions range from midway-type rides to high-tech extravaganzas, we've developed categories for them:

Super Headliners The best attractions in the theme parks. Mind-boggling in size, scope, and imagination. The cutting edge of attraction technology and design.

Headliners Full-scale, multimillion-dollar themed adventures and theater presentations. Modern in technology and design, employing a range of special effects.

Major Attractions Themed adventures on a more modest scale but incorporating the newest technologies. Or, larger-scale attractions of older design.

Minor Attractions Midway-type rides, small "dark rides," small theater presentations, transportation rides, and elaborate walk-through attractions.

Diversions Passive and interactive exhibits. Includes playgrounds, video arcades, and street theater.

2. Arrive Early! Arrive Early! Arrive Early!

This is the critical key to touring efficiently and avoiding long lines. The earlier a park opens, the greater your advantage, because most vacationers won't wake up early and go to a park before it opens. Take advantage of early-entry privileges if you're eligible.

3. Avoid Bottlenecks

Crowds create time-gobbling bottlenecks. To avoid them: Eat off-hours. Don't shop near closing time when throngs moving toward the exit fill shops en route. Reconsider taking new or slow-loading rides; both have long lines.

• Touring Plans: What They Are •
and How They Work

General Overview of the Touring Plans

Our touring plans are step-by-step guides for seeing the maximum with a minimum of time in line. All were tested by our staff and everyday Disney World patrons. When the two groups were compared, visitors touring without the plan averaged 3⅔ hours more waiting per day than people using our plan, and they experienced 37 percent fewer attractions.

Touring plans for the Magic Kingdom begin on page 145; EPCOT, page 202; and Disney-MGM, page 239. The Pleasure Island touring plan starts on page 272. For your convenience, a one-day touring plan for Universal Studios Florida begins on page 262.

What You Can Realistically Expect
from the Touring Plans

There are more attractions at the Magic Kingdom and EPCOT than you can see in one day, even if you never wait in line. The one-day touring plans, however, allow you to see as much as possible. Depending on circumstances, you may not complete the plan. For the Magic Kingdom and EPCOT, the two-day plans are more comprehensive, efficient, and relaxing.

Variables That Will Affect the Success
of the Touring Plans

Factors affecting the plans' success are how quickly you move among rides; when and how many food and toilet breaks you take; where and how you eat; your ability to navigate the parks; how fast rides are brought to capacity; and the time you arrive for a theater performance. Small groups almost always move faster than large ones, and adults generally move faster than families with young children. Switching off (see page 58) slows families. Plus, some children simply can't meet the "early to rise" dictate of the plans.

Tour continuously and expeditiously until around noon. After that hour, breaks and setbacks won't affect the plans significantly.

If You Lose the Thread

Anything from a blister to a broken attraction can derail a touring plan. If the plan is interrupted:

1. Skip one step for every 25 minutes you're delayed.
2. Forget the touring plan and organize the remainder of your day using the optimum touring times given in the attraction profiles.

Touring Plans and the Obsessive/Compulsive Reader

We suggest that you follow the touring plans religiously, especially in the mornings, if you're visiting Disney World during busier, more crowded times of year. The consequence of touring spontaneity in peak season is literally hours of otherwise avoidable standing in line. During quieter times, there's no need to be compulsive about the plans.

A Clamor for Customized Touring Plans

Our touring plans are intended to be flexible. Adapt them to your group's preferences. If you don't like scary rides, skip them. If you want to ride Space Mountain three times in a row, go for it. Will it make the plan less effective? Sure, but the plan was created only to help you have fun.

Understanding
Walt Disney World Attractions

Avoid frustration and time in line by understanding Disney World's attractions.

• Cutting Your Time in Line •
by Understanding the Rides

Disney World has many different rides, but most fall into three categories: continuous loaders, interval loaders, and cycle rides.

Continuous Loaders

Some rides never stop. They're like a conveyor belt that goes round and round. These are continuous loaders. The Haunted Mansion in the Magic Kingdom and Spaceship Earth at EPCOT are examples. They have lots of cars on the conveyor belt and can move more than 2,000 people an hour. Lines at continuous loaders keep moving.

Interval Loaders

Interval loaders have vehicles (cars, boats, or such) that load and unload at set intervals (sometimes controlled manually, sometimes by computer). Space Mountain in Tomorrowland is such a ride, with space capsules being released at 36-, 26-, or 21-second intervals depending on crowds. If demand is high, some rides of this type can add vehicles and move even more people. Those that can't (20,000 Leagues Under the Sea, for example, with only nine submarines) move fewer people.

Interval loaders can be very efficient if the dispatch interval is relatively short and if the ride can accommodate lots of vehicles at one time (Pirates of the Caribbean, with many boats and a short interval, can move almost 3,000 people an hour).

Cycle Rides

In these "stop-and-go" rides, people waiting to ride exchange places with those who just have ridden. The whole system shuts down during loading and unloading. These rides, with unavoidable down time, can handle fewer people than continuous or interval loaders in the same amount of time. The classic cycle ride Dumbo, the Flying Elephant, is one of the Magic Kingdom's most popular, but its lines generally are long and slow. Both Dumbo and Cinderella's Golden Carrousel, another cycle ride, also suffer from having a very limited number of vehicles. That adds to the bottleneck.

The Bottom Line

If riding a certain attraction is important to you, don't worry about the ride type or the wait. Ride and enjoy. (Do remember that cycle rides generally are least busy in early morning or late at night.) But if you have limited time, avoid cycle rides and their built-in crowds. Instead, choose continuous or interval loaders, especially those that can add vehicles when crowds are heavy (Star Tours at Disney-MGM Studios, for example).

Also, steer clear of cycle rides run by only one person, who must do it all: load, unload, check safety restraints, and operate the ride. Such staffing slows the ride greatly. Sometimes, to make up for it, the ride time is cut, so you may wait a long time and be rewarded with a shortened experience.

• Cutting Your Time in Line •
by Understanding the Shows

Many featured attractions at Disney World are theater presentations. Most operate in three phases:

1. Guests are in the theater viewing the presentation.
2. Guests have passed through the turnstile into a holding area. They'll be admitted to the theater as soon as the presentation in progress ends. Several attractions offer a preshow in their waiting area.

3. A line forms outside. As many people as there are theater seats will be admitted to the lobby when it clears.

Theater capacity, the show's popularity, and park attendance determine how long lines will be at a theater. Except for holidays and other days of heavy attendance, the longest wait for a show usually doesn't exceed the length of one complete performance.

Since almost all theater attractions run continuously, stopping only long enough for the previous audience to leave and the waiting audience to enter, a performance will be in progress when you arrive.

No Disney World theaters (except Main Street Cinema in the Magic Kingdom and amphitheater productions) will seat latecomers.

Most theaters hold many people. When a new audience is admitted, the outside line usually disappears. Exceptions are *Country Bear Jamboree* in the Magic Kingdom; *The Making of Me* in the Wonders of Life pavilion and *Honey, I Shrunk the Audience* in the Imagination pavilion at EPCOT; and *Voyage of the Little Mermaid* and *MuppetVision 4-D* at Disney-MGM.

3

Selecting Your Hotel

The Basic Considerations

Whether short-timer or full-vacationer, every Disney World visitor needs a place to stay. The basic question is whether to stay *in* Walt Disney World. Luxury accommodations can be found in and out of the World. Budget lodging is another story. Rooms in Disney World range from about $80 to beyond $500 a night. Outside the World, rooms cost as low as $30 a night at some independent motels.*

Beyond affordability is convenience. There's no real hardship in staying outside the World and driving (or taking the hotel shuttle, if available) to the theme parks. Meals can be less expensive, and rooming outside leaves you more receptive to other Orlando attractions. Universal Studios Florida, Kennedy Space Center, Sea World, and Cypress Gardens, among others, are well worth your attention.

If there are young children in your party, review *Walt Disney World with Kids* (pages 55–62) before choosing your lodging. Similarly, seniors, honeymooners or romantics, and disabled guests should refer to the applicable sections of *Special Tips for Special People* (see pages 63–70) before choosing a hotel.

• Benefits of Staying in the World •

Walt Disney World resort hotel and campground guests have exclusive privileges. Some are advertising gimmicks; others are

---

*Rates vary depending on room location (view) and/or season and are subject to change.

real and potentially valuable. Here are the privileges and what they mean:

1. Convenience The commute is short and frequent by Disney's bus, boat, and monorail. This is especially advantageous if you stay in a hotel connected by the monorail or boat. There are, however, dozens of hotels just outside Disney World that are within five minutes of theme-park parking lots.

2. Early Entry at Theme Parks Guests at Walt Disney World resorts (excluding those at the independent hotels of Disney Village Hotel Plaza) may enter a designated theme park one hour earlier than the general public each day. Disney guests also are offered specials on admission, among them a passport good for the duration of your visit.

Early-entry privileges can be quite valuable during peak season, when the theme parks are mobbed. If you're willing to get up before sunrise and get to the park as early as 6:30 a.m., you'll be rewarded with uncrowded, stress-free touring. Early entry also is handy off-season, when the parks open and close early.

3. Preferential Treatment in Making Advance Dinner Show Reservations

4. Lunch and Dinner Reservations Disney resort guests can make priority seating/reservations for lunch, dinner, and character dining by phone up to 60 days in advance.

5. Babysitting and Child-Care Alternatives Babysitting, child care, and children's programs are offered to Disney resort guests. Each hotel connected by the monorail, as well as several other Disney hotels, offers "clubs," themed child-care centers where potty-trained children ages 3 to 12 can stay while parents go out.

Though somewhat expensive, the clubs are highly regarded by children and parents. On the negative side, they're open only in the evening, and not all Disney hotels have them. If you're staying at a Disney hotel without a child-care club, use one of the private, in-room babysitting services such as Fairy Godmother or Kinder-Care (see pages 60–62). In-room babysitting is also available at hotels outside the World.

6. Overnight Kennel Privileges for Pets

7. Guaranteed Theme-Park Admissions This is useful on days of unusually heavy attendance. In practice, no guest is ever turned away from a theme park until its parking lot fills. The privilege doesn't extend to Blizzard Beach, Typhoon Lagoon, and River Country.

8. Children Sharing a Room with Their Parents There's no extra charge per night for children under 18 in a room with their parents. Many hotels outside the World also offer this.

9. Free Parking in Theme-Park Lots This saves about $5 per day.

10. Recreational Privileges Disney guests get preferential treatment for tee times at golf courses.

• How to Get Discounts on Lodging •
at Walt Disney World

There are so many guest rooms in and around Walt Disney World that competition is brisk and everyone, including Disney, deals to keep them filled. This has led to a more flexible discount policy for Disney World hotels. Here are tips for getting those breaks:

1. Value Season vs. Regular Season The same room is $20–$40 cheaper in Value seasons than in Regular or Holiday seasons.*

1997 Value Seasons	1997 Regular & Holiday Seasons
January 1–February 8	December 19–December 31, 1996
April 20–June 6*	February 9–April 19
August 17– December 18	June 7–August 16
	December 19–December 31

*Caribbean Beach, Port Orleans, and Dixie Landings resorts are on a slightly different calendar. All-Star Resorts discount rooms only during January and September.

2. Ask about Specials When you talk to Disney reservationists, inquire specifically about specials. Ask, "What special rates or discounts are available at Disney hotels during the time of our visit?" One reader saved $440 by asking about discounts "for that room" during her stay.

3. Disney's Ocala Information Center The Disney Information Center off I-75 in Ocala, Fla., routinely books Disney hotel rooms at discounts of up to 43 percent! The discounts are offered as an incentive to walk-in travelers who may not have considered lodging at a Disney property or even going to Disney World. The rooms available vary according to date and season, but you can almost always count on a good deal. You must reserve your room in person at the center, but if you call in advance (phone (904) 854-0770) and say you're on your way, they'll usually tell you what discounts are available. The center is open daily from 9 a.m. until 6 p.m.

4. Travel Agents Once ineligible for commissions on Disney bookings, travel agents now are active players and good sources of information on specials.

5. Magic Kingdom Club Membership in the Magic Kingdom Club, offered as a benefit by employers, credit unions, and organizations, includes a 10–30 percent discount on Disney lodging and 5–7 percent off theme-park tickets. Ask your personnel department if the club is offered. Two-year individual memberships in the program are about $65. For information, call (714) 781-1550 or write:

> Magic Kingdom Club
> Gold Card
> P.O. Box 3850
> Anaheim, CA 92803-3850

6. Organizations and Auto Clubs Disney works with programs with several auto clubs and organizations. Recently, for instance, AAA members were offered 10–20 percent off on Disney hotels.

7. Room Upgrades Sometimes an upgrade is as good as a discount. If you visit during a slower time, book the least expensive room your discounts will allow. Checking in, ask very politely about being upgraded to a "water-" or "pool-view" room. Often, you'll be accommodated at no additional charge.

8. Extra Nights Discounts   During slower times, book your Disney hotel for half as long as you intend to stay. The hotel often offers extra nights at a discount to get you to stay longer.

• Walt Disney World Lodging •

The Grand Floridian, Polynesian, Contemporary, Wilderness Lodge, and Shades of Green resorts are near the Magic Kingdom. The Swan and Dolphin hotels, Yacht and Beach Club resorts, and Disney's Boardwalk are near EPCOT. The Villas at the Disney Institute are on the far northeast side of Disney World; All-Star Resorts occupy a similar position on the far southwest side. Centrally located are the Caribbean Beach Resort, Old Key West Resort, Port Orleans, and Dixie Landings.

Choosing a Walt Disney World Hotel

Refer to this section if you want to stay in Walt Disney World but don't know which hotel to choose.

What It Costs to Stay in a Disney Resort Hotel	
Grand Floridian	$275–515 per night
Boardwalk Inn Resort	$240–450
Yacht Club Resort	$235–430
Dolphin Resort	$235–350
Beach Club Resort	$235–325
Polynesian Resort	$225–405
Swan Resort	$205–345
Contemporary Resort	$205–310
Old Key West Resort	$205–310
Wilderness Lodge	$169–310
Port Orleans Resort	$98–144
Caribbean Beach Resort	$98–144
Dixie Landings Resort	$98–144
All-Star Resorts	$79–89

1. Cost First, look at your budget, then refer to the price listings in this section.

Boardwalk Villas, Old Key West Resort, and Villas of the Disney Institute offer condo-type lodging with one-, two-, and three-bedroom units complete with kitchens, living rooms, VCRs, and washers and dryers. Prices range from about $230 per night for a one-bedroom Club Suite at the Disney Institute to over $800 per night for a three-bedroom unit at the Old Key West Resort or the Boardwalk Villas. Fully equipped house trailers are available at the Fort Wilderness Campground for $195 to $230. A limited number of suites are available at the more expensive Disney resorts, but they don't have kitchens.

Rooms in the seven hotels of Walt Disney World Village Hotel Plaza are commodious but can be more expensive than those at hotels served by the monorail. We find few bargains there, and it's less exciting than inside the World. Plaza guests don't have early-entry privileges or free parking at the theme parks. But the hotels operate their own buses to the parks.

What It Costs to Stay in the Village Hotel Plaza			
The Hilton	814 rooms	bus service	$185–245 per night
Courtyard Disney Village	323 rooms	bus service	$95–165 per night
Hotel Royal Plaza	396 rooms	bus service	$97–150 per night
Guest Doubletree Suites	229 rooms	bus service	$99–239 per night
Travelodge Hotel	325 rooms	bus service	$119–169 per night
Grosvenor Resort	630 rooms	bus service	$99–160 per night
Buena Vista Palace	808 rooms	bus service	$130–250 per night
Buena Vista Palace	220 suites	bus service	$235–350 per night

Not included in this discussion is Shades of Green. It was leased by the U.S. Department of Defense in 1994 for use by active-duty and retired service personnel. Rates at Shades of Green, one of the nicest Disney World hotels, are based on the guest's rank: the higher the rank, the greater the cost. All rooms, however, go for a fraction of what military personnel would pay at other Disney resorts.

2. Location If you use your own car, the location of your Disney hotel isn't especially important unless you plan to spend most of your time at the Magic Kingdom. (In this case, Disney transportation is always more efficient than your car, because it bypasses the Transportation and Ticket Center and deposits you at the theme-park entrance.) If you plan to use Disney transportation:

Most convenient to the Magic Kingdom are the three resorts linked by monorail: Grand Floridian, Contemporary, and Polynesian.

Contemporary Resort is also a 10- to 15-minute walk from the Magic Kingdom. Contemporary Resort guests reach EPCOT by monorail but must transfer at the Transportation and Ticket Center. Buses connect the resort to Disney-MGM Studios.

The Polynesian Resort is served by the monorail and is within walking distance of the Transportation and Ticket Center, where you can catch an express monorail to EPCOT. This makes the Polynesian the only Disney resort with direct monorail access to both EPCOT and the Magic Kingdom. To minimize your walk to the TTC, reserve a room in the Pago Pago, Moorea, or Oahu buildings.

Most convenient to EPCOT and Disney-MGM are the Boardwalk Inn, Boardwalk Villas, Yacht and Beach Club resorts, and Swan and Dolphin resorts. Though all are within easy walking distance of EPCOT's International Gateway, boat service is also available. Vessels also connect to Disney-MGM. EPCOT hotels are best for guests planning to spend most of their time at EPCOT and/or Disney-MGM Studios.

If you plan to use Disney transportation to see all three major parks and the swimming parks, book a centrally located resort with good transit connections. Recommended are the Polynesian, EPCOT resorts, Caribbean Beach, Old Key West, Dixie Landings, and Port Orleans.

Though not centrally located, All-Star Resorts have very good bus service to all theme and swimming parks. Wilderness Lodge and Fort Wilderness Campground have the most inconvenient transportation. The Villas of the Disney Institute also have transportation shortcomings.

If you plan to play golf, the Villas at the Disney Institute and the Old Key West Resort are built around courses. Near but not on a course are the Grand Floridian, Polynesian, Dixie Landings, and Port Orleans. For boating and water sports, book the Polynesian, Contemporary, Grand Floridian, or Wilderness Lodge. The lodge is also the best choice for hikers, cyclists, and joggers.

3. Room Quality Most Disney World guests don't spend much time in their hotel rooms, though they're among the best-designed and -appointed anywhere. Plus, they're meticulously maintained. Top of the line are the spacious and luxurious rooms of the Grand Floridian. Bringing up the rear are the small, garish rooms of the All-Star Resorts. But even these are sparkling clean and livable.

Here's how rooms at Disney hotels (along with the Swan and the Dolphin, which are Westin and Sheraton hotels, respectively) stack up for quality:

Hotel	Room Quality Rating
1. Grand Floridian Resort	97
2. Boardwalk Inn	95
3. Beach Club Resort	95
4. Yacht Club Resort	95
5. Boardwalk Villas	88
6. Contemporary Resort	87
7. Polynesian Resort	87
8. Wilderness Lodge	87
9. Villas at the Disney Institute	87
10. Old Key West Resort (studio)	86
11. Dolphin Resort (Sheraton)	86
12. Swan Resort (Westin)	86
13. Port Orleans Resort	85
14. Dixie Landings Resort	85
15. Caribbean Beach Resort	79
16. All-Star Resorts	74

Groups and larger families should ask how many persons can be accommodated in a guest room. Groups requiring two or more rooms should consider condos or villas in or out of the World.

4. Theme All Disney hotels are themed to make you feel you're in a special place or a period of history.

Hotel	Theme
All-Star Resorts	Sports and music
Beach Club	New England beach club of the 1870s
Boardwalk Inn	East Coast boardwalk hotel of the early 1900s
Boardwalk Villas	East Coast beach cottage of the early 1900s
Caribbean Beach	Caribbean islands
Contemporary Resort	The future as perceived by past and present generations
Dixie Landings	Life on the Mississippi in the antebellum South
Dolphin Resort	Modern Florida resort
Grand Floridian	Turn-of-the-century luxury hotel in Florida
Old Key West Resort	Key West
Polynesian Resort	Hawaiian/South Sea islands
Port Orleans	Turn-of-the-century New Orleans and Mardi Gras
Swan Resort	Modern Florida resort
Villas at the Disney Institute	Combination rustic villas and country club atmosphere
Wilderness Lodge	National park grand lodge of the early 1900s in the American Northwest
Yacht Club	New England seashore hotel of the 1880s

5. Dining EPCOT resorts are best for quality and selection in dining. Each is within an easy walk of the others and of the ten ethnic restaurants in the World Showcase at EPCOT.

The only other place in Disney World where restaurants and hotels are similarly concentrated is Walt Disney World Village Hotel Plaza. The Hilton, Courtyard by Marriott, the Grosvenor, and Buena Vista Palace offer dining and are in walking distance of dining at Pleasure Island and Disney Marketplace.

Guests at the Contemporary, Polynesian, and Grand Floridian can eat there or commute to restaurants in the Magic Kingdom (not recommended) or to restaurants in other monorail-linked hotels. Riding the monorail among hotels (or to the Magic Kingdom) takes about ten minutes each way, not counting the wait for the train.

All other Disney resorts are somewhat isolated. This means you dine at your hotel unless you have a car and can go elsewhere. Or, you eat in the theme parks. Disney transportation works fine for commuting from the hotels to the parks, but it's hopelessly time-consuming for moving among hotels.

Of the more isolated resorts, the Wilderness Lodge serves the best and most varied food. Next is the Villas at the Disney Institute, but food there is expensive. Port Orleans, Dixie Landings, Old Key West, and Caribbean Beach have full-service restaurants of acceptable quality, food courts, and in-room pizza delivery. None of the isolated resorts offers enough variety for the average person to be happy eating in his/her hotel every day. All-Star Resorts don't have a full-service restaurant, only two food courts.

6. Amenities and Recreation All Disney resorts provide elaborate swimming pools, themed shops and stores, restaurants or food courts, a bar or lounge, and access to the five Disney golf courses. The more you pay, the more you get.

Nine resorts offer evening child care: Swan and Dolphin, Grand Floridian, Yacht and Beach Club resorts, Polynesian, Wilderness Lodge, and Boardwalk Inn and Villas. All other Disney resorts offer in-room babysitting.

7. Night Life The boardwalk at Boardwalk Inn and Villas has an upscale dance club, a New Orleans club with dueling pianos and sing-along, a brew pub, and a sports bar. Other Disney resorts offer only lounges that stay open late.

Camping at Walt Disney World

Disney's Fort Wilderness Campground is a spacious resort for both tent and RV campers. Fully equipped, air-conditioned trailers are also for rent. Fort Wilderness has economy sites, a group camping area, RV hookups, evening entertainment, horseback riding, bike and jogging trails, swimming, and a petting farm. River Country is nearby. Access to the Magic Kingdom and Discovery Island is by boat; access other destinations by private car or shuttle.

• Selecting and Booking a Hotel Outside • of Walt Disney World

There are three primary "out-of-the-World" areas to consider:

1. International Drive This area, about 15 to 20 minutes east of Walt Disney World, parallels I-4 on its southern side and offers a wide selection of hotels and restaurants. Accommodations range from $30 to $200 per night. The chief drawbacks of the International Drive area are its terribly congested roads, numerous traffic signals, and inadequate access to westbound I-4. The biggest bottleneck is the intersection of International Drive and Sand Lake Road. In some sections of International Drive, the traffic can be circumvented by using local streets one or two blocks to the southeast.

Discount stores, boutiques, restaurants, and entertainment facilities are walking distance from many International Drive hotels.

Hotels in the International Drive area are listed in the Orlando Official Accommodations Guide published by the Orlando/Orange County Convention and Visitors Bureau. For a copy, call (800) 255-5786 or (407) 363-5874.

2. Lake Buena Vista and the I-4 Corridor There are a number of hotels along FL 535 and north of I-4 between Walt Disney World and I-4's intersection with the Florida Turnpike. These properties are easily reached from the Interstate and are near numerous restaurants. Driving time from here to Disney World is 5 to 15 minutes. Most hotels in this area are listed in the Orlando Official Accommodations Guide.

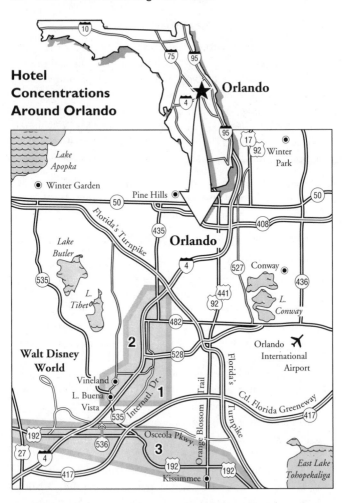

Hotel Concentrations Around Orlando

3. US 192 This is the highway to Kissimmee, southeast of Walt Disney World. In addition to a number of large, full-service hotels are many small, independent motels that are a good value. Several dozen properties on US 192 are closer to the Magic Kingdom, EPCOT, and Disney-MGM than the more expensive hotels in Walt Disney World Village and the Disney Village Hotel Plaza. Traffic on US 192 is extremely heavy but usually moves smoothly. Though the situation is improving, US 192 is somewhat inferior in terms of number and quality of restaurants.

Hotels on US 192 and in Kissimmee are listed in the Kissimmee–St. Cloud Tour & Travel Sales Guide. Call (800) 327-9159.

Driving Time to the Theme Parks for Visitors Lodging outside Walt Disney World

Here's the approximate commuting time to the major theme parks' parking lots from several off-World lodging areas. Add a few minutes to pay your parking fee and park. Once parked at the Transportation and Ticket Center (Magic Kingdom parking lot), it's an average of 20 to 30 minutes more to the Magic Kingdom. To get to the main entrance from EPCOT's lot, add 7 to 10 minutes. At Disney-MGM, expect to spend 5 to 10 minutes getting from your car to the entrance. If you haven't bought your theme-park admission in advance, tack on another 10 to 20 minutes.

Driving Time to the Theme Parks			
Minutes From	To: Magic Kingdom Parking Lot	EPCOT Parking Lot	Disney-MGM Studios Parking Lot
Downtown Orlando	26	23	24
North International Dr. and Universal Studios	20	17	18
Central International Dr. and Sand Lake Road	18	15	16
South International Dr. and Sea World	15	12	13
FL 535	10	7	8
FL 192, north of I-4	10–15	7–12	5–10
FL 192, south of I-4	10–18	7–15	5–13

• Getting a Good Deal on a Room outside • Walt Disney World

Hotel development at Walt Disney World has sharpened the competition among lodgings throughout the Disney World/Orlando/Kissimmee area. Hotels outside the World struggle to fill their rooms. Unable to compete with Disney on convenience or perks, off-World hotels lure patrons with bargains. The extent of the bargain depends on the season, the day of the week, and area events. Here are tips and strategies for getting a good deal on a room outside Walt Disney World.

1. Orlando MagiCard Orlando MagiCard is a discount program sponsored by the Orlando/Orange County Convention and Visitors Bureau. Cardholders are eligible for discounts of 10–40 percent at about 75 participating hotels. The MagiCard is also good for discounts at area attractions. It's free, valid for up to six persons, and available to anyone 18 or older.

To obtain a MagiCard and a list of participating hotels and attractions, call (800) 255-5786 or (407) 363-5874. It's also available at the Convention and Visitors Bureau at 8445 International Drive in Orlando.

2. Exit Information Guide EIG (Exit Information Guide) publishes a book of discount coupons for bargain rates at hotels throughout Florida. The book is free in many restaurants and motels along interstate highways leading to Florida. The guide is available for $3 (credit cards accepted; $5 USD for Canadian delivery) by contacting:

Exit Information Guide
4205 NW 6th Street
Gainesville, FL 32609
(904) 371-3948

3. Wholesalers, Consolidators, and Reservation Services
Wholesalers and consolidators buy rooms, or options on rooms, from hotels at a low rate. They then resell the rooms at a profit through travel agents or tour packagers or directly to the public. When wholesalers and consolidators deal directly with the public, they frequently represent themselves as "reservation services." Here are two that frequently offer substantial discounts:

Accommodations Express	(800) 444-7666
Hotel Reservations Network	(800) 964-6835

4. If You Make Your Own Reservation Always call the specific hotel, not the chain's national 800 number. Reservationists at the 800 number often don't know about local specials. Always ask about specials before you inquire about corporate rates. Don't be reluctant to bargain. If you're buying a hotel's weekend package, for example, and want to stay longer, you can often obtain at least the corporate rate for the extra days. Bargain, however, before you check in.

5. Condominium Deals A large number of condo resorts and time-shares in the Kissimmee/Orlando area rent to vacationers for a week or less. Look for bargains, especially during off-peak periods. Reservations and information can be obtained from:

Concord Condos & Vacation Homes	(800) 251-1112
Condolink	(800) 733-4445
Hospitality Vacation Homes	(800) 969-7077
Kissimmee–St. Cloud Reservations	(800) 333-5477
Vistana Resort	(800) 877-8787

Hotels and Motels:
Rated and Ranked

• Room Ratings •

To evaluate properties according to relative quality, style, state of repair, cleanliness, and size of their **standard rooms,** we have grouped the hotels and motels into classifications denoted by stars. Star ratings in this guide apply to Orlando area properties only and don't necessarily correspond to ratings awarded by other travel critics. We have tied our ratings to levels of quality established by specific American hotel corporations.

Star ratings apply to *room quality only* and describe the property's standard accommodations. At most hotels and motels, a "standard" room has either one king or two queen beds. In an all-suite property, the standard accommodation is either a one- or

Room Star Ratings		
★★★★★	*Superior Rooms*	Tasteful and luxurious by any standard
★★★★	*Extremely Nice Rooms*	What you would expect at a Hyatt Regency or Marriott
★★★	*Nice Rooms*	Holiday Inn or comparable quality
★★	*Adequate Rooms*	Clean, comfortable, and functional, without frills— like a Motel 6
★	*Super Budget*	

two-room suite. Star ratings are assigned without regard to whether a property has restaurant(s), recreational facilities, entertainment, or other extras.

In addition to stars, we also use a numerical rating system. Our rating scale is 0 to 100, with 100 as the best possible rating and zero (0) as the worst. Numerical ratings are presented to show the difference we perceive between one property and another.

The location column identifies the area around Walt Disney World where you will find a property. The designation "WDW" means the property is inside Walt Disney World. A "1" means the property is on or near International Drive. Properties on US 192 (aka Irlo Bronson Memorial Highway, Vine Street, and Space Coast Parkway) are indicated by "3." All others are marked "2" and for the most part are located along the I-4 corridor.

Properties on US 192 also carry location designations with their names, such as the Holiday Inn Maingate East. The consensus in Orlando seems to be that the main entrance to Walt Disney World is the broad interstate-type road that runs from US 192. This is called Maingate. Coming from US 27 toward the Maingate area, properties before the Maingate turnoff are called Maingate West; properties after the Maingate turnoff are called Maingate East.

• How the Hotels Compare •

Cost estimates are based on the hotel's published (rack) rates for standard rooms. Each "$" represents $30. Thus a cost of "$$$" means that a room (or suite) will be about $90 a night.

Here's a hit parade of the nicest rooms in town. It was compiled by checking several rooms randomly at each hotel, but not all. If you arrive and are assigned a room inferior to what you were led to expect, demand to be moved.

How the Hotels Compare

Hotel	Location	Room Star Rating	Room Quality Rating	Cost	Phone (A/C 407)
WDW Grand Floridian Resort	WDW	★★★★★	97	$$$$$$$$$$-	934-7639
WDW Beach Club Resort	WDW	★★★★½	95	$$$$$$$$	934-7639
WDW Boardwalk Inn	WDW	★★★★½	95	$$$$$$$$	934-7639
WDW Yacht Club Resort	WDW	★★★★½	95	$$$$$$$$	934-7639
Shades of Green	WDW	★★★★½	94	open to military only	824-3400
Marriott Orlando World Center	2	★★★★½	92	$$$$$+	239-4200
Renaissance Orlando Resort	2	★★★★½	92	$$$$$$$$-	351-5555
Peabody Orlando	1	★★★★½	91	$$$$$$$$-	352-4000
Hyatt Regency Grand Cypress	2	★★★★	89	$$$$$$+	239-1234
Homewood Suites Maingate	3	★★★★	88	$$$$$-	396-2229
WDW Boardwalk Villas	WDW	★★★★	88	$$$$$$$+	934-7639
Doubletree Guest Suites	WDW	★★★★	87	$$$$+	934-1000
Hawthorne Suites Orlando	1	★★★★	87	$$$+	351-6600
Hilton Inn Gateway (tower rooms)	3	★★★★	87	$$$$+	396-4400
WDW Contemporary Resort	WDW	★★★★	87	$$$$$$$+	934-7639

How the Hotels Compare (*continued*)

Hotel	Location	Room Star Rating	Room Quality Rating	Cost	Phone (A/C 407)
WDW Polynesian Resort	WDW	★★★★	87	$$$$$$$+	934-7639
WDW Villas at the Disney Institute	WDW	★★★★	87	$$$$$$$$$$+	934-7639
WDW Wilderness Lodge	WDW	★★★★	87	$$$$$$-	934-7639
Buena Vista Suites	1	★★★★	86	$$$$	239-8588
Embassy Suites Orlando International	1	★★★★	86	$$$$$-	352-1400
Embassy Suites Resort	2	★★★★	86	$$$$$	239-1144
WDW Dolphin Resort	WDW	★★★★	86	$$$$$$$$+	934-7639
WDW Old Key West Resort	WDW	★★★★	86	$$$$$$$+	934-7639
WDW Swan	WDW	★★★★	86	$$$$$$$$-	934-7639
WDW Dixie Landings Resort	WDW	★★★★	85	$$$+	934-7639
WDW Port Orleans Resort	WDW	★★★★	85	$$$+	934-7639
Melia Orlando Suites & Villas	3	★★★★	84	$$$+	397-0555
Omni Rosen Hotel	1	★★★★	84	$$$$$-	800-800-9840
Radisson Inn Lake Buena Vista	2	★★★★	84	$$	239-8400
Villas at Resort World	2	★★★★	84	$$$$$-	800-423-8604

		How the Hotels Compare *(continued)*			

Hotel	Location	Room Star Rating	Room Quality Rating	Cost	Phone (A/C 407)
Best Western Grosvenor Resort	WDW	★★★★	83	$$$$+	828-4444
Buena Vista Palace	WDW	★★★★	83	$$$$$	827-2727
Enclave Suites	1	★★★★	83	$$$+	351-1155
Hilton Disney Village	WDW	★★★½	82	$$$$$$	827-4000
Hyatt Orlando	3	★★★½	82	$$$$+	396-1234
Residence Inn Lake Cecile	3	★★★½	82	$$$	396-2056
Summerfield Suites	1	★★★½	82	$$$$$$$+	352-2400
Summerfield Suites Lake Buena Vista	2	★★★½	82	$$$$$$$+	238-0777
Radisson Twin Towers Hotel	1	★★★½	81	$$$$	800-327-2110
Embassy Suites Plaza International	1	★★★½	80	$$$$+	800-362-2779
Orlando Marriott	1	★★★½	80	$$$$-	351-2420
Westgate Lakes	2	★★★½	80	$$$	352-8051
Residence Inn Orlando	1	★★★½	79	$$$+	345-0117
WDW Caribbean Beach Resort	WDW	★★★½	79	$$$+	934-7639
Travelodge Hotel Disney Village	WDW	★★★½	78	$$$$	828-2424
Courtyard by Marriott	1	★★★½	77	$$$+	800-321-2211
Courtyard Disney Village	WDW	★★★½	77	$$$$-	828-8888

How the Hotels Compare *(continued)*

Hotel	Location	Room Star Rating	Room Quality Rating	Cost	Phone (A/C 407)
Wyndham Garden Hotel	2	★★★½	77	$$$+	239-8500
Courtyard Maingate	3	★★★½	75	$$$+	396-4000
Hilton Inn Gateway (garden rooms)	3	★★★½	75	$$$+	396-4400
Quality Suites Maingate East	3	★★★	75	$$$$-	396-8040
Holiday Inn Sun Spree Resort	2	★★★	74	$$$-	239-4500
Quality Suites International Drive	1	★★★	74	$$$+	363-0332
Ramada Plaza Resort Maingate at the Parkway	3	★★★	74	$$$-	396-7000
The Castle Hotel (Holiday Inn Sun Spree Resort)	1	★★★	74	$$$$$+	800-952-2785
WDW All-Star Resort	WDW	★★★	74	$$+	939-5000
Ramada Resort Florida Center	1	★★★	73	$$+	351-4600
Country Hearth Inn	1	★★★	72	$$$+	352-0008
Days Inn Lake Buena Vista Resort	2	★★★	72	$$$-	800-423-3297
Holiday Inn Hotel & Suites Maingate East	3	★★★	72	$$$$+	396-4488
Holiday Inn Maingate	3	★★★	72	$$$$-	396-7300

How the Hotels Compare *(continued)*

Hotel	Location	Room Star Rating	Room Quality Rating	Cost	Phone (A/C 407)
Quality Inn Lake Cecile	3	★★★	72	$$-	396-4455
Travelodge Suites Eastgate	3	★★★	72	$$+	396-7666
Radisson Inn International	1	★★★	71	$$+	345-0505
Wilson World Maingate	3	★★★	71	$$+	396-6000
Clarion Plaza Hotel	1	★★★	70	$$$$+	352-9700
Comfort Suites Orlando	2	★★★	70	$$+	351-5050
Days Inn Lake Buena Vista Village	2	★★★	70	$$+	239-4646
Howard Johnson Universal Tower	1	★★★	70	$$$-	351-2100
Radisson Inn Maingate	3	★★★	70	$$+	396-1400
Sheraton World Resort	1	★★★	70	$$$+	352-1100
Travelodge Maingate East	3	★★★	70	$+	396-4222
Floridian of Orlando	1	★★★	69	$$-	351-5009
Holiday Inn Express	1	★★★	69	$$$-	351-4430
Holiday Inn Universal Studios	1	★★★	69	$$$+	351-3333
Howard Johnson Fountain Park	3	★★★	69	$$$-	396-1111

How the Hotels Compare *(continued)*

Hotel	Location	Room Star Rating	Room Quality Rating	Cost	Phone (A/C 407)
Hampton Inn International Drive	1	★★★	68	$$$-	345-1112
Hampton Inn Sandlake	1	★★★	68	$$-	363-7886
Hampton Inn Universal Studios	1	★★★	68	$$+	351-6716
Hotel Royal Plaza	WDW	★★★	68	$$$+	828-2828
Howard Johnson Park Square	2	★★★	68	$$$-	239-6900
Sheraton Lakeside Inn	3	★★★	68	$$$-	396-2222
Wellesley Inn	1	★★★	68	$$$-	345-0026
Days Inn Lake Buena Vista	2	★★★	67	$$+	239-4441
Hampton Inn Maingate	3	★★★	67	$$+	396-8484
Holiday Inn Maingate West	3	★★★	67	$$+	396-1100
La Quinta Inn International	1	★★★	67	$$+	351-1660
Westgate Towers	3	★★★	67	$$$$$$+	396-2500
Days Suites Maingate East	3	★★★	66	$$$+	396-7900
Delta Orlando Resort	1	★★★	66	$$$$	351-3340
Ramada Resort Maingate	3	★★★	66	$$$-	396-4466
Holiday Inn International Resort	1	★★★	65	$$$$-	351-3500

How the Hotels Compare (continued)

Hotel	Location	Room Star Rating	Room Quality Rating	Cost	Phone (A/C 407)
Las Palmas Hotel	1	★★★	65	$$$-	351-3900
Quality Inn Plaza	1	★★★	65	$$-	345-8585
Days Inn Maingate West	3	★★½	64	$$+	396-1000
Econo Lodge International	1	★★½	64	$$-	800-327-0750
Econo Lodge Maingate West	3	★★½	64	$+	396-9300
Larson's Lodge Maingate	3	★★½	64	$$+	396-6100
Red Roof Inn Kissimmee	3	★★½	64	$$+	396-0065
Wynfield Inn Maingate	3	★★½	64	$$+	800-346-1551
Best Western Maingate	3	★★½	63	$$	396-0100
Best Western Plaza International	1	★★½	63	$$$-	345-8195
Gateway Inn	1	★★½	63	$$	351-2000
Lakeside Resort	3	★★½	63	$$	396-1828
Rodeway Inn International	1	★★½	63	$$-	351-4444
Days Inn	3	★★½	62	$$-	800-544-5713
Howard Johnson Maingate	3	★★½	62	$$-	800-638-7829
Inns of America International	1	★★½	62	$$	800-826-0778
Inns of America Maingate	3	★★½	62	$$-	800-826-0778
Ramada Inn Westgate	3	★★½	62	$+	941-424-2621
Comfort Inn International	1	★★½	61	$$+	351-4100

How the Hotels Compare (continued)

Hotel	Location	Room Star Rating	Room Quality Rating	Cost	Phone (A/C 407)
Howard Johnson South Int'l Drive	1	★★½	61	$$+	351-5100
MIC Lakefront Inn	1	★★½	61	$+	345-5340
Ramada Limited Universal Maingate	1	★★½	61	$$$-	354-3996
Riande Continental Plaza	1	★★½	61	$$-	352-8211
Best Western Eastgate	3	★★½	60	$$-	396-0707
Comfort Inn at Lake Buena Vista	2	★★½	60	$$+	239-7300
Comfort Inn Maingate	3	★★½	60	$$-	396-7500
Days Inn Orlando Lakeside	1	★★½	60	$$	351-1900
Howard Johnson Lodge	1	★★½	60	$$+	351-2900
Resort Suites	3	★★½	60	$+	396-1780
Wynfield Inn Westwood	1	★★½	60	$$+	800-346-1551
Days Inn Convention Center	1	★★½	59	$$$-	352-8700
Days Inn International Drive	1	★★½	59	$$$-	800-325-2525
Days Inn Universal Studios	1	★★½	59	$$-	351-3800

How the Hotels Compare *(continued)*

Hotel	Location	Room Star Rating	Room Quality Rating	Cost	Phone (A/C 407)
Park Inn International	3	★★½	59	$+	396-1376
Red Carpet Inn East	3	★★½	59	$+	396-1133
Sleep Inn Maingate	3	★★½	59	$$-	396-1600
Buena Vista Motel	3	★★½	58	$+	396-2100
Famous Host Inn	3	★★½	58	$+	396-8883
Knights Inn Maingate	3	★★½	58	$$-	396-4200
Quality Inn International	1	★★½	58	$$-	351-1600
Golden Link Motel	3	★★½	57	$	396-0555
Knights Inn Maingate East	3	★★½	57	$$-	396-8186
Ramada Limited	3	★★½	57	$+	396-2212
Sun Motel	3	★★½	57	$+	396-2673
Crystal Tree Inn	1	★★½	56	$$-	352-8383
Econo Lodge Maingate Central	3	★★½	56	$+	800-553-2666
Econo Lodge Maingate Hawaiian	3	★★½	56	$$	396-2000
Fairfield Inn International	1	★★½	56	$$	363-1944
HoJo Inn Maingate	3	★★½	56	$$+	396-1748
Central Motel	3	★★	55	$+	396-2333
Monte Carlo	3	★★	55	$+	396-4700
Red Roof Inn Orlando	1	★★	55	$$+	352-1507
Rodeway Inn Eastgate	3	★★	55	$+	396-7700

How the Hotels Compare *(continued)*

Hotel	Location	Room Star Rating	Room Quality Rating	Cost	Phone (A/C 407)
Traveler's Inn	3	★★	55	$+	396-1668
Travelodge Orlando Flags	1	★★	55	$$-	800-722-7462
Days Inn Maingate East	3	★★	54	$$	396-7900
Economy Inns of America	3	★★	54	$+	800-826-0778
Key Motel	3	★★	54	$-	396-6200
Kissimmee Super 8 Motel	3	★★	54	$$-	396-1144
Motel 6 International Drive	1	★★	53	$+	351-6500
King's Inn & Suites	3	★★	52	$+	396-4762
Motel 6 Maingate East	3	★★	51	$+	396-6333
Motel 6 Maingate West	3	★½	45	$+	396-6427

• Good Deals and Bad Deals •

Now let's take a look at the best combinations of quality and value in a room. As before, rankings are made without consideration of location or availability of restaurant(s), recreational facilities, entertainment, and/or amenities. Each lodging is awarded a value rating on a 0–100 scale. The higher the rating, the better the value.

Value ratings aim to give you some sense of value received for dollars spent. A ★★½ room at $30 may have the same value rating as a ★★★★ room at $85, but that doesn't mean the rooms will be of comparable quality. Regardless of whether it's a good deal, a ★★½ room is still a ★★½ room.

You will note the scarcity of Disney hotels on the best-deal list. This is because our ratings focus exclusively on the quality of the guest room, not on the amenities associated with Disney hotels. If you factor in these extras, the rates charged at Disney hotels appear to many to be a fair value for the money.

Listed below are the best room buys for the money, regardless of location or star classification, based on averaged rack rates. Note that a suite sometimes can cost less than a hotel room.

The Top 30 Best Deals					
Hotel	Location	Room Star Rating	Room Quality Rating	Cost	Phone (A/C 407)
Radisson Inn Lake Buena Vista	2	★★★★	84	$$	239-8400
Golden Link Motel	3	★★½	57	$	396-0555
Travelodge Maingate East	3	★★★	70	$+	396-4222
Quality Inn Lake Cecile	3	★★★	72	$$-	396-4455
Key Motel	3	★★	54	$-	396-6200
Floridian of Orlando	1	★★★	69	$$-	351-5009

The Top 30 Best Deals *(continued)*

Hotel	Location	Room Star Rating	Room Quality Rating	Cost	Phone (A/C 407)
Hampton Inn Sandlake	1	★★★	68	$$-	363-7886
Buena Vista Motel	3	★★½	58	$+	396-2100
Famous Host Inn	3	★★½	58	$+	396-8883
Quality Inn Plaza	1	★★★	65	$$-	345-8585
MIC Lakefront Inn	1	★★½	61	$+	345-5340
Resort Suites	3	★★½	60	$+	396-1780
Westgate Lakes	2	★★★½	80	$$$	352-8051
Hawthorne Suites Orlando	1	★★★★	87	$$$+	351-6600
WDW Dixie Landings Resort	WDW	★★★★	85	$$$+	934-7639
WDW Port Orleans Resort	WDW	★★★★	85	$$$+	934-7639
Ramada Inn Westgate	3	★★½	62	$+	941-424-2621
Ramada Limited	3	★★½	57	$+	396-2212
Melia Orlando Suites & Villas	3	★★★★	84	$$$+	397-0555
Enclave Suites	1	★★★★	83	$$$+	351-1155
Travelodge Suites Eastgate	3	★★★	72	$$+	396-7666
Days Inn	3	★★½	62	$$-	800-544-5713
Howard Johnson Maingate	3	★★½	62	$$-	800-638-7829
Park Inn International	3	★★½	59	$+	396-1376
Red Carpet Inn East	3	★★½	59	$+	396-1133
Residence Inn Lake Cecile	3	★★★½	82	$$$	396-2056

The Top 30 Best Deals *(continued)*					
Hotel	Location	Room Star Rating	Room Quality Rating	Cost	Phone (A/C 407)
WDW All-Star Resort	WDW	★★★	74	$$+	939-5000
Holiday Inn Maingate West	3	★★★	67	$$+	396-1100
Best Western Eastgate	3	★★½	60	$$-	396-0707
Monte Carlo	3	★★	55	$+	396-4700

4

Walt Disney World with Kids

Considerations and Situations

Children and parents brighten at the prospect of visiting Disney World. But it's a big trip for both, and lack of planning may steal the magic from Walt's magic kingdoms. Here are some important considerations:

Age Disney entertainment is generally oriented to older children and adults. Kids need to be a fairly mature seven years old to *appreciate* the Magic Kingdom, and a year or two older to get much out of EPCOT or Disney-MGM.

Time of Year to Visit Avoid the hot, crowded summer months, especially with preschoolers. Try to go in October, November (except Thanksgiving), early December, January, February, or April (except Easter). If your school-age children are good students, take them out of school so you can visit during the off season. Arrange study assignments relating to the educational aspects of Disney World. *Nothing* will enhance your Walt Disney World vacation as much as avoiding summer and holidays.

Building Naps and Rest into Your Itinerary Disney World is huge. Don't try to see everything in one day. At any season, tour in the early morning and return to your hotel around 11:30 a.m. for lunch, a swim, and a nap. Return to the park in late afternoon or early evening.

Where to Stay If you can afford to stay in Walt Disney World, do it and save time and hassle in commuting. In or out of the World, it's imperative that your young children have a midday rest break.

Your hotel should be within a 20-minute one-way commute of the theme parks. If you're traveling with children 12 and younger, we recommend the Polynesian, Grand Floridian, or Wilderness Lodge resorts (in that order) if they fit your budget. Less expensive are Dixie Landings, Port Orleans, or Caribbean Beach. Bargain accommodations are available at All-Star Resorts.

Least Common Denominators Somebody in your group will run out of steam first, and the whole family will be affected. Pushing the tired or discontented beyond their capacity will spoil the day for them—and you.

Setting Limits and Making Plans Avoid arguments and disappointment by establishing guidelines for each day, and get everybody committed in advance.

Be Flexible Any day at Walt Disney World includes surprises; be prepared to adjust.

Overheating, Sunburn, and Dehydration These are young children's most common problems at Disney World. Carry sunscreen, and use it generously, even on children in canopied strollers. Avoid overheating by taking periodic breaks in the shade or an air-conditioned restaurant or show. Sodas and fountains aren't enough. Carry plastic water bottles, and push fluids.

Blisters Wear comfortable, well-broken-in shoes and two pairs of thin socks (preferable to one pair of thick socks). Preschoolers may not know blisters are forming. Inspect their feet at least twice a day. Precut Moleskin bandages; they won't sweat off. Before a blister forms, air out the hot spot and protect it with Moleskin.

First Aid Each theme park has a First Aid Center.

Things You Forgot or Things You Ran Out Of Rain gear, diapers, diaper pins, formula, film, aspirin, topical sunburn treatments, and other sundries are sold at all the major theme and swimming parks. Rain gear is cheap; most other items aren't.

Caring for Infants at the Theme Parks Centralized facilities for infant and toddler care provide everything necessary for changing diapers, preparing formulas, and warming bottles. Food and baby supplies are sold. The Magic Kingdom's Baby Center is next to the Crystal Palace at the end of Main Street. At EPCOT, Baby Services is near Odyssey Restaurant, to the right of the World of Motion in Future World. At Disney-MGM, Baby Care is in the Guest Services Building, left of the entrance.

Strollers Bring your own or rent one for a modest daily fee at any major theme park. Obtain one for any child age six and younger that fits. If you rent a stroller at the Magic Kingdom and go later to EPCOT or Disney-MGM, return your Magic Kingdom stroller and present your receipt at the next park. You'll be issued another stroller without additional charge. If you return to your hotel for a break, leave your stroller near an attraction by the park's entrance and reclaim it when you return.

Strollers at the Magic Kingdom and EPCOT are large and sturdy, with sun canopies and cargo baskets. At Disney-MGM, they're the collapsible type. Only collapsible strollers are permitted on Disney monorails and buses. When you enter a show or ride, you'll have to park your stroller, usually in an open, unprotected area. It's unlikely to be stolen, but it may be moved by Disney cast members "tidying up." Tie a scarf or ribbon on it for easy identification.

Rent a stroller to the right of the entrance at the Magic Kingdom, on the left side of the Entrance Plaza at EPCOT, and at Oscar's Super Service just inside the entrance of Disney-MGM Studios.

• Disney, Kids, and Scary Stuff •

Disney rides and shows are adventures. Though all of the endings are happy, the adventures may intimidate or frighten young children. Monsters and special effects at Disney-MGM are more real and sinister than those at other theme parks. Think twice about exposing a preschooler to machine-gun battles, earthquakes, and the creature from *Alien*.

Preschoolers should start with Dumbo and work up to the Jungle Cruise in late morning. Skip Pirates of the Caribbean.

Attractions Where Switching-Off Is Common	
Magic Kingdom	
Tomorrowland	Space Mountain
	Alien Encounter
Frontierland	Splash Mountain
	Big Thunder Mountain Railroad
EPCOT	
Future World Wonders of Life pavilion	Body Wars
Disney-MGM Studios	Star Tours
	"Twilight Zone" Tower of Terror

• Waiting Line Strategy •

Switching Off (The Baby Swap)   Several attractions may frighten young children or have minimum height and/or age requirements. Some couples bypass these attractions, while others take turns riding. Skipping some of Disney's best rides or waiting twice in line is unnecessary.

Solve the problem with "switching off" (The Baby Swap). To switch off, there must be at least two adults. Everybody waits in line together. When you reach a Disney attendant, say you want to switch off. The greeter will allow everyone, including the children, to enter. When you reach the loading area, one adult will ride while the other stays with the kids. The riding adult disembarks and takes over the children while the other adult rides.

• Attractions That Eat Even Adults •

Many attractions at Walt Disney World cause motion sickness or other problems for older children and adults. We refer to them as attractions that eat adults.

• The Disney Characters •

The large and friendly costumed versions of Mickey, Minnie, Donald, Goofy, and others—known as "Disney characters"—

Attractions That Eat Even Adults	
Magic Kingdom	
Tomorrowland	Space Mountain
	Alien Encounter
Fantasyland	Mad Tea Party
Frontierland	Big Thunder Mountain Railroad
	Splash Mountain
EPCOT	
Future World	Body Wars
Disney-MGM Studios	Star Tours
	Tower of Terror

link Disney animated films and the theme parks. About 250 have been brought to life and mix with patrons or perform in shows or parades in the major theme parks and hotels.

Prepare your child to meet the characters. Almost all are quite large, and several are huge. All can intimidate a preschooler. Don't thrust your children at the characters; let them approach gradually. You may need to make the first contact to show your children that the characters are harmless.

Some costumes offer poor visibility, and children approaching on a character's blind side may not be seen or may be stepped on or bowled over. Children should approach from the front, and parents should stay with them, stepping back only to take photos.

At the Magic Kingdom characters are encountered more frequently than anywhere else in Walt Disney World. There's almost always one next to City Hall on Main Street and usually one or more in Town Square or around the railroad station. If it's rainy, check the veranda of Tony's Restaurant. Characters appear in all the "lands" but are more apt to be in Fantasyland and Mickey's Toontown Fair. At the Toontown Fair, Mickey meets fans in his office. Goofy, Chip 'n Dale, and Pluto, each with his own greeting area, are also available for autographs, photos, and hugs. Cinderella greets diners at King Stefan's Banquet Hall on the second floor of the Castle (reservation required). Also look for characters in the Central Hub and by Splash Mountain in Frontierland.

Characters are featured in the afternoon and evening parades and play a major role in Castle Forecourt shows (entrance to the castle on the moat side) and at the Galaxy Palace Theater in Tomorrowland.

At EPCOT In keeping with the park's theme, Goofy roams Future World in a metallic cape reminiscent of Buck Rogers, and Mickey in Ben Franklin costume greets guests in front of *The American Adventure.*

Don't expect to encounter either the number or variety of characters at EPCOT that you would in the Magic Kingdom, but your kids generally can interact more with them at EPCOT. Two of EPCOT's original characters, Dreamfinder and Figment, stay around the Journey to Imagination pavilion in Future World, and assorted characters appear at the Showcase Plaza each morning. Characters also occasionally visit *The American Adventure* pavilion and the United Kingdom in the World Showcase. Character shows are performed daily at the American Gardens Theater in the World Showcase.

At Disney-MGM Studios Characters most frequently are in front of the Animation Building, along Mickey Avenue (leading to the sound stages), and at the end of New York Street on the back lot. Mickey and "his friends" pose for keepsake photos (about $10) on Hollywood Boulevard and Sunset Boulevard. Characters are also prominent in shows, with *Voyage of the Little Mermaid* running almost continuously, and an abbreviated version of *Beauty and the Beast* performed several times daily at the Theater of the Stars.

• Babysitting •

Child-care Centers Child care isn't available inside the theme parks, but each hotel connected by the monorail and EPCOT resorts (Swan and Dolphin hotels, Yacht and Beach Club resorts) offers child care for potty-trained children older than three. Generally, children can be left between 4 p.m. and midnight. Snacks, blankets, and pillows are provided. Play is supervised but not organized, and toys, videos, and games are plentiful. Guests at any Disney resort or campground may use the service.

The most elaborate child-care "club" or "camp" is the Neverland Club at the Polynesian Resort. This and one at Wilderness Lodge include a buffet dinner. At other locations, you arrange for room service to deliver your children's meals. At Camp Dolphin in the Dolphin hotel, children may eat at the Coral Cafe or the Soda Shop next door.

Readers invariably praise the Neverland Club. Cost is $8 per child per hour, with a three-hour minimum.

If you aren't staying at a Disney resort offering a child-care club, and you *do not* have a car, use in-room babysitting.

Kinder-Care Learning Centers also operate child-care facilities at Walt Disney World. Originally developed for use by Disney employees, Kinder-Care also accepts guests' children on a

Child-care Clubs

Hotel	Name of Program	Ages	Phone
Buena Vista Palace	All about Kids	All	(407) 827-2727
Boardwalk Inn & Villas	Little Toots	4–12	(407) 939-5100
Contemporary Resort	Mouseketeer Clubhouse	4–12	(407) 824-1000, ext. 3038
Grand Floridian	Mouseketeer Club	4–12	(407) 824-3000, ext. 2985
The Hilton	Vacation Station	4–12	(407) 827-4000
Polynesian Resort	Neverland Club	4–12	(407) 824-2170
WDW Dolphin	Camp Dolphin	3–12	(407) 934-4241
WDW Swan	Camp Swan	3–12	(407) 934-1621
Wilderness Lodge Resort	Cub's Den	4–12	(407) 824-1083
Yacht and Beach Clubs	Sandcastle Club	4–12	(407) 934-7000

* Clubs operate afternoon and evenings. Reservations required.

space-available basis. Kinder-Care provides services similar to hotels' clubs, except that the daytime *Learning While Playing Development Program* is more structured and educational. Children from ages 1 (provided they're walking and can eat table food) through 12 are eligible. Reservations: (407) 827-5437.

In-Room Babysitting   In-room babysitting is available through Kinder-Care (phone (407) 827-5444) or the Fairy Godmother service.

Though expensive, Fairy Godmother is on call 24 hours a day and provides the area's most flexible and diversified service. Godmothers will come to any hotel at any hour. They'll take your children to the theme parks. There's no age limit for the Godmothers, who also tend the elderly. All sitters are female nonsmokers. Cost is $7 an hour for up to three children (in the same family), with a four-hour minimum and a $5 travel fee. Godmothers will sit a group of children from different families for $5 an hour per family. Reservations: (407) 277-3724 or (407) 275-7326.

• Walt Disney World Learning •
Programs for Children

Four learning programs are available for children age 15 and younger. They are Kidventure (phone (407) 824-3784), Wildlife Adventure (phone (407) 354-1855), Art Magic: Bringing Illusion to Life (phone (407) 354-1855), and Show Biz Magic (phone (407) 354-1855). The well-presented and enjoyable programs are expensive but include admission to any theme park visited, classroom materials, and lunch. Class size is limited.

Disney Day Camp at the Disney Institute

Disney Day Camp, for ages seven to nine, offers one or two half-day field trips focusing on art, entertainment, international cultures, and nature. Morning sessions are 8:30 a.m. until noon; afternoon programs, 1:30 to 5 p.m. Prices vary; lunch is optional. Reservations: (407) 827-4800.

Special Tips
for Special People

Walt Disney World for Couples

So many couples marry or honeymoon at Walt Disney World that a department has been formed to meet their needs. *Disney's Fairy Tale Weddings & Honeymoons* offers a range of wedding venues and services, as well as honeymoon packages. They're all expensive. Contact:

Disney's Fairy Tale Weddings & Honeymoons
P.O. Box 10020
Lake Buena Vista, FL 32830-0020
Phone: (407) 828-3400

Romantic Getaways

Walt Disney World is a favorite getaway for honeymooners and other couples. But not all Disney hotels are equally romantic. We recommend these Disney lodgings for romantics:

1. Polynesian Resort
2. Wilderness Lodge Resort
3. Grand Floridian Beach Resort
4. Boardwalk Inn
5. Yacht and Beach Club resorts
6. Contemporary Resort (tower rooms)

Romantic Places to Eat

Quiet, romantic restaurants with good food are rare in the theme parks. Only the Coral Reef and the San Angel Inn at

EPCOT satisfy both requirements. Hotels offer a wider selection: Narcoossee's, at the Grand Floridian; Fulton's Crab House, on the riverboat at Pleasure Island; Cap'n Jack's Oyster Bar and Rainforest Cafe, at Disney Village Marketplace; Ariel's, at the Beach Club; Yachtsman Steakhouse, at the Yacht Club; Sum Chows and Kimonos, at the Swan and Dolphin; and 'Ohana, at the Polynesian Resort.

Eat later in the evening and choose among the restaurants listed, but always expect to encounter children—well-behaved or otherwise.

Romantic Stuff to Do

1. Lounges. There's a nice but pricey lounge atop the Contemporary Resort that's great for watching sunsets or evening fireworks. If you want just the view, access an outside promenade through the glass doors at the end of the lounge. Another wonderful getaway with a view is Mizner's Lounge on the Alcazar level of the Grand Floridian. Each evening, a dance band plays '20s and '30s music on the adjacent landing.

2. The Floating Electrical Pageant. One of Disney's most romantic entertainments, the parade of spectacularly lighted barges starts after dark. Watch from the pier or beach at the Polynesian Resort.

3. Take a boat ride. Small launches shuttle guests to and from the Grand Floridian, Polynesian Resort, Magic Kingdom, Wilderness Lodge, and Fort Wilderness Campground well into the night. Disney launches also cruise the canal connecting Disney-MGM and EPCOT.

   During daytime at the Fort Wilderness dock, rent boats for exploring Bay Lake and the Seven Seas Lagoon. The adjacent campground is honeycombed with footpaths for lovely walks in early morning or evening.

   If you enjoy hiking and boating, visit Juniper Springs Recreation Area in the Ocala National Forest. About an hour and a half north of Walt Disney

World, the forest is extraordinarily beautiful. Information: (904) 625-2808.

4. Picnic during temperate months on the beaches of Bay Lake and the Seven Seas Lagoon or at Fort Wilderness Campground. Room service at resorts can prepare your lunch. Drinks, including wine and beer, are less expensive in hotel convenience shops.

5. Dine and dance on the Boardwalk, which offers nice restaurants and an upscale dance club.

6. Rent a bike at Wilderness Lodge and explore Fort Wilderness Campground. Maps are available at the rental shed.

Walt Disney World for Seniors

Most seniors enjoy Disney World much more when they tour with folks their own age. Personal tastes rule; there are no attractions we categorically advise against. But there are some you should weigh before you go:

Magic Kingdom

Space Mountain This roller coaster in the dark vibrates a lot. Put your glasses in your fanny pack. (We can't guarantee they'll stay in your pocket.)

Big Thunder Mountain Railroad Although sedate compared with Space Mountain, this ride is very jarring, especially the side-to-side shaking.

Splash Mountain This ride combines Disney whimsy with the thrill of a log flume. There's one big drop near the end and a bit of a splash.

The Swiss Family Treehouse This isn't a thrill ride, but it involves lots of stair climbing and an unsteady pontoon bridge.

Mad Tea Party An adaptation of a carnival ride: big tea cups spin until you're nauseated.

EPCOT

Body Wars This ride jolts more than Star Tours at Disney-MGM and is more apt to cause motion sickness than the Mad Hatter's tea cups. It includes a graphic anatomy lesson.

Disney-MGM Studios

Star Tours   If you're prone to motion sickness, this flight simulation will affect you.

Tower of Terror   Although most thrills are visual, the Tower features a gut-wrenching simulation of an elevator in free fall.

Getting Around

A seven-hour visit to one of the theme parks normally includes four to eight miles on foot. If you aren't up for that much walking, let an athletic member of your party push you in a rented wheelchair. EPCOT and the Magic Kingdom also offer electric carts.

Wheelchair users and their immediate parties use priority entrances at most attractions.

Your rental receipt is good for a replacement wheelchair in any park during the same day.

Lodging

If you can afford it, stay in Walt Disney World. Rooms are some of the area's nicest, always clean and well-maintained. And transportation is always available, at no extra cost, to any destination in Disney World.

Disney hotels assign rooms closer to restaurants and transportation to guests of any age who can't tolerate much walking. They also carry guests to and from their rooms in golf carts.

Seniors intending to spend more time at EPCOT and Disney-MGM than at the Magic Kingdom should consider the Yacht and Beach Club resorts, the Swan, the Dolphin, or the Boardwalk Inn.

Contemporary Resort is excellent for mobile seniors who want to be on the monorail system (wheelchairs can't access the monorail platform; they enter by escalators), as are the Grand Floridian and Polynesian Resort. The latter, however, occupy many acres and may entail considerable walking. For a restful, rustic feeling, choose the Wilderness Lodge. If you want a kitchen and comforts of home, book Old Key West Resort or Boardwalk Villas.

RVers will like Fort Wilderness Campground. Within 20 minutes of Disney World are several KOA campgrounds. None offers the wilderness setting or amenities that Disney does, but they cost less.

Something Extra

We think at least one behind-the-scenes tour should be part of every senior's visit. Most are at EPCOT and offer in-depth looks at Disney World operations. Especially worthwhile are Hidden Treasures and Gardens of the World. If you don't have the time for these lengthy tours, join the shorter Greenhouse Tour at The Land pavilion, also in EPCOT.

Walt Disney World for Disabled Guests

Wholly or partially nonambulatory guests may rent wheelchairs. Most rides, shows, attractions, rest rooms, and restaurants accommodate the nonambulatory disabled. For specific inquiries or problems, call (407) 824-4321. If you're in the Magic Kingdom and need special assistance, go to City Hall on Main Street. At EPCOT, inquire at Guest Relations, left of Spaceship Earth. At Disney-MGM, go to Guest Services, left of the main entrance.

A limited number of easy-to-operate electric carts are available for rent at the Magic Kingdom and EPCOT.

Close-in parking for the disabled is available at all Disney World lots. Request directions when you pay.

An information booklet for disabled guests is available at all wheelchair rental locations. Theme-park maps distributed free to each guest pinpoint wheelchair-accessible attractions.

Peter Smith, a paraplegic, has written an excellent book, *Handicapped in Walt Disney World.* The 300-page, indexed guide ($10.95) covers trip planning and on-site touring. The book is sold at Disney World or through Southpark Publishers in Dallas, Texas (phone (214) 296-5659).

Even if an attraction doesn't accommodate wheelchairs, nonambulatory guests may still ride if they can transfer from their wheelchair to the vehicle of the ride. Disney staff isn't trained or permitted to assist in transfers.

Because most queuing areas won't accommodate wheelchairs, nonambulatory guests and their party should request boarding instructions from an attendant as soon as they arrive at an attraction. The group usually gets priority entry.

Visitors with Dietary Restrictions Visitors on special or restricted diets, including those requiring kosher meals, can be assisted at City Hall in the Magic Kingdom, Guest Relations in EPCOT, or Guest Services in Disney-MGM Studios.

Sight- and/or Hearing-Impaired Guests The Magic Kingdom, EPCOT, and Disney-MGM provide complimentary tape cassettes and portable tape players to assist sight-impaired guests. They're available at City Hall in the Magic Kingdom, Guest Relations at EPCOT, and Guest Services at Disney-MGM. A deposit is required.

6

Arriving and Getting Around

Getting There

• Directions •

Motorists can reach any Walt Disney World attraction or destination via World Drive, off US 192, or via EPCOT Drive, off I-4 (see map, pages 4–5).

From I-10 Take I-10 east across Florida to I-75 southbound. Exit I-75 onto the Florida Turnpike. Exit at Clermont and take US 27 south. Turn left onto US 192 and follow the signs to Disney World.

From I-75 southbound Follow I-75 south to the Florida Turnpike. Exit at Clermont and take US 27 south. Turn left onto US 192. Follow the signs.

From I-95 southbound Follow I-95 south to I-4. Go west on I-4, passing through Orlando. Exit at EPCOT Drive. Follow the signs.

From Daytona or Orlando Go west on I-4 through Orlando. Exit at EPCOT Drive. Follow the signs.

From the Orlando International Airport Take FL 528 (toll) west from the airport for about 12 miles to the intersection with I-4. Go west on I-4 and exit at EPCOT Drive.

From Miami, Fort Lauderdale, and southeastern Florida Go north on the Florida Turnpike to I-4 westbound. Exit I-4 at EPCOT Drive.

From Tampa and southwestern Florida Take I-75 northbound to I-4. Go east on I-4 and exit on US 192 northbound. Follow the signs.

The entrance to Walt Disney World Village is separate from entrances to the theme parks. To reach it, take the FL 535 exit off I-4. Go north. Follow the signs.

• Getting to Walt Disney World from the Airport •

Independent shuttles (shared with other Disney World–bound passengers) cost $22–35 per person, round trip. Mears Motor Transportation Service (phone (407) 423-5566) charges $25 per adult and $17 per child. Cabs are about $32–42 *one way.*

Getting Oriented

A good map—the Disney Transportation Guide—is available by calling (407) 824-4321. It's folded, with the overall resort map on one side and Disney Transportation routes on the other. After you arrive, get one from guest services at one of the theme parks or Disney hotels.

• **Finding Your Way Around** •

To avoid getting lost in sprawling Disney World, think of the complex as five major areas, or clusters:

1. The first encompasses all hotels and theme parks around Seven Seas Lagoon. This includes the Magic Kingdom, hotels connected by monorail, Shades of Green resort, and three golf courses.
2. The second includes developments on and around Bay Lake: Wilderness Lodge Resort, Fort Wilderness Campground, Discovery Island, River Country, and two golf courses.
3. EPCOT, Disney-MGM Studios, EPCOT resorts, and the Caribbean Beach Resort make up the third cluster.
4. The fourth encompasses Walt Disney World Village, Disney World Village Hotel Plaza, Disney Village Marketplace, Disney Institute, another golf course, Pleasure Island, Typhoon Lagoon, and Port Orleans, Dixie Landings, and Old Key West resorts.
5. The fifth and newest contains Disney All-Star Resorts and Blizzard Beach.

How to Travel
Around the World

Disney World day guests not staying in the complex can use the monorail system, most of the bus system, and some of the boat system. Make sure your car is parked in the lot of the theme park (or other Disney destination) where you plan to finish your day. This is critical if you stay at a park until closing.

Driving to the Magic Kingdom

Most Magic Kingdom day guests park in the Transportation and Ticket Center (TTC) parking lot. Its sections are named for Disney characters. On the reverse of your parking receipt are aisle numbers and section names. Mark where you have parked. You'll probably need this reminder to find your car later.

After parking, walk to a loading station and catch a tram to the Transportation and Ticket Center, where you can buy theme-park admissions. If you want to go to the Magic Kingdom, ride the ferry across Seven Seas Lagoon or catch the monorail. If the monorail queue is long, take the ferry. The monorail trip takes about 3½ to 5 minutes. The ferry takes 6½ minutes.

If you drive to another theme park on the same day, show your earlier parking receipt and park free.

Going to EPCOT from the Magic Kingdom In the morning, take the monorail to the TTC and transfer to the EPCOT monorail. In the afternoon, take the ferry to the TTC. If you plan to spend the remainder of the day at EPCOT and your car is in the TTC lot, drive your car over. If you plan to return to the Magic Kingdom or don't have a car at the TTC, commute via the EPCOT monorail.

> At all Disney parks, if you leave and intend to return to that park or visit another on the same day, have your hand stamped for free re-entry.

Going to Disney-MGM from the Magic Kingdom Either take a Disney bus or drive. If you plan to conclude your day at the Studios, drive. If you intend to return to the Magic Kingdom, take the bus. The Studios bus loads immediately left of the Magic Kingdom exit. You don't have to return to the TTC.

Leaving the Magic Kingdom at Day's End If you conclude your day at the Magic Kingdom and need to return to the TTC, first try the ferry. If it's mobbed, take either the "express" or "local" (stops at hotels) monorail.

Driving to EPCOT

Park in the EPCOT lot unless you plan to conclude your day at the Magic Kingdom. Sections are named for pavilions in the park's Future World area. Access to EPCOT is direct from the tram.

Going to the Magic Kingdom from EPCOT Take the monorail to the TTC and transfer to the Magic Kingdom express monorail. If you don't plan to return to EPCOT and have a car in the EPCOT lot, drive to the TTC and take the ferry or monorail.

Going to Disney-MGM Studios from EPCOT If you plan to finish the day at the Studios, drive. If you plan to return to EPCOT, leave the park through the main entrance and bus to the Studios. Or leave through the International Gateway in World Showcase and catch a boat at the nearby Yacht and Beach Club resorts. The latter option is best if you're returning to EPCOT for dinner at a World Showcase restaurant.

Driving to Disney-MGM

Going to the Magic Kingdom from Disney-MGM Regardless of where you intend to conclude the day, it's easier to bus to the Magic Kingdom. Because the bus unloads at the park's entrance instead of the TTC, you avoid reparking, taking the tram to the TTC, and catching the monorail or ferry. It's the same when you return to the Studios.

Going to EPCOT from Disney-MGM Drive to the EPCOT parking lot if you don't intend to return to the Studios. If you plan to return, take a bus or boat to EPCOT. Take the bus if you want to start at EPCOT's main entrance, the boat if you're headed for World Showcase.

Taking a Shuttle Bus from Your Out-of-the-World Hotel

Many lodgings near Disney World provide trams and buses. They save you the parking fees and drop you near theme-park entrances, but they may not get you there as early as you want or be available when you want to return. Also, most don't add vehicles at peak hours (you might have to stand), and some stop at other hotels before arriving at Disney World. Check particulars at your hotel.

If you're depending on hotel shuttles, leave the park at least 45 minutes before closing. If you stay until closing and are tired, hail a cab at stands near the Bus Information buildings at EPCOT, Disney-MGM, and the TTC. If cabs aren't available, the staff at Bus Information will call one. If you're at the Magic Kingdom at closing, take the monorail to a resort and get a cab there.

• Transportation Trade-offs for Guests • at Walt Disney World Resorts and Campground

The Walt Disney World transportation system is large, diversified, and generally efficient, but it can be overwhelmed during peak traffic, especially park opening and closing times, and it's difficult to figure out how bus, boat, and monorail systems interconnect.

If a resort offers boat or monorail service, its bus service will be limited. This means you'll have to transfer at the TTC for many Disney World destinations. If you're staying at a Magic Kingdom resort served by monorail (Polynesian, Contemporary, Grand Floridian), you'll commute efficiently to the Magic Kingdom by monorail. If you want to visit EPCOT, however, you must take the monorail to the TTC and transfer to the EPCOT monorail. (Guests at the Polynesian can eliminate the transfer by walking about 10 minutes to the TTC and catching the direct monorail to EPCOT.)

If you're staying at an EPCOT resort, walk or commute by boat to the International Gateway at EPCOT. Although buses run directly from EPCOT resorts to the Magic Kingdom, there's no direct bus service to EPCOT's main entrance or to Disney-MGM. To reach the Studios from EPCOT resorts, take a boat.

Caribbean Beach, Dixie Landings, Wilderness Lodge, Port Orleans, Old Key West, and All-Star resorts, plus the Villas of the Disney Institute, offer direct buses to all theme parks. The rub is that guests sometimes must walk a long way to catch a bus that makes numerous stops en route to the parks. Morning riders may have to stand. Evening riders may be put on indirect routes that add many minutes to the commute.

Since Disney Village Hotel Plaza terminated its contract with Disney Transportation Operations and hired another carrier, shuttle service has become a problem for guests. Before booking a plaza hotel, check the nature and frequency of its shuttle.

• Walt Disney World Bus Service •

Buses in the Disney World system have illuminated panels above the front windshield that flash the bus's destination. At theme parks, waiting areas are labeled by destination. At resorts, go to any bus stop and wait for the bus with your destination displayed.

Service from resorts to theme parks is fairly direct. You may have intermediate stops, but you won't have to transfer. Service to swimming parks, Disney Village Marketplace, Pleasure Island, and other Disney hotels may require transfers.

Buses to parks run about every 20 minutes, beginning about 7 a.m. on days when the parks' opening is 9 a.m. Buses to Disney-MGM or EPCOT go to the park entrance. Until one hour before the park opens, buses to the Magic Kingdom deliver early riders to the TTC, where they must transfer. Buses go directly to the park on early-entry mornings.

If you're commuting to an early-entry theme park, count on its opening to eligible guests an hour to an hour and a half before the official time. Buses to the early-entry park begin running about two hours before opening.

For your return bus in the evening, leave the park 40 minutes to an hour before closing. If you get caught in the exodus, don't worry. Buses, boats, and monorails operate for two hours after parks close.

• Walt Disney World Monorail Service •

Picture the monorail system as three loops. Loop A is an express route running counterclockwise that connects the Magic Kingdom with the TTC. Loop B runs clockwise alongside Loop A, making all stops, with service to (in this order) the TTC, Polynesian Resort, Grand Floridian Resort, Magic Kingdom, and Contemporary Resort. The long Loop C dips southeast, connecting the TTC with EPCOT. Hub for all loops is the TTC, where you usually park when visiting the Magic Kingdom.

Monorail service to Magic Kingdom resorts usually starts two hours before official opening time on early-entry days and an hour and a half before opening on other days. If you're staying at a Magic Kingdom resort and want to be among the first in the Magic Kingdom on a non-early-entry morning when the official opening is 9 a.m., board the monorail at the times indicated below. On an early-entry morning (when the opening is 9 a.m.), go 45–60 minutes earlier. If the official opening is 8 a.m., bounce everything up another hour.

From Contemporary Resort	7:45–8 a.m.
From Polynesian Resort	7:50–8:05 a.m.
From Grand Floridian	8:00–8:10 a.m.

If you're a day guest (no early-entry privileges), you'll be allowed on the monorail at the TTC between 8:15 and 8:30 a.m. when the official opening is 9 a.m. If you want to board earlier, take the walkway from the TTC to the Polynesian Resort and board there.

The monorail loop connecting EPCOT with the TTC opens at 7:30 a.m. when EPCOT's official opening is 9 a.m. To be at EPCOT when the park opens, catch the EPCOT monorail at the TTC no later than 8:05 a.m.

You can't go directly from the Magic Kingdom to EPCOT. You must catch the express monorail (Loop A) to the TTC and transfer to Loop C. If lines are short, the trip takes 25–35 minutes. In late afternoon, the wait to board Loop A may be a half hour or more. The total commute then is 45–55 minutes.

Monorails usually run two hours after closing. If the monorail is too crowded or has quit running for the day, catch a bus.

If you want to ride in the front with the conductor, all you have to do is ask.

7

Bare Necessities

• Credit Cards and Money •

Credit Cards

- MasterCard, VISA, and American Express are accepted for theme-park admission.
- No credit cards are accepted in parks' fast-food restaurants.
- Disney shops, sit-down restaurants, and resorts accept only MasterCard, VISA, and American Express credit cards.

Financial Matters

Cash Branches of Sun Bank are on Main Street in the Magic Kingdom and at 1675 Buena Vista Drive. Service at EPCOT and Disney-MGM is limited to an automatic teller machine.

A License to Print Money

One of Disney's more sublime ploys for separating you from your money is the printing and issuing of Disney Dollars. Available in denominations of $1 (Mickey Moolah), $5 (Goofy Greenbacks), and $10 (Minnie Money), the colorful cash can be used for purchases at Disney World, Disneyland, and Disney Stores nationwide. Disney Dollars also can be exchanged one-for-one for U.S. currency. Disney money is available all over Disney World.

Unspent dollars usually end up in a drawer, which is what Disney accountants hoped would happen.

• Problems and Unusual Situations •

Attractions Closed for Repairs

Check in advance to learn what attractions may be closed during your visit. Major attractions may be unavailable, but ticket prices will be unchanged.

Car Trouble

Security or tow-truck patrols will help if you lock the keys in your car or return to a dead battery. The nearest auto repair centers are Felix's Exxon on US 192 east of I-4 (phone (407) 396-2252) and Maingate Exxon, US 192 west of I-4 (phone (407) 396-2721). Disney security will help you contact either.

Lost and Found

If you lose or find something in the Magic Kingdom, City Hall handles it. At EPCOT, Lost and Found is in the entrance plaza. At Disney-MGM, it's at Guest Services. If you discover your loss after you've left the parks, call (407) 824-4245.

Medical Matters

If You Need a Doctor Mediclinic provides 24-hour service. Doctors are available for house calls to all hotels and campgrounds (Disney and non-Disney). Cost is $98 per visit, more after 10 p.m. Or you can go (no appointments) to the clinic, 2901 Parkway Boulevard, Suite 3-A, in Kissimmee. Minimum charge is $65. Hours are 9 a.m. to 9 p.m. every day. Call Mediclinic at (407) 396-1195.

Also available is the Buena Vista Walk-In Clinic on FL 535 North near the entrance to Walt Disney World Village. Patients are seen on a walk-in basis only between 8 a.m. to 8 p.m. daily. Call (407) 828-3434 for fees or details.

Prescription Medicine The closest pharmacy is in Goodings Supermarket on FL 535 in Lake Buena Vista (phone (407) 827-1200). For $5 extra, Turner Drugs (phone (407) 828-8125) will deliver to your hotel. The fee is charged to your hotel account.

Rain

Weather bad? Go to the parks anyway. Crowds are lighter, and most attractions are covered. Showers, especially during warmer months, are short.

Rain gear is a bargain. Ponchos cost less than $5; umbrellas, about $9.50.

• Services and Shopping •

Cameras and Film

Camera Centers at the parks sell disposable cameras (about $9; $16 with flash) and rent full-size VHS Sharp video camcorders at $25 per day with a $300 refundable deposit. Credit cards are accepted for the deposit; picture I.D. is required. Gear can be rented at one center, returned at another.

Film is widely available. Developing is provided by most Disney hotel gift shops and the Camera Centers. Outlets displaying the Photo Express sign offer two-hour developing. Express centers at EPCOT and the Studios often run late.

Disney Souvenirs

The greatest variety and best deals in Disney souvenirs are at World of Disney, a 40,000-square-foot character superstore at Disney Village Marketplace. Less crowded than shops in the theme parks, it's accessible by bus or boat.

There are stuffed toys of Disney characters, Disney books and records, character hats, and items that are hard if not impossible to find outside Disney shops.

T-shirts, the most popular souvenir, are sold areawide. Those in Disney World are expensive ($15–37) but high-quality, 100 percent cotton. Shirts outside the World ($7–18) usually are of lower quality, 50/50 cotton and polyester.

The only retailer selling discounted items *from* Walt Disney World is Character Warehouse (phone (407) 345-5285) in Mall Two of the Belz Factory Outlet World at the north end of International Drive. Prices are good, but selection generally is limited to closeouts. Hours are 10 a.m. to 9 p.m. Monday through Saturday and 10 a.m. to 6 p.m. Sunday.

A good selection of cotton/poly shirts and other character merchandise is available at Bargain World (phone (407) 345-8772) at 6454 International Drive, 8520 International Drive, and 5781 and 7586 US 192.

Pet Care

Pets aren't allowed in the major or minor theme parks. But *never* leave an animal in a hot car while you tour; the pet will die. Kennels and holding facilities are provided near the TTC, left of the EPCOT entrance plaza, left of the Disney-MGM entrance plaza, and at Fort Wilderness Campground. Small pets (mice, hamsters, birds) must have escape-proof cages.

Kennels open one hour before the park and close one hour after. They're staffed 24 hours a day. Disney resort guests may board a pet for $9 per pet per night. Other guests are charged $11 per pet per night. Day care for all is $6. Multiday boarding isn't available. Owners must feed and exercise their pets.

Excuse Me, But Where Can I Find . . .

Someplace to Put These Packages? Lockers are on the ground floor of the Main Street railroad station in the Magic Kingdom, right of Spaceship Earth in EPCOT, right of the Disney-MGM entrance at Oscar's Super Service, and on the east and west ends of the TTC.

Package Pick-up is available at all theme parks. Ask the salesperson to send your purchases to Package Pick-up. When you leave the park, they'll be waiting for you. EPCOT has two exits and two Package Pick-ups—specify which you want.

A Mixed Drink or Beer? Alcoholic beverages aren't sold in the Magic Kingdom. They're available at other parks and resorts.

A Grocery Store? Stock up on snacks at Goodings Supermarket in Crossroads Shopping Center on FL 535. The entrance is across FL 535 from the entrance to Disney Village Marketplace and Village Hotels.

Suntan Lotion? This and other sundries are sold in the Emporium on Main Street in the Magic Kingdom, in most shops at

Disney-MGM, and in many shops in EPCOT's Future World and World Showcase.

A Smoke? Cigarettes are sold throughout the theme parks, but smoking is prohibited in all attractions, waiting areas, and shops.

Feminine Hygiene Products? They're available in women's rest rooms throughout Disney World.

Dining In and Around Walt Disney World

Dining outside Walt Disney World

If your visit to Disney World is short, eating at the parks or your hotel will save time. Sit-down meals anywhere will gobble hours you could spend touring. The shorter your time, the more you'll save by eating fast foods.

When we're researching the *Unofficial Guide,* we eat few meals outside of Disney World. Because you might like to try the local scene, we asked Scott Joseph, wine and food critic of the *Orlando Sentinel,* to recommend restaurants.

Where to Eat Outside Walt Disney World

American

Cafe Tu Tu Tango; 8625 International Drive, Orlando; inexpensive to moderate; (407) 248-2222.

Chatham's Place; 7575 Dr. Phillips Boulevard, Orlando; moderate to expensive; (407) 345-2992.

Manuel's on the 28th; 390 N. Orange Avenue, Orlando; expensive; (407) 246-6580.

Pebbles; 12551 FL 535, Crossroads Shopping Center, Lake Buena Vista; moderate to expensive; (407) 827-1111.

Where to Eat Outside Walt Disney World *(continued)*

American *(continued)*

Sam Snead's Tavern; 2461 S. Hiawassee Road, Orlando; inexpensive to moderate; (407) 295-9999.

Wild Jack's; 7364 International Drive, Orlando; moderate; (407) 352-4407.

Beef

Butcher Shop Steakhouse; 8445 International Drive, Mercado Mediterranean Village, Orlando; moderate; (407) 363-9727.

Charlie's Steak House; 6107 S. Orange Blossom Trail, Orlando; moderate; (407) 851-7130.

Chinese

Ming Court; 9188 International Drive, Orlando; expensive; (407) 351-9988.

Cuban

Numero Uno; 2499 S. Orange Avenue, Orlando; inexpensive; (407) 841-3840.

French

Le Coq Au Vin; 4800 S. Orange Avenue, Orlando; moderate; (407) 851-6980.

Le Provence; 50 E. Pine Street, Orlando; moderate; (407) 843-1320.

German

Old Munich; 5731 S. Orange Blossom Trail, Orlando; moderate; (407) 438-8997.

Indian

Passage to India; 5532 International Drive, Orlando; moderate; (407) 351-3456.

Where to Eat Outside Walt Disney World *(continued)*

Italian

Capriccio; 9801 International Drive, Orlando;
  moderate to expensive; (407) 345-4450.

Rosario's; 4838 W. Irlo Bronson, Kissimmee; moderate;
  (407) 396-2204.

Tarantino's; 917 N. Bermuda Avenue, Kissimmee;
  inexpensive to moderate; (407) 870-2622.

Middle Eastern

Aladdin's Cafe; 1015 E. Semoran Boulevard, Casselberry;
  moderate; (407) 331-0488.

Seafood

Hemingway's; 1 Grand Cypress Boulevard, Hyatt Regency
  Grand Cypress, Orlando; expensive; (407) 239-1234.

Thai

Siam Orchid; 7575 Republic Drive, Orlando;
  moderate to expensive; (407) 351-0821.

Dining in Walt Disney World

More than five dozen full-service restaurants operate in Disney World, including 20 inside the theme parks. Collectively, they offer exceptional variety. Most are expensive and many serve less-than-distinguished fare, but the scene is improving. Good deals can be found, and there are ethnic delights rare outside of America's largest cities.

• Fast Food in the Theme Parks •

This chapter deals primarily with full-service restaurants in the theme parks and hotels. Fast-food eateries are described in sections on the theme parks. To help you compare, however, we've compiled a quick-reference list on this page (tax is included).

• Tips for Saving Money on Food •

If you want to eat at full-service restaurants, do it at lunch. Menus are largely the same, but the prices are lower. Money-saving early-bird meals are offered at some restaurants. The special includes choice of soup or salad, entree, and dessert and is served between 4:30 and 6 p.m.

What Will Fast Food Cost?	
Soft drinks, iced tea, lemonade: small, $1.55; large, $1.85	
Coffee: small, $1; large, $1.20	Salads: $3.50–6
Potato chips: 80¢	Popcorn: $1.75
Sandwiches: $3.50–6	Bottled water: $2
Ice cream: $1.50–2	Fries: $1.30

• Reservations •

When you call to make dinner reservations, the reservationist may assign you "priority seating." This means only that you'll be seated ahead of walk-ins. It doesn't mean a table has been held for you. You're likely to wait (sometimes up to an hour) to be seated. Customers don't like this, but restaurants do. They run closer to capacity under this policy.

If you can, call (407) 939-3463 well before you leave home and try to make a reservation for the restaurant(s) of your choice. If "priority seating" is mentioned, plan to dine where reservations are taken or to go early or late to your first-choice eatery.

Disney resort guests may obtain priority seating/reservations by dialing 55 or 56 from their room one to three days in advance. Day guests may make reservations at the park on the day of the meal or at the door of the restaurant, starting when the park opens.

EPCOT has a priority seating/reservations service at Guest Services, left of the geodesic dome. Because the park is large, it's convenient to sign up here and avoid making a special trip to the desired restaurant. At Disney-MGM, a priority seating/reservations desk is on the corner of Hollywood and Sunset boulevards. Magic Kingdom restaurants don't have a central reservations service.

• Theme-Park Restaurants •

Getting into a theme-park restaurant depends on its popularity and seating capacity and the crowd in the park when you visit. Each restaurant serves lunch from 11 a.m. to 4 p.m. and dinner from 4 p.m. until one hour before the park closes.

• Dress •

Informal dress is acceptable at all theme-park restaurants. Hotel restaurants tolerate shorts and T-shirts, but you'd feel more comfortable dressed up a bit. Only Victoria & Albert's at the Grand Floridian requests jackets for men.

• A Few Caveats •

1. However creative and enticing the menu descriptions, avoid fancy food. Order dishes the kitchen's unlikely to botch.
2. Don't order baked, broiled, poached, or grilled seafood unless the restaurant specializes in it or has at least a 3½-star rating in our restaurant profile.
3. Theme-park restaurants rush their customers. If you want to relax over your expensive meal, don't order it all at once. Order drinks. Study the menu while you sip, then order appetizers. Order your entree only after the appetizers have been served. Dawdle over coffee and dessert.

• Where the Author and Research Team Eat •

We avoid eating in the Magic Kingdom. When we have no choice, we choose simple fast food or eat a family-style character meal at the Liberty Tree Tavern.

At EPCOT, we enjoy chicken *mole* at San Angel Inn in Mexico, the buffet and draft beer at Restaurant Akershus in Norway, and many dishes at Restaurant Marrakesh in Morocco, the Biergarten in Germany, and Teppanyaki in Japan.

At Disney-MGM, we eat at the Hollywood Brown Derby or Mama Melrose's and go to the Sci-Fi or Prime Time for dessert.

The best deals in Disney World are the skillet dinners at the Wilderness Lodge's Whispering Canyon and the clambake at Cape May Cafe in the Beach Club. Chef Mickey's at the Contemporary and 1900 Park Fare at the Grand Floridian offer good character buffets. Park Fare's food is better.

We also like Kimonos (Japanese) at the Swan, Ariel's at the Beach Club, and Fulton's Crab House and the Portobello Yacht Club on Pleasure Island.

• The Full-Service Restaurants • of Walt Disney World

Star Rating The star rating represents the entire dining experience: style, service, ambiance, and presentation and quality of food. Five stars is the highest rating and indicates that the restaurant offers the best of everything. Four-star restaurants are above average, and three-star restaurants offer meals that are good, though not memorable. Two-star restaurants serve mediocre fare, and one-star restaurants are below average.

Cost We include a main dish with vegetable or side dish and a choice of soup or salad. Appetizers, desserts, drinks, and tips aren't included. Cost is rated inexpensive, moderate, or expensive.

Inexpensive	=	$14 or less per person
Moderate	=	$15–25 per person
Expensive	=	More than $25 per person

Quality Rating If you want the best food, and cost isn't an issue, look no further than the quality ratings. They're based on a scale of 0 to 100, with 100 as the best and zero (0) as the worst. The rating is based on preparation, presentation, taste, freshness, and creativity of the food served.

Value Rating If you're looking for both quality and a good deal, check the value rating. They range from A to F, as follows:

A	=	Exceptional value, a real bargain
B	=	Good value
C	=	Fair value, you get exactly what you pay for
D	=	Somewhat overpriced
F	=	Extremely overpriced

New Places

Five new restaurants will be added to Disney's culinary lineup, but they had not opened by press time. Four of the restaurants—Spoodles, The Flying Fish, The Big River Grille & Brewing Works, and ESPN Club—will be at the Boardwalk. Spoodles will be a Mediterranean-style eatery, The Flying Fish should be self explanatory, The Big River Grille will be a brewpub serving American fare, and ESPN Club will serve mainly sandwiches and appetizers.

The fifth new restaurant, Rain Forest Cafe, will open at the Disney Village. Part of a growing chain, the restaurant will emphasize environmentally correct cuisine and feature fantastic decor (a volcano that actually erupts!).

Walt Disney World Restaurants by Cuisine

Type of Restaurant	Location	Overall Rating	Price	Quality Rating	Value Rating
American					
California Grill	Contemporary	★★★★½	Moderate	96	C+
Planet Hollywood	Pleasure Island	★★★½	Moderate	87	C
Hollywood & Vine Cafeteria	Disney-MGM	★★★	Inexpensive	84	B
The Hollywood Brown Derby	Disney-MGM	★★★	Expensive	84	C
Seasons	Disney Institute	★★★	Moderate	84	B
Baskervilles	Grosvenor Resort	★★★	Moderate	82	C
Olivia's Cafe	Old Key West Resort	★★★	Moderate	81	C
Yacht Club Galley	Yacht Club	★★★	Moderate	81	C
The Garden Grill Restaurant	EPCOT	★★½	Moderate	79	C
Whispering Canyon Cafe	Wilderness Lodge	★★½	Moderate	79	B
Liberty Tree Tavern	Magic Kingdom	★★½	Mod/Exp	74	D
Boatwright's Dining Hall	Dixie Landings	★★½	Moderate	73	D
King Stefan's Banquet Hall	Magic Kingdom	★★½	Moderate	73	D
'50s Prime Time Cafe	Disney-MGM	★★	Moderate	69	D
Coral Isle Cafe	Polynesian	★★	Moderate	68	C
Grand Floridian Cafe	Grand Floridian	★★	Moderate	68	D
Gulliver's Grill at Garden Grove	Swan	★★	Expensive	67	D
Sci-Fi Dine-In Theater Restaurant	Disney-MGM	★★	Moderate	67	D
Crockett's Tavern	Fort Wilderness	★★	Moderate	66	C

Walt Disney World Restaurants by Cuisine *(continued)*

Type of Restaurant	Location	Overall Rating	Price	Quality Rating	Value Rating
Tangaroa Terrace	Polynesian	★★	Moderate	66	C
Barbecue					
Fireworks Factory	Pleasure Island	★★★½	Moderate	89	C
Buffet					
Cape May Cafe	Beach Club	★★★	Moderate	84	B
Crystal Palace	Magic Kingdom	★★½	Moderate	79	C
Chef Mickey's	Contemporary	★★	Moderate	67	C
Canadian					
Le Cellier	EPCOT	★★	Inexpensive	72	D
Chinese					
Sum Chows	Dolphin	★★★★½	Expensive	97	C
Nine Dragons Restaurant	EPCOT	★★½	Expensive	74	F
English					
Rose & Crown Dining Room	EPCOT	★★★	Moderate	83	C
French					
Chefs de France	EPCOT	★★★½	Moderate	87	C-
Bistro de Paris	EPCOT	★★★½	Expensive	86	D
Au Petit Cafe	EPCOT	★★★	Moderate	82	C
German					
Biergarten Restaurant	EPCOT	★★½	Moderate	75	C
Gourmet					
Victoria & Albert's	Grand Floridian	★★★★½	Expensive	96	D
Arthur's 27	Buena Vista Palace	★★★★	Expensive	90	C

Walt Disney World Restaurants by Cuisine *(continued)*

Type of Restaurant	Location	Overall Rating	Price	Quality Rating	Value Rating
Italian					
Portobello Yacht Club	Pleasure Island	★★★½	Expensive	88	D
Palio	Swan	★★★	Moderate	81	C
Flagler's	Grand Floridian	★★★	Moderate	79	D
Tony's Town Square Restaurant	Magic Kingdom	★★½	Moderate	78	D
L'Originale Alfredo di Roma Ristorante	EPCOT	★★½	Expensive	74	D
Mama Melrose's Ristorante Italiano	Disney-MGM	★★½	Expensive	74	D
Japanese					
Kimonos	Swan	★★★★	Moderate	90	C
Teppanyaki	EPCOT	★★★½	Expensive	85	C
Tempura Kiku	EPCOT	★★★	Moderate	83	C
Benihana— The Japanese Steakhouse	Hilton	★★½	Moderate	75	C
Mexican					
San Angel Inn Restaurant	EPCOT	★★★	Expensive	84	D
Moroccan					
Restaurant Marrakesh	EPCOT	★★★	Moderate	81	C
Norwegian					
Restaurant Akershus	EPCOT	★★★½	Moderate	89	B
Polynesian					
'Ohana	Polynesian	★★★	Moderate	79	C

Walt Disney World Restaurants by Cuisine *(continued)*

Type of Restaurant	Location	Overall Rating	Price	Quality Rating	Value Rating
Seafood					
Ariel's	Beach Club	★★★★	Expensive	91	C
Narcoossee's	Grand Floridian	★★★★	Expensive	91	D
Fireworks Factory	Pleasure Island	★★★½	Moderate	89	C
Fulton's Crab House	Pleasure Island	★★★½	Expensive	89	C
Artist Point	Wilderness Lodge	★★★½	Moderate	86	C
Cap'n Jack's Oyster Bar	Village Marketplace	★★★	Inexpensive	84	B
Coral Reef	EPCOT	★★★	Expensive	84	D
Harry's Safari Bar and Grill	Dolphin	★★★	Expensive	81	D
Bonfamille's Cafe	Port Orleans	★★★	Moderate	80	C
Captain's Tavern	Caribbean Beach	★★	Moderate	67	C
Finn's Grill	Hilton	★	Moderate	55	D
Steak					
Narcoossee's	Grand Floridian	★★★★	Expensive	91	D
Harry's Safari Bar and Grill	Dolphin	★★★	Expensive	81	D
Yachtsman Steakhouse	Yacht Club	★★★	Expensive	80	D
Concourse Steakhouse	Contemporary	★★½	Moderate	72	C-
The Outback	Buena Vista Palace	★★	Expensive	67	D
Tex-Mex					
Juan & Only's Bar and Jail	Dolphin	★★★	Moderate	80	B

The Magic Kingdom

• Early Entry •

Three days each week (usually Monday, Thursday, and Saturday) the Magic Kingdom opens an hour early to Disney World hotel and campground guests (excluding those at Walt Disney World Village Hotel Plaza). If you aren't a Disney resort guest, avoid the Magic Kingdom on those days. Crowds balloon with resort guests exercising early-entry privileges, and congestion is nearly unmanageable by 10 a.m., especially in summer or holiday periods.

If you're a Disney resort guest, arrive at the park for early entry an hour and 40 minutes before the official opening time. When you're admitted, you'll be allowed into all Fantasyland attractions except *Legend of the Lion King* and all Tomorrowland attractions except Space Mountain, Tomorrowland Transit Authority, and AstroOrbiter, which open a half hour later, and the *Carousel of Progress,* which opens at the official time.

Early-entry guests should be aboard a bus to the park two hours before official opening. Take advantage of early entry, then leave the midmorning crowding and go to another park for the remainder of the day.

The early-entry schedule changes often. Call Walt Disney World Information (phone (407) 824-4321) in advance to verify which days will be early entry during your stay. Guests seeking early entry must show their identification card (issued on check-in) when they present their admission pass.

• **Getting Oriented** •

The Magic Kingdom/Transportation and Ticket Center parking lot opens about two hours before the park's official opening. After paying a fee and parking, guests are transported to the TTC by tram. From there, they take a monorail or ferry to the park's entrance.

Guests at the Contemporary, Polynesian, or Grand Floridian resorts can commute directly to the Magic Kingdom by monorail. From Wilderness Lodge or Fort Wilderness Campground, access is by boat. Guests of other Disney resorts can reach the park by bus. All Disney guests, regardless of how they arrive, are taken directly to the park entrance, bypassing the TTC.

Stroller and wheelchair rentals are to the right of the train station; lockers (cleaned out nightly) are on the ground floor of the station. City Hall, on your left as you enter Main Street, serves as the center for information, lost and found, some reservations, and entertainment.

A guide map to the park is available at City Hall. It lists all attractions, shops, and eating places; pinpoints first aid, baby care, and assistance for the handicapped; and gives photography tips. It also lists times for special events, live entertainment, and other activities that day.

Main Street ends at a central hub, from which branch the entrances to five other sections of the Magic Kingdom: Adventureland, Frontierland, Liberty Square, Fantasyland, and Tomorrowland. Mickey's Toontown Fair is wedged between Fantasyland and Tomorrowland and doesn't connect to the central hub.

• **Starting the Tour** •

Be open-minded and adventuresome about Magic Kingdom attractions. Don't dismiss one until **after** you have tried it.

Take advantage of what Disney does best: the fantasy adventures of Splash Mountain and the Haunted Mansion, and the AudioAnimatronic (talking robots) attractions, including *Hall of Presidents* and Pirates of the Caribbean. In the descriptions of attractions which follow, we give ratings based on a scale of zero to five stars. Five stars is the best rating.

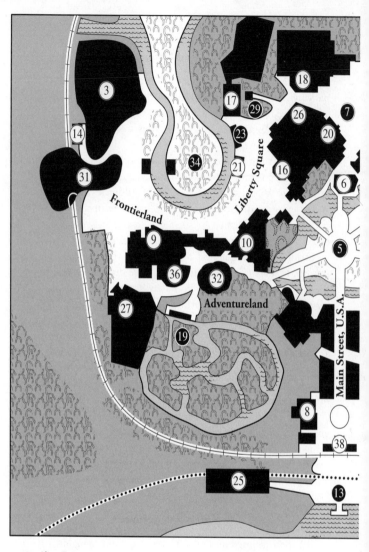

1. *Alien Encounter*
2. AstroOrbiter
3. Big Thunder Mountain Railroad
4. *Carousel of Progress*
5. Central hub
6. Cinderella Castle
7. Cinderella's Golden Carrousel
8. City Hall
9. *Country Bear Jamboree*
10. Diamond Horseshoe Saloon
11. Dreamflight
12. Dumbo, the Flying Elephant
13. Ferry dock
14. Frontierland Railroad Station
15. Grand Prix Raceway
16. *The Hall of Presidents*
17. The Haunted Mansion
18. It's a Small World
19. Jungle Cruise
20. *Legend of the Lion King*

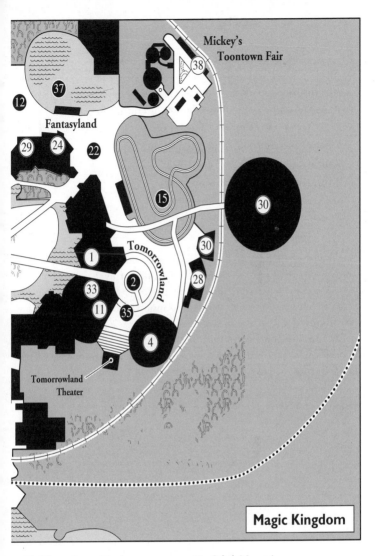

Magic Kingdom

21. Liberty Square Riverboat	31. Splash Mountain
22. Mad Tea Party	32. Swiss Faimily Treehouse
23. Mike Fink Keelboats	33. *The Timekeeper*
24. Mr. Toad's Wild Ride	34. Tom Sawyer Island
25. Monorail station	35. Tomorrowland Transit Authority
26. Peter Pan's Flight	36. *Tropical Serenade*
27. Pirates of the Caribbean	*(Enchanted Tiki Birds)*
28. Skyway	37. 20,000 Leagues Under the Sea
29. Snow White's Adventures	38. WDW Railroad Station
30. Space Mountain	

Not to Be Missed at the Magic Kingdom	
Adventureland	Pirates of the Caribbean
Frontierland	Big Thunder Mountain Railroad
	Splash Mountain
Liberty Square	The Haunted Mansion
Fantasyland	Peter Pan's Flight
Tomorrowland	Space Mountain
	The Timekeeper
Special events	Evening Parade

Don't burn daylight shopping; most of the goods are available elsewhere. Limit the time you spend on carnival-type rides; you probably have something similar near your hometown. (Don't, however, mistake Space Mountain and Big Thunder Mountain Railroad for amusement-park rides. They may be roller coasters, but they're pure Disney genius.) Similarly, eat a good breakfast early and avoid lines at eateries. Snack on vendor foods during the day.

Main Street, U.S.A.

Begin and end your Magic Kingdom visit on Main Street, which opens a half hour before and closes a half hour to an hour after the rest of the park. The Walt Disney World Railroad stops at the Main Street Station; board here for a grand tour of the park or a ride to Frontierland or Mickey's Toontown Fair.

Main Street is a re-creation of a turn-of-the-century, small-town American street. Its buildings are real. All interiors, furnishings, and fixtures are true to the period. Along the street are shops and eating places, a cinema, and a fire station. Horse-drawn trolleys, double-decker buses, fire engines, and horseless carriages transport visitors along Main Street to the central hub.

Walt Disney World Railroad

What It Is: Scenic railroad ride around theme park's perimeter; also transportation to Frontierland and Mickey's Toontown Fair

Scope & Scale: Minor attraction

When to Go: Anytime

Special Comments: Main Street is usually the least-congested station.

Author's Rating: Plenty to see; ★★½ [Ratings are based on a scale of zero to five stars. Five stars is the best rating.]

Overall Appeal by Age Group:

Pre-school	Grade School	Teens	Young Adults	Over 30	Senior Citizens
★★★★	★★★	★★½	★★★	★★★½	★★★½

Duration of Ride: About 19 minutes for a complete circuit

Avg. Wait in Line per 100 People Ahead of You: 8 minutes

Assumes: Two or more trains operating

Loading Speed: Fast

Description and Comments   A transportation ride blending sights and experiences with an energy-saving way to get around the park. The train provides glimpses of all lands except Adventureland.

Touring Tips   Save the train until after you have seen the featured attractions or need transportation. On busy days, lines form at the Frontierland Station, but rarely at Main Street and Mickey's Toontown Fair stations. Strollers aren't allowed on the train. Wheelchair access is only at Frontierland and Mickey's Toontown Fair stations.

Main Street Eateries and Shops

Description and Comments   Some of the Magic Kingdom's better food and specialty/souvenir shopping in a nostalgic, happy setting. The Emporium offers the park's best selection of Disney souvenirs.

Touring Tips   The shops are fun, but the merchandise (except for certain Disney souvenirs) is available elsewhere. If seeing the attractions is your goal, save Main Street until day's end. If you want to shop, avoid noon and near closing, when crowds are heavy.

The Crystal Palace, at the central hub end of Main Street, has a good cafeteria often overlooked by lunch (but not dinner) crowds.

Adventureland

Adventureland is the first land to the left of Main Street. It combines African safari and New Orleans/Caribbean themes.

Swiss Family Treehouse

What It Is: Outdoor walk-through treehouse

Scope & Scale: Minor attraction

When to Go: Before 11:30 a.m. and after 5 p.m.

Special Comments: Requires climbing a lot of stairs.

Author's Rating: A visual delight; ★★★

Overall Appeal by Age Group:

Pre-school	Grade School	Teens	Young Adults	Over 30	Senior Citizens
★★★★	★★★★	★★★★	★★★★	★★★★	★★★★

Duration of Tour: 10–15 minutes

Avg. Wait in Line per 100 People Ahead of You: 7 minutes

Assumes: Normal staffing

Description and Comments   A fantastic replication of the shipwrecked family's home.

Touring Tips   A self-guided tour involves many stairs but no ropes or ladders. Tourists who stop for extra-long looks or to rest may create bottlenecks. Visit in late afternoon or early evening if you're on a one-day tour schedule, or first thing on your second day.

Jungle Cruise

What It Is: Outdoor safari-theme boat ride adventure

Scope & Scale: Major attraction

When to Go: Before 10 a.m. or two hours before closing

Author's Rating: An enduring Disney masterpiece; ★★★½

Overall Appeal by Age Group:

Pre-school	Grade School	Teens	Young Adults	Over 30	Senior Citizens
★★★★½	★★★★½	★★★★	★★★★	★★★★	★★★★

Duration of Ride: 8–9 minutes

Avg. Wait in Line per 100 People Ahead of You: 3½ minutes

Assumes: 10 boats operating

Loading Speed: Moderate to fast

Description and Comments   A cruise through jungle waterways. Passengers encounter elephants, lions, hostile natives, and a menacing hippo. Boatman's spiel adds to the fun.

Touring Tips   Among the park's oldest attractions. Good staff and improved management have speeded lines up, but it's very difficult to estimate the length of wait for the Jungle Cruise. It's usually longer than it looks.

Pirates of the Caribbean

What It Is: Indoor pirate-theme adventure boat ride

Scope & Scale: Headliner

When to Go: Before noon or after 5 p.m.

Special Comments: Frightens some children.

Author's Rating: Disney AudioAnimatronics at its best. Not to be missed; ★★★★★

Overall Appeal by Age Group:

Pre-school	Grade School	Teens	Young Adults	Over 30	Senior Citizens
★★★	★★★★★	★★★★★	★★★★★	★★★★★	★★★★★

Duration of Ride: About 7½ minutes

Avg. Wait in Line per 100 People Ahead of You: 1½ minutes

Assumes: Both waiting lines operating

Loading Speed: Fast

Description and Comments   Scenes along boat's course depict a pirate raid on an island settlement, from bombardment of the fortress to debauchery after the victory.

Touring Tips   One of the park's most elaborate and imaginative attractions. Engineered to move large crowds fast, Pirates is good to see during later afternoon. It has two lines, both covered.

Tropical Serenade (Enchanted Tiki Birds)

What It Is: Audio-animatronic Pacific Island musical theater show

Scope & Scale: Minor attraction

When to Go: Before 11 a.m. and after 3:30 p.m.

Author's Rating: Very, very unusual; ★★½

Overall Appeal by Age Group:

Pre-school	Grade School	Teens	Young Adults	Over 30	Senior Citizens
★★½	★★★	★★	★★★	★★★	★★★

Duration of Presentation: 15½ minutes

Preshow Entertainment: Talking birds

Probable Waiting Time: 15 minutes

Description and Comments   Sit-down theater where more than 200 robotic birds, flowers, and Tiki-god statues sing and whistle through a musical program.

Touring Tips   Usually not too crowded. Go in late afternoon; you'll appreciate the break in air-conditioning.

Adventureland Eateries and Shops

Description and Comments   Plentiful specialty shopping. Restaurants less crowded during lunch than elsewhere in the park.

Touring Tips   El Pirata y El Perico, serving Mexican fast food and hot dogs, is often overlooked.

Frontierland

Frontierland adjoins Adventureland as you tour clockwise. Focus is on the Old West, with stockade-type structures and pioneer trappings.

Splash Mountain

What It Is: Indoor/outdoor water-flume adventure boat ride
Scope & Scale: Super headliner
When to Go: At park opening time or just before closing
Special Comments: Children must be 3' 8" tall; younger than 7 years must ride with an adult. Switching-off option provided (see page 58).
Author's Rating: A wet winner. Not to be missed; ★★★★★
Overall Appeal by Age Group:

Pre-school	Grade School	Teens	Young Adults	Over 30	Senior Citizens
†	★★★★★	★★★★★	★★★★★	★★★★★	★★★½

† Many preschoolers are too short to ride; others are intimidated by watching from the waiting line. Those who ride generally give high marks (3–5 stars).

Duration of Ride: About 10 minutes
Avg. Wait in Line per 100 People Ahead of You: 3½ minutes
Assumes: Operation at full capacity
Loading Speed: Moderate

Description and Comments   Amusement-park flume ride, Disney-style. Highly imaginative. Combines steep chutes with excellent special effects. Covers more than half a mile, splashing through swamps, caves, and backwoods bayous before climaxing in a five-story plunge and Brer Rabbit's triumphant return home.

More than 100 audio-animatronic characters regale riders with songs, including "Zip-a-Dee-Doo-Dah."

Touring Tips   This happy, exciting, and adventuresome ride vies with Space Mountain as the park's most popular ride. Even as the park opens, hundreds are poised to rush to Splash Mountain. Crowds build fast in the morning, and two-hour waits can be expected once the park fills. Get in line first thing, no later than 45 minutes after opening. If you miss Splash Mountain in the morning, lines are shorter during afternoon or evening parades, or just before the park closes.

As with Space Mountain in Tomorrowland, crowds race to Splash Mountain when the park opens. Your best strategy is to go to the end of Main Street and turn left to the Crystal Palace. In front of the restaurant is a bridge that provides a shortcut to Adventureland. Stand at the barrier rope, and be ready to sprint or walk fast when the rope drops. Cross the bridge to Adventureland, bear right, and keep truckin' to Frontierland.

At Splash Mountain, if you ride in the front seat, you will almost certainly get wet. Riders elsewhere get splashed. Since you don't know what seat you'll be assigned, be prepared. On a cool day, carry a plastic garbage bag. Tear holes in the bottom and sides to make a water-resistant sack dress. Tuck the bag in under your bottom. Leave your camera with a nonriding member of your group or wrap it in plastic.

The scariest part of this ride is the steep chute you see when standing in line, but the drop looks worse than it is. Despite reassurances, however, many children wig out after watching it. One reader's kids tried to hold their breath throughout the ride, thinking they would be going underwater.

Big Thunder Mountain Railroad

What It Is: Tame, western-mining-themed roller coaster

Scope & Scale: Headliner

When to Go: Before 10 a.m., during parades, or in the hour before closing

Special Comments: Children must be 3' 4" tall; younger than 7 must ride with an adult. Switching-off option provided (see page 58).

Author's Rating: Great effects, relatively tame ride.
   Not to be missed; ★★★★

Overall Appeal by Age Group:

Pre-school	Grade School	Teens	Young Adults	Over 30	Senior Citizens
★★★	★★★★	★★★★	★★★★	★★★★	★★★

Duration of Ride: Almost 3½ minutes

Avg. Wait in Line per 100 People Ahead of You: 2½ minutes

Assumes: 5 trains operating

Loading Speed: Moderate to fast

Description and Comments   Roller coaster through and around a "mountain." Idea is that you're on a runaway mine train during Gold Rush. Roller coaster is about 5 on a "scary scale" of 10. First-rate examples of Disney creativity are showcased: realistic mining town, falling rocks, and earthquake. People who don't like roller coasters and some seniors and preschoolers won't enjoy this ride.

Touring Tips   Emphasis is on the sights instead of the roller-coaster thrill.

   The opening of nearby Splash Mountain in 1992 forever changed traffic flow to Big Thunder Mountain Railroad. Adventuresome guests ride Splash Mountain first, then go next door to Big Thunder. This means larger crowds in Frontierland all day and longer waits for Big Thunder Mountain. The best way to experience Magic Kingdom "mountains" is to ride Space Mountain when the park opens, Big Thunder Mountain immediately afterward, then Splash Mountain.

Country Bear Jamboree

What It Is: Audio-animatronic country hoedown theater show

Scope & Scale: Major attraction

When to Go: Before 11:30 a.m. and during the two hours
   before closing

Special Comments: Shows change at Christmas and during
   summer.

Author's Rating: A Disney classic; ★★★

Overall Appeal by Age Group:

Pre-school	Grade School	Teens	Young Adults	Over 30	Senior Citizens
★★★★	★★★★	★★★	★★★½	★★★★	★★★★

Duration of Presentation: 15 minutes

Preshow Entertainment: None

Probable Waiting Time: This attraction is very popular but has a relatively small capacity. Waiting time on a busy day between noon and 5:30 p.m. averages 30–50 minutes.

Description and Comments   A cast of charming robotic bears sing and stomp through a western-style hoedown. Repeat visitors find that the humorous and upbeat show hasn't been revised for many moons; some are disappointed.

Touring Tips   The *Jamboree* is very popular and draws large crowds even early in the day. Go before 11:30 a.m. or right before a parade.

Tom Sawyer Island and Fort Sam Clemens

What It Is: Outdoor walk-through exhibit/rustic playground

Scope & Scale: Minor attraction

When to Go: Midmorning through late afternoon

Special Comments: Closes at dusk.

Author's Rating: The place for rambunctious kids; ★★★

Overall Appeal by Age Group:

Pre-school	Grade School	Teens	Young Adults	Over 30	Senior Citizens
★★★★★	★★★★★	★★★½	★★★	★★★	★★★

Description and Comments   Tom Sawyer Island is a getaway within the park, with hills, cave, windmill, tipsy barrel bridge, and paths to explore. It delights and relaxes adults while providing harmless freedom for children. There's even a "secret" escape tunnel.

Touring Tips   Tom Sawyer Island isn't a top attraction, but it's one of the park's better-conceived. Attention to detail is excellent. It's a must for families with children ages 5 through 15. If your group is adults, visit on your second day or stop by on your first after you've seen the attractions you most wanted to see.

Go between noon and dusk, when the island closes. Although kids could spend a whole day there, plan at least 20 minutes. Access is by raft from Frontierland; two operate simultaneously, and the trip is efficient. Despite its limited menu, our favorite Magic Kingdom restaurant for lunch is Aunt Polly's Landing, on Tom Sawyer Island.

Davy Crockett's Explorer Canoes

What It Is: Outdoor scenic canoe ride

Scope & Scale: Minor attraction

When to Go: Before noon or after 5 p.m.

Special Comments: Skip it if the lines are long; closes at dusk.

Author's Rating: The most fun way to see Rivers of America;
★★★

Overall Appeal by Age Group:

Pre-school	Grade School	Teens	Young Adults	Over 30	Senior Citizens
★★★★	★★★★	★★★★	★★★★	★★★★	★★★★

Duration of Ride: 9–15 minutes, depending on how fast you paddle

Avg. Wait in Line per 100 People Ahead of You: 28 minutes

Assumes: 3 canoes operating

Loading Speed: Slow

Description and Comments   Paddle-yourself ride around Tom Sawyer Island and Fort Sam Clemens on the same route as the Liberty Square Riverboat and Mike Fink Keelboats. Canoes operate only during peak months.

Touring Tips   The canoes are one of three ways to see the same territory. Because canoes and keelboats are slower in loading, we usually ride the riverboat. Walk around Tom Sawyer Island and Fort Sam Clemens for a different view of the same sights.

Diamond Horseshoe Saloon Revue

What It Is: Live western song and dance show

Scope & Scale: Minor attraction

When to Go: Check the daily entertainment schedule

Special Comments: No Disney characters in this show

Author's Rating: Fast-paced and funny; ★★★

Overall Appeal by Age Group:

Pre-school	Grade School	Teens	Young Adults	Over 30	Senior Citizens
★★	★★★	★★	★★★	★★★	★★★

Duration of Show: About 40 minutes

Avg. Wait in Line per 100 People Ahead of You: No wait

Description and Comments   The *Diamond Horseshoe Revue* is a PG-rated cattle town saloon show, with comedy, song, and can-can dancing. Audience members are conscripted to join the cast.

Touring Tips   Reservations aren't required; walk in and have a seat. If you don't want to be in the show, sit upstairs. Cold sandwiches, chips, cookies, and soft drinks are sold at the bar. Lunch crowds overlook the Diamond Horseshoe, especially between shows. The best times to see the show are over lunch and after the afternoon parade.

Frontierland Eateries and Shops

Description and Comments   Coonskin caps and western-theme shopping. Fast-food eateries usually are very crowded between 11:30 a.m. and 2 p.m. An exception is the relaxing Aunt Polly's Landing outdoors on Tom Sawyer Island. We recommend it for lunch, though fare is limited to cold fried chicken served with potato salad and a biscuit, and ham-and-cheese and peanut butter sandwiches. Prices are reasonable, the river view fine.

Touring Tips   Don't waste time shopping unless that's what you came for. Skip Aunt Polly's if the wait to board the raft is long.

Liberty Square

Liberty Square re-creates colonial America at the time of the American Revolution. Architecture is federal or colonial. A real 130-year-old live oak (dubbed the "Liberty Tree") lends dignity and grace to the setting.

The Hall of Presidents

What It Is: Audio-animatronic historical theater presentation

Scope & Scale: Major attraction

When to Go: Anytime

Author's Rating: Impressive and moving; ★★★

Overall Appeal by Age Group:

Pre-school	Grade School	Teens	Young Adults	Over 30	Senior Citizens
★	★★½	★★★	★★★½	★★★★	★★★★

Duration of Presentation: Almost 23 minutes

Preshow Entertainment: None

Probable Waiting Time: Lines look awesome but usually are swallowed up when the show in progress lets out. Even during busiest times, waits rarely exceed 40 minutes.

Description and Comments A 20-minute, strongly inspirational and patriotic program highlights milestones in American history. The performance climaxes with a roll call of presidents, with words of encouragement from Presidents Lincoln and Clinton. A very moving show coupled with one of Disney's best and most ambitious robotic efforts. The production was updated in 1994. Narration is by Maya Angelou.

Touring Tips Detail and costumes are masterful. If your children fidget during the show, notice that the presidents do, too. The attraction is one of the park's most popular, especially among seniors, drawing large crowds between 11 a.m. and about 5 p.m. Don't be put off by lines; the theater holds more than 700 people. On less busy days, you'll probably have no wait to enter the lobby.

Liberty Square Riverboat

What It Is: Outdoor scenic boat ride

Scope & Scale: Major attraction

When to Go: Anytime

Author's Rating: Slow, relaxing, and scenic; ★★½

Overall Appeal by Age Group:

Pre-school	Grade School	Teens	Young Adults	Over 30	Senior Citizens
★★★	★★★	★★½	★★★	★★★	★★★

Duration of Ride: About 16 minutes

Average Wait to Board: 10–14 minutes

Assumes: Normal operations

Description and Comments   Large-capacity paddle wheeler that cruises around Tom Sawyer Island and Fort Sam Clemens. This beautiful riverboat provides a lofty perspective of Frontierland and Liberty Square.

Touring Tips   One of three boat rides on the same waters. Davy Crockett's Explorer Canoes and the Mike Fink Keelboats are slower in loading; ride the riverboat.

The Haunted Mansion

What It Is: Big, friendly spookhouse

Scope & Scale: Major attraction

When to Go: Before 11:30 a.m. or after 8 p.m.

Special Comments: Frightens some very young children.

Author's Rating: Some of Disney World's best special effects. Not to be missed; ★★★★

Overall Appeal by Age Group:

Pre-school	Grade School	Teens	Young Adults	Over 30	Senior Citizens
Varies	★★★★★	★★★★½	★★★★½	★★★★½	★★★★½

Duration of Ride: 7-minute ride plus a 1½-minute preshow

Avg. Wait in Line per 100 People Ahead of You: 2½ minutes

Assumes: Both "stretch rooms" operating

Loading Speed: Fast

Description and Comments Fun more than scary. Disney's description sums it up: "Come face to face with 999 happy ghosts, ghouls, and goblins in a 'frightfully funny' adventure." Some children become anxious about what they think they'll see. Almost nobody is scared by the actual sights.

Touring Tips Lines ebb and flow more than at other Magic Kingdom high spots because the mansion is near *The Hall of Presidents* and Liberty Square Riverboat. Those attractions disgorge 750 and 450 people, respectively, when each show or ride ends, and many of those folks head straight for the mansion. Slip in between crowds.

Mike Fink Keelboats

What It Is: Outdoor scenic boat ride

Scope & Scale: Minor attraction

When to Go: Before 11:30 a.m. or after 5 p.m.

Special Comments: Don't ride if the lines are long; closes at dusk.

Author's Rating: ★★

Overall Appeal by Age Group:

Pre-school	Grade School	Teens	Young Adults	Over 30	Senior Citizens
★★★½	★★★	★★★	★★★	★★★	★★★

Duration of Ride: 9½ minutes

Avg. Wait in Line per 100 People Ahead of You: 15 minutes

Assumes: 2 boats operating

Loading Speed: Slow

Description and Comments Small keelboats that circle Tom Sawyer Island and Fort Sam Clemens on the same route as Davy Crockett's Explorer Canoes and the Liberty Square Riverboat. The riverboat is fastest. Keelboat's top deck is exposed to the elements.

Liberty Square Eateries and Shops

Description and Comments   American crafts and souvenirs in shops. One restaurant, the Liberty Tree Tavern; it's often overlooked by lunch crowds.

Touring Tips   Liberty Tree Tavern now offers character meals with a fixed menu served family style. Characters aside, the meal may be the Magic Kingdom's best. Reservations are required.

Fantasyland

Fantasyland is the heart of the Magic Kingdom, an enchanting place spread gracefully like a miniature alpine village beneath the lofty towers of Cinderella Castle.

It's a Small World

What It Is: Indoor boat ride with world brotherhood theme

Scope & Scale: Major attraction

When to Go: Anytime

Author's Rating: Exponentially "cute"; ★★★

Overall Appeal by Age Group:

Pre-school	Grade School	Teens	Young Adults	Over 30	Senior Citizens
★★★★	★★★½	★★½	★★★	★★★	★★★½

Duration of Ride: About 11 minutes

Avg. Wait in Line per 100 People Ahead of You: 1¾ minutes

Assumes: Busy conditions with 30 or more boats operating

Loading Speed: Fast

Description and Comments Happy, upbeat attraction with a catchy tune you won't soon forget. Small boats carry visitors on a tour around the world, with singing and dancing dolls show-casing dress and culture of each nation. Almost everyone enjoys It's a Small World, but it stands, with *Enchanted Tiki Birds,* as an attraction that some could take or leave, while others consider it a masterpiece.

Touring Tips Cool off here during the heat of the day. Lines are shortest between 11 a.m. and 5 p.m.

Skyway to Tomorrowland

What It Is: Scenic transportation to Tomorrowland
Scope & Scale: Minor attraction
When to Go: Before noon or during special events
Special Comments: If there's a line, it will be quicker to walk.
Author's Rating: Nice view; ★★½
Overall Appeal by Age Group:

Pre-school	Grade School	Teens	Young Adults	Over 30	Senior Citizens
★★★★	★★★★	★★★½	★★★½	★★★½	★★★½

Duration of Ride: About 5 minutes one way
Avg. Wait in Line per 100 People Ahead of You: 10 minutes
Assumes: 45 or more cars operating
Loading Speed: Moderate to slow

Description and Comments Part of the Magic Kingdom internal transportation system, the Skyway is a chairlift connecting to Tomorrowland. The view is great.

Touring Tips We take this scenic trip in the morning, during afternoon or evening parades, or just before closing (ride opens later and closes earlier than others in Fantasyland), when crowds are light and views dramatic. Strollers aren't accommodated.

Peter Pan's Flight

What It Is: Indoor fantasy adventure
Scope & Scale: Minor attraction
When to Go: Before 10 a.m. or after 6 p.m.
Author's Rating: Happy, mellow, and well done. Not to be missed; ★★★★
Overall Appeal by Age Group:

Pre-school	Grade School	Teens	Young Adults	Over 30	Senior Citizens
★★★★	★★★★	★★★½	★★★★	★★★★	★★★★

Duration of Ride: A little over 3 minutes
Avg. Wait in Line per 100 People Ahead of You: 5½ minutes
Assumes: Normal operation
Loading Speed: Moderate to slow

Description and Comments   Peter Pan's Flight is superbly designed and absolutely delightful, with a happy theme uniting unforgettable Disney characters, beautiful effects, and charming music. Some consider it the best among three similar rides (Peter Pan, Snow White, and Mr. Toad).

Touring Tips   Lines are long all day. Try before 10 a.m., during a parade, or just before the park closes.

Legend of the Lion King

What It Is: Live mixed-media and puppet theater show

Scope & Scale: Major attraction

When to Go: Before 11 a.m. and during parades

Special Comments: The most recent addition to Fantasyland

Author's Rating: Uplifting and fun; ★★★

Overall Appeal by Age Group:

Pre-school	Grade School	Teens	Young Adults	Over 30	Senior Citizens
★★★★	★★★★	★★★½	★★★★	★★★★	★★★★

Duration of Presentation: About 16 minutes

Preshow Entertainment: 7-minute preshow

Probable Waiting Time: 12 minutes

Description and Comments   An example of Disney's integrated marketing strategy, the attraction stimulates demand for *The Lion King* movie and video. It's a close cousin to *Voyage of the Little Mermaid* at the Disney-MGM Studios. The story is poignant and engaging, with some dark moments, ending on a happy and triumphant note. Imaginative puppetry, animation, and special effects create an effective collage.

Touring Tips   Popularity of *Legend of the Lion King* has grown; so have lines. Budget a 40-minute wait, and go about 10 a.m. or during parades or other live events. The theater holds about 500 people, swallowing most of the line each time one show ends and another begins.

Cinderella's Golden Carrousel

What It Is: Merry-go-round

Scope & Scale: Minor attraction

When to Go: Before 11 a.m. or after 8 p.m.

Special Comments: Adults enjoy the beauty and nostalgia of this ride.

Author's Rating: A beautiful children's ride; ★★½

Overall Appeal by Age Group:

Pre-school	Grade School	Teens	Young Adults	Over 30	Senior Citizens
★★★★	★★½	★	★★½	★★★	★★★

Duration of Ride: About 2 minutes

Avg. Wait in Line per 100 People Ahead of You: 5 minutes

Assumes: Normal staffing

Loading Speed: Slow

Description and Comments One of the most elaborate and lovely merry-go-rounds anywhere, especially with the lights on.

Touring Tips Watch from the sidelines unless your group includes young children.

Mr. Toad's Wild Ride

What It Is: Disney version of a spook-house track ride

Scope & Scale: Minor attraction

When to Go: Before 11 a.m. or after 6 p.m.

Author's Rating: Just O.K.; ★★

Overall Appeal by Age Group:

Pre-school	Grade School	Teens	Young Adults	Over 30	Senior Citizens
★★★½	★★★½	★★★	★★½	★★½	★★½

Duration of Ride: About 2¼ minutes

Avg. Wait in Line per 100 People Ahead of You: 5½ minutes

Assumes: Both tracks operating

Loading Speed: Slow

Description and Comments This spook house doesn't live up to many visitors' expectations or to Disney's reputation for quality. The big facade suggests an elaborate ride, but the building is divided into halves, with similar versions of the same ride in each half. There is a separate line for each.

Touring Tips We receive a lot of mail disagreeing with our appraisal of this ride. Clearly, Mr. Toad has his advocates. If you're on a tight schedule, don't wait very long for Mr. Toad.

Ride if you allotted two days for the Magic Kingdom or want to add your opinion to the controversy. To be a supertoad, try both sides.

Snow White's Adventures

What It Is: Disney version of a spook-house track ride

Scope & Scale: Minor attraction

When to Go: Before 11 a.m. and after 6 p.m.

Special Comments: Terrifying to many young children.

Author's Rating: Worthwhile if wait isn't long; ★★★

Overall Appeal by Age Group:

Pre-school	Grade School	Teens	Young Adults	Over 30	Senior Citizens
★★★	★★★	★★½	★★★	★★★	★★★

Duration of Ride: Almost 2½ minutes

Avg. Wait in Line per 100 People Ahead of You: 6¼ minutes

Assumes: Normal operation

Loading Speed: Moderate to slow

Description and Comments   Mine cars travel through a spook house showing Snow White as she narrowly escapes harm at the hands of the wicked witch. Action and effects are a cut above Mr. Toad's Wild Ride, but not as good as Peter Pan's Flight.

Touring Tips   We get more mail about this ride than any other Disney attraction. It terrifies many kids age 6 and younger. After a 1995 upgrade of the ride, Snow White plays a greater role, but the relentless and ubiquitous witch continues to be the focal character. Many readers say their young children won't ride *any* attraction that operates in the dark after experiencing Snow White's Adventures. One mother wrote that preschoolers expect forest animals and dwarfs but get a terrifying witch—and lots of her.

Experience Snow White if lines aren't long, or on a second day at the park.

20,000 Leagues Under the Sea

What It Is: Submarine-theme adventure boat ride

Scope & Scale: Major attraction

When to Go: Before 9:30 a.m., during parades, or just before closing

Special Comments: Better if experienced after dark

Author's Rating: Not very convincing; ★★½

Overall Appeal by Age Group:

Pre-school	Grade School	Teens	Young Adults	Over 30	Senior Citizens
★★★★	★★★	★★★	★★★	★★★	★★★½

Duration of Ride: About 8½ minutes

Avg. Wait in Line per 100 People Ahead of You: 8 minutes

Assumes: 9 submarines operating

Loading Speed: Slow

Description and Comments   This attraction, based on the Disney movie of the same title, is one of several rides that are successful at both Disneyland in California and Walt Disney World. It's a submarine voyage that encounters ocean-floor farming, robotic marine life, sunken ships, squid attacks, and other adventures. The ride struggles to maintain its appeal alongside such marvels as Pirates of the Caribbean and Splash Mountain.

Touring Tips   Slow loading. Ride the first hour the park is open.

Dumbo, the Flying Elephant

What It Is: Disneyfied midway ride

Scope & Scale: Minor attraction

When to Go: Before 10 a.m. and after 9 p.m.

Author's Rating: An attractive children's ride; ★★★

Overall Appeal by Age Group:

Pre-school	Grade School	Teens	Young Adults	Over 30	Senior Citizens
★★★★★	★★★★	★★	★½	★½	★½

Duration of Ride: 1½ minutes

Avg. Wait in Line per 100 People Ahead of You: 20 minutes

Assumes: Normal staffing

Loading Speed: Slow

Description and Comments   Tame, happy children's ride based on the lovable flying elephant. Despite being little different from rides at state fairs and amusement parks, Dumbo is the favorite Magic Kingdom attraction of many younger children. They'll wait patiently for more than an hour to take the 1½ minute ride.

Touring Tips   Bypass this slow-loading ride unless you're on a very relaxed schedule.

Mad Tea Party

What It Is: Midway-type spinning ride

Scope & Scale: Minor attraction

When to Go: Before 11 a.m. and after 5 p.m.

Special Comments: Make your teacup spin faster by turning the wheel in the center.

Author's Rating: Fun, but not worth the wait; ★★

Overall Appeal by Age Group:

Pre-school	Grade School	Teens	Young Adults	Over 30	Senior Citizens
★★★★	★★★★	★★★★	★★★	★★	★★

Duration of Ride: 1½ minutes

Avg. Wait in Line per 100 People Ahead of You: 7½ minutes

Assumes: Normal staffing

Loading Speed: Slow

Description and Comments   Riders whirl feverishly in big teacups. Teenagers like to lure adults onto the teacups, then turn the wheel in the middle, making the cups spin faster, until the adults are on the verge of throwing up.

Touring Tips   This ride, well-done but not unique, is notoriously slow in loading. Skip it on a busy schedule—if the kids will let you. Ride the morning of your second day if your schedule is more relaxed.

Fantasyland Eateries and Shops

Description and Comments   Many Magic Kingdom visitors want to know, "What's in the Cinderella Castle?" The answer is: You can't see it all, but you can inspect a fair-sized chunk if you eat at King Stefan's Banquet Hall. The atmosphere is fine, but except for breakfast, we haven't had the best food at King Stefan's. If your kids *really* want to see the castle, make reservations at King Stefan's and order dessert only.

You don't have to eat at King Stefan's to see Cinderella, who greets diners in the waiting area of the restaurant. Enter through the left door by the hostess stand. She can tell you when Cinderella will appear.

Fantasyland shops offer abundant specialty and souvenir shopping. Mickey's Christmas Carol sells exceptional Christmas decorations.

Touring Tips   We don't recommend King Stefan's if you're in a hurry or mind paying fancy prices for ho-hum food.

Other Fantasyland lunch options include Lumière's Kitchen (parents can get special lunches for children) and Pinocchio Village Haus, which in early morning serves good coffee and pastries.

Mickey's Toontown Fair

Mickey's Toontown Fair is the first new "land" to be added to the Magic Kingdom since its opening and the only land that doesn't connect to the central hub. Attractions include meeting Mickey Mouse, Mickey's house, Minnie Mouse's house, and a child-size roller coaster.

Mickey's Toontown Fair is sandwiched on three acres between Fantasyland and Tomorrowland. It's by far the smallest "land" and more like an attraction. Though you can enter from Fantasyland, Mickey's Toontown Fair generally receives guests arriving by Walt Disney World Railroad.

This land is the Magic Kingdom's greeting headquarters for Disney characters, which are available on a reliable schedule.

Mickey's Country House

What It Is: Walk-through tour of Mickey's House

Scope & Scale: Minor attraction

When to Go: Before 11:30 a.m. and after 4:30 p.m.

Author's Rating: Well done; ★★½

Overall Appeal by Age Group:

Pre-school	Grade School	Teens	Young Adults	Over 30	Senior Citizens
★★★★★	★★★★½	★★★½	★★★½	★★★½	★★★½

Duration of Attraction: 15–30 minutes (depending on the crowd)

Avg. Wait in Line per 100 People Ahead of You: 20 minutes

Assumes: Normal staffing

Touring Speed: Slow

Description and Comments   Mickey's House is the start of a self-guided tour through the famous mouse's house, into his back-yard, and past Pluto's doghouse.

Touring Tips   Discerning observers will see immediately that Mickey's House is a cleverly devised queuing area for visitors to Mickey's office for the Mouse Encounter. It also heightens antic-ipation and displays a lot of Disney memorabilia.

If meeting Mickey is your child's priority, take the railroad from Main Street to the Mickey's Toontown Fair station as soon as you enter the park.

Minnie's Country House

What It Is: Walk-through exhibit

Scope & Scale: Minor attraction

When to Go: Before 11:30 a.m. and after 4:30 p.m.

Author's Rating: Great detail; ★★

Overall Appeal by Age Group:

Pre-school	Grade School	Teens	Young Adults	Over 30	Senior Citizens
★★★★	★★★½	★★½	★★½	★★½	★★½

Duration of Tour: 10 minutes

Avg. Wait in Line per 100 People Ahead of You: 12 minutes

Touring Speed: Slow

Description and Comments   Minnie's Country House offers a self-guided tour through the rooms and backyard of Mickey's main squeeze. Similar to Mickey's Country House, only more feminine, Minnie's also showcases Disney memorabilia. Among its highlights are the fanciful appliances in Minnie's kitchen.

Touring Tips   The main difference between Mickey's and Min-nie's houses is that Mickey is at home to receive guests. Minnie never was home during our visits.

Barnstormer at Goofy's Wiseacres Farm

What It Is: Small roller coaster

Scope & Scale: Minor attraction

When to Go: Before 10:30 a.m., during the parades and *Fantas-mic!* in the evening, and just before the park closes

Author's Rating: Great for little ones, but not worth the wait
    for adults; ★★

Overall Appeal by Age Group:

Pre-school	Grade School	Teens	Young Adults	Over 30	Senior Citizens
★★★★	★★★½	★★½	★★½	★★½	★★

Duration of Ride: About 50 seconds

Avg. Wait in Line per 100 People Ahead of You: 10 minutes

Assumes: Normal staffing

Loading Speed: Slow

Description and Comments   Goofy's Barnstormer is a very small
roller coaster. The ride is zippy but supershort. In fact, of the 52
seconds the ride is in motion, 32 seconds are consumed in exiting
the loading area, being ratcheted up the first hill, and braking
into the off-loading area. Riders spend just 20 seconds careening
around the track.

Touring Tips   The cars of this dinky coaster are too small for
most adults. Unfortunately, the ride *is* visually appealing. All kids
want to ride, subjecting the whole family to glacially moving
lines. If you don't have kids with you, skip Goofy's Barnstormer.

Donald's Boat

What It Is: Interactive fountain and playground

Scope & Scale: Diversion

When to Go: Anytime

Special Comments: Kids will get wet.

Author's Rating: Spontaneous, yeah!; ★★½

Overall Appeal by Age Group:

Pre-school	Grade School	Teens	Young Adults	Over 30	Senior Citizens
★★★★	★★★	★	★½	★½	★½

Description and Comments   Spurts of water erupt randomly
from tiny holes in the deck of Donald's Boat, which purportedly
is springing leaks. Children walk around on deck, plugging holes
with their hands and feet and trying to guess where the water
will pop up next.

Touring Tips   Young children love this attraction and will play in the fountains until they're drenched. Ponchos don't help, because water shoots up as well as rains down. Our advice: get naked! Bare skin dries faster than wet clothes. Strip your munchkins to the legal limit and turn them loose. If you really want to plan ahead, bring extra underwear and a towel.

Tomorrowland

Tomorrowland is a mix of rides and experiences relating to the technological development of humankind and what life will be in the future. If this sounds like EPCOT's theme, it's because Tomorrowland was a breeding ground for ideas that spawned EPCOT. Yet Tomorrowland and EPCOT are very different in more than scale. EPCOT is educational. Tomorrowland is more for fun, depicting the future as envisioned in science fiction.

Exhaustive renovation of Tomorrowland was completed in 1995. The new design is ageless, reflecting a nostalgic vision of the future imagined by dreamers and scientists in the 1920s and '30s, with fanciful mechanical rockets and metallic cities. Disney calls the renovated Tomorrowland the "Future That Never Was." *Newsweek* dubbed it "retro-future."

In the new Tomorrowland, *Alien Encounter* replaces *Mission to Mars.* The *Carousel of Progress* has been jazzed up and moved forward in time, and *American Journeys,* with the addition of audio-animatronic characters and a plot, has been recast as *Transportarium.* The Starjets ride, now sporting a campy Jules Verne look as the AstroOrbiter, is higher off the ground but still goes in circles. The WEDway People Mover has become the Tomorrowland Transit Authority. Venerable Space Mountain holds its own, but Grand Prix Raceway and the Skyway to Fantasyland seem out of place.

Space Mountain

What It Is: Roller coaster in the dark

Scope & Scale: Super headliner

When to Go: First thing when the park opens, during the hour before closing, or between 6 and 7 p.m.

Special Comments: Great fun and action, much wilder than Big Thunder Mountain. Children must be 3' 8" tall to ride

and, if younger than 7, must be accompanied by an adult.
Switching-off is available.

Author's Rating: A great roller coaster with excellent special
effects. Not to be missed; ★★★★

Overall Appeal by Age Group:

Pre-school	Grade School	Teens	Young Adults	Over 30	Senior Citizens
†	★★★★★	★★★★★	★★★★½	★★★★	†

† Some preschoolers loved Space Mountain; others were fright-
ened. Our sample of senior riders was too small to develop an
accurate rating.

Duration of Ride: Almost 3 minutes

Avg. Wait in Line per 100 People Ahead of You: 3 minutes

Assumes: 2 tracks operating at 21-second dispatch intervals

Loading Speed: Moderate to fast

Description and Comments   Totally enclosed in a mammoth
futuristic structure, Space Mountain is a creative and engineering
marvel. The theme is a spaceflight through dark recesses of the
galaxy. Effects are superb, and the ride is the fastest and wildest in
the Disney repertoire. As a roller coaster, Space Mountain is a
lulu, much more thrilling than Big Thunder Mountain.

Touring Tips   Ride only if you can handle a fairly wild roller
coaster. What sets Space Mountain apart is that the cars plummet through darkness. In 1994, however, lighting was added.
Riders now can see the track in front of the car and much of the
coaster's superstructure. We hope the additional lighting is temporary. Half the fun is not knowing where the car will go next.

Each rider has his own seat. Parents can't sit next to their
child.

Space Mountain is the favorite attraction of many visitors.
Each morning before the park opens, particularly during summer and holiday periods, several hundred SM "junkies" crowd
rope barriers at the central hub awaiting the signal to sprint the
250 yards to the ride. The "Space Mountain Morning Mini
Marathon," as our researchers called it, pits parents against off-
spring, brother against sister, coeds against truck drivers, nuns
against beauticians. Disney personnel tell you not to run, but if
you want to ride Space Mountain without a long wait, you have

to show well in the marathon, because five minutes after the park's opening, Space Mountain's line is longer than any other in the Magic Kingdom.

If you dash: Arrive early; be one of the first in the park (easy if you have early-entry privileges). Go to the end of Main Street, cut right past the Plaza Restaurant, and stop under an archway saying "The Plaza Pavilion Terrace Dining," where a Disney worker will be standing behind a rope barrier. You're about 100 yards closer to Space Mountain here, on a route through the Plaza Pavilion, than your competition waiting to dash from the central hub. From this point, middle-aged folks walking fast can beat most teens sprinting from the hub. Plus, you wait in the shade.

If you don't catch Space Mountain in early morning, try again during the hour before closing, when would-be riders are often held in line outside the entrance until all those previously in line have ridden, thus emptying the attraction. The appearance from outside is that the line is enormous, when in fact the only people waiting are those visible. This crowd-control technique, known as "stacking," discourages visitors from getting in line and ensures that the ride will be able to close on schedule.

Splash Mountain siphons off some guests who would have made Space Mountain their first stop. Even so, a mob rushes to Space Mountain as soon as the park opens. If you especially like thrill attractions and only have one day, see *Alien Encounter* first in the morning, followed by Space Mountain, Big Thunder Mountain Railroad, and Splash Mountain.

If you're an early-entry guest and Big Thunder and Splash mountains are high on your list, see *Alien Encounter* and ride Space Mountain (as well as Fantasyland attractions) until 10–15 minutes before the general public is admitted. At that time, go to the boundary between Fantasyland and Liberty Square and wait for the park to open. When it does, move quickly along the Liberty Square and Frontierland waterfronts to Big Thunder and Splash mountains.

If you aren't eligible for early entry, visit the Magic Kingdom on a Tuesday, Wednesday, Friday, or Sunday and make Space Mountain and *Alien Encounter* your first two attractions. If you aren't eligible for early entry but your schedule requires you to visit on an early-entry day, ride Splash Mountain and Big

Thunder Railroad first, then catch Space Mountain and *Alien Encounter* during a parade or just before the park closes.

Grand Prix Raceway

What It Is: Drive-'em-yourself miniature cars
Scope & Scale: Major attraction
When to Go: Before 11 a.m. and after 5 p.m.
Special Comments: Must be 4' 4" tall to drive.
Author's Rating: Boring for adults (★); great for preschoolers
Overall Appeal by Age Group:

Pre-school	Grade School	Teens	Young Adults	Over 30	Senior Citizens
★★★½	★★★	★	½	½	½

Duration of Ride: Approximately 4¼ minutes
Avg. Wait in Line per 100 People Ahead of You: 4½ minutes
Assumes: 285-car turnover every 20 minutes
Loading Speed: Slow

Description and Comments   An elaborate miniature raceway with gasoline-powered cars that travel up to 7 mph. The raceway, with sleek cars, racing noises, and Grand Prix billboards, is alluring. Unfortunately, the cars poke along on a track. Ho-hum for most adults and teens. The height requirement often excludes young children who would enjoy the ride.

Because cars jam up at the end, it can take as long to get off as to get on.

Touring Tips   This ride is appealing visually but definitely one adults can skip. Preschoolers, however, love it. If your pre-schooler is too short to drive, ride along and allow your child to steer the car on its guide rail while you work the gas pedal. Go as slowly as possible to prolong the ride.

The line for the Grand Prix is routed across a pedestrian bridge that leads to the loading areas. For a shorter wait, turn right off the bridge to the first loading area.

Skyway to Fantasyland

What It Is: Scenic overhead transportation to Fantasyland
Scope & Scale: Minor attraction

When to Go: Before noon and during special events

Special Comments: If there's a line, it's probably quicker
  to walk.

Author's Rating: Nice view; ★★½

Overall Appeal by Age Group:

Pre-school	Grade School	Teens	Young Adults	Over 30	Senior Citizens
★★★★	★★★★	★★★½	★★★½	★★★½	★★★½

Duration of Ride: Approximately 5 minutes one way

Avg. Wait in Line per 100 People Ahead of You: 10 minutes

Assumes: 45 or more cars operating

Loading Speed: Moderate

Description and Comments   A skylift that transports you from
Tomorrowland to the far corner of Fantasyland near its boundary with Liberty Square. The view is one of the Magic Kingdom's best, but walking is usually faster.

Touring Tips   Unless lines are short, the Skyway won't save you
time as transportation. As a ride, however, it affords incredible
views. The Skyway sometimes opens later and closes earlier than
other Tomorrowland rides. Strollers aren't allowed.

AstroOrbiter

What It Is: Buck Rogers–style rockets revolving around
  a central axis

Scope & Scale: Minor attraction

When to Go: Before 11 a.m. or after 5 p.m.

Special Comments: This attraction is not as innocuous
  as it appears.

Author's Rating: Not worth the wait; ★★

Overall Appeal by Age Group:

Pre-school	Grade School	Teens	Young Adults	Over 30	Senior Citizens
★★★★	★★★	★★½	★½	★	★

Duration of Ride: 1½ minutes

Avg. Wait in Line per 100 People Ahead of You: 13½ minutes

Assumes: Normal staffing

Loading Speed: Slow

Description and Comments   Though recently upgraded and visually appealing, AstroOrbiter is still a slow-loading carnival ride. The fat little rockets simply fly in circles. The best thing about AstroOrbiter is the view aloft.

Touring Tips   If you ride with preschoolers, seat them first, then board. The AstroOrbiter flies higher and faster than Dumbo and frightens some children. It can also turn adults green.

Tomorrowland Transit Authority

What It Is: Scenic tour of Tomorrowland

Scope & Scale: Minor attraction

When to Go: During the hot, crowded period of the day (11:30 a.m.–4:30 p.m.)

Special Comments: A good way to check out the crowd at Space Mountain

Author's Rating: Scenic, relaxing, informative; ★★★

Overall Appeal by Age Group:

Pre-school	Grade School	Teens	Young Adults	Over 30	Senior Citizens
★★★	★★★	★★½	★★½	★★★	★★★

Duration of Ride: 10 minutes

Avg. Wait in Line per 100 People Ahead of You: 1½ minutes

Assumes: 39 trains operating

Loading Speed: Fast

Description and Comments   A once-unique prototype of a linear induction-powered mass-transit system, the people mover's tram cars carry riders on a leisurely tour of Tomorrowland that includes a peek inside Space Mountain.

Touring Tips   A relaxing ride where lines move quickly. It's good to take during busier times of day, when the kids need a short nap or when mom needs to nurse the baby. Ride repeatedly without disembarking.

Carousel of Progress

What It Is: Audio-animatronic theater production

Scope & Scale: Major attraction

When to Go: Anytime

Author's Rating: Nostalgic, warm, and happy; ★★★

Overall Appeal by Age Group:

Pre-school	Grade School	Teens	Young Adults	Over 30	Senior Citizens
★★★	★★★½	★★★½	★★★½	★★★★	★★★★½

Duration of Presentation: 18 minutes

Preshow Entertainment: Documentary on the attraction's long history

Probable Waiting Time: Less than 10 minutes

Description and Comments   Updated and improved during the Tomorrowland renovation, *Carousel of Progress* cheerfully looks at how technology and electricity have changed the lives of an audio-animatronic family over several generations. It's thoroughly delightful, showcasing a likable family and a happy tune that bridges the generations.

Touring Tips   This attraction is a great favorite of repeat visitors and is included on all of our one-day touring plans. *Carousel of Progress* handles big crowds effectively and is a good choice during busier times of day.

Dreamflight

What It Is: Travel-theme indoor ride

Scope & Scale: Minor attraction

When to Go: Anytime

Author's Rating: Pleasant but not compelling; ★★

Projected Overall Appeal by Age Group:

Pre-school	Grade School	Teens	Young Adults	Over 30	Senior Citizens
★★★½	★★★½	★★★½	★★★½	★★★½	★★★½

Duration of Ride: About 6 minutes

Avg. Wait in Line per 100 People Ahead of You: 3 minutes

Assumes: Normal operation

Loading Speed: Fast

Description and Comments   Presented by Delta Airlines, Dreamflight fancifully depicts the history of flight. This new addition to Tomorrowland could have been more interesting. As is, it's just "nice."

Touring Tips Very seldom is there a line. Go during the heat of day.

The Timekeeper

What It Is: Time-travel movie adventure

Scope & Scale: Major attraction

When to Go: Anytime

Special Comments: Audience must stand throughout presentation.

Author's Rating: Outstanding. Not to be missed; ★★★★

Overall Appeal by Age Group:

Pre-school	Grade School	Teens	Young Adults	Over 30	Senior Citizens
★★★	★★★½	★★★½	★★★½	★★★★	★★★★

Duration of Presentation: About 20 minutes

Preshow Entertainment: Robots, lasers, and movies

Probable Waiting Time: 8–15 minutes

Description and Comments Developed as *Le Visionarium* for Euro Disneyland, *The Timekeeper* adds AudioAnimatronic characters and a storyline to the long-successful 360° Circle-Vision technology. The preshow introduces Timekeeper (a humanoid) and 9-Eye (a time-traveling robot so named because she has nine cameras that serve as eyes). Afterward, the audience enters the main theater, where Timekeeper places 9-Eye into a time machine and dispatches her on a crazed journey into the past and future. What 9-Eye sees on her odyssey is projected onto huge screens that surround the audience. The robot travels to prehistoric Europe, then forward to meet French author and visionary Jules Verne, who hitches a ride into the future. Circle-Vision film technology, AudioAnimatronics, and high-tech special effects establish *The Timekeeper* as one of Tomorrowland's premier attractions.

Touring Tips *The Timekeeper* draws large crowds from mid-morning on. Because the theater accommodates more than 1,000 guests per showing, there's never much of a wait.

Alien Encounter

What It Is: Theater-in-the-round science fiction horror show

Scope & Scale: Major attraction

When to Go: Before 10 a.m. or after 6 p.m.

Special Comments: Frightens children.

Author's Rating: ★★★

Overall Appeal by Age Group:

Pre-school	Grade School	Teens	Young Adults	Over 30	Senior Citizens
★★★	★★★★½	★★★★	★★★★	★★★★	★★★

Duration of Presentation: About 12 minutes

Preshow Entertainment: About 6 minutes

Probable Waiting Time: 12–40 minutes

Description and Comments   Heralded as the showpiece of the "new" Tomorrowland, *Alien Encounter* is staged in the former home of *Mission to Mars*. Guests witness "interplanetary teleportation," a technique that breaks travelers down into electrons for transmission to distant locations. In this case, the demonstration goes awry (of course), and an extremely unsavory alien arrives in the theater. Mayhem ensues.

Alien Encounter is the antithesis of most Disney attractions: There is no uplifting message and no happy ending. There is death in *Alien Encounter*, and its tone is dark and foreboding. While the "Twilight Zone" Tower of Terror at Disney-MGM is suspenseful and subtle, *Alien Encounter* is uncomfortable and gross. The discomfort begins at the preshow, where in a teleportation experiment, a cuddly audio-animatronic character is hideously fried and deformed, then vomited screaming into outer space.

Alien Encounter has its advocates, but for us it's mean and twisted. The coup de grace is the hawking of T-shirts in the adjacent gift shop bearing the image of the little creature that was tortured and maimed.

Touring Tips   Disney's most disturbing and frightening attraction, *Alien Encounter* was initially rejected by Walt Disney Co. Chairman Michael Eisner for not being scary enough. Though reader reaction to *Alien Encounter* is mixed, almost everyone agrees it isn't for young children. *Alien Encounter* stays busy all day.

Tomorrowland Eateries and Shops

Description and Comments   Cosmic Ray's Starlight Cafe is the largest and most efficient Magic Kingdom fast-food restaurant. The Plaza Pavilion, however, serves better food, including a good Italian sub. Several shops provide opportunities for buying souvenirs.

Touring Tips   Forget shopping until your second day unless it's your top priority.

Live Entertainment in the Magic Kingdom

Daily live entertainment—bands, character appearances, parades, singing, dancing, and ceremonies—further enliven the Magic Kingdom. For events on the day you visit, check the schedule in your handout map. If you don't receive one as you enter, get one at City Hall. Remember: If you're on a tight schedule, it's impossible to see featured attractions **and** the live performances. Our one-day touring plans exclude the live shows, because some parades and performances siphon crowds away from popular rides, shortening lines.

Here's an incomplete list of events scheduled with some regularity for which reservations aren't required.

Sword in the Stone A ceremony with audience participation based on the Disney animated feature of the same name. Merlin the Magician selects youngsters to test their strength by removing Excalibur from the stone. Staged several times daily behind Cinderella Castle.

Bay Lake and Seven Seas Lagoon Electrical Pageant This is one of our favorites among the Disney floating extras, but you have to leave the Magic Kingdom to see it. The pageant is a stunning electric light show afloat on small barges and accompanied by electronic music. It's performed at nightfall on World Showcase Lagoon and Bay Lake. Exit the Magic Kingdom and take the monorail to the Polynesian Resort. Get a drink and walk to the end of the pier. The show begins about 9 p.m. during summer.

Fantasy in the Sky A stellar fireworks display after dark on nights the park is open late. Watch from the terrace of Plaza Pavilion restaurant in Tomorrowland.

Disney Character Shows & Appearances On most days, a character poses for photos from 9 a.m. until 10 p.m. next to City Hall. Mickey, Chip 'n Dale, Pluto, and Goofy are available most of the day at Mickey's Toontown Fair. Daily shows at Castle Forecourt Stage and Tomorrowland Galaxy Palace Theater feature characters. They also roam the park throughout the day but can almost always be found in Fantasyland and Mickey's Toontown Fair.

• Parades •

Parades are spectaculars with dozens of Disney characters and amazing special effects. In late 1991, the beloved Main Street Electrical Parade was unplugged, and the afternoon parade was replaced by an eye-popping celebration of carnivals worldwide. The new parades are larger, more colorful, and more elaborate. The afternoon parade is outstanding; the evening parade, not to be missed.

Parades disrupt traffic in the park. It's nearly impossible, for example, to get to Adventureland from Tomorrowland, or vice versa, during a parade.

Afternoon Parade

Usually at 3 p.m., it includes bands, floats, and marching characters. The latest edition is called *Mickey Mania.*

Evening Parade(s)

The evening parade is a high-tech production featuring electro-luminescence and fiberoptics, light-spreading thermoplastics, and clouds of underlit liquid nitrogen smoke. For those who flunked chemistry, the parade also offers music, Mickey Mouse, and twinkling lights. Depending on closing time, it's staged once at 9 p.m.; or twice when the park is open late, at 8 and 10 p.m. or at 9 and 11 p.m.

During slower times of year, the evening parade is held only on weekends, and sometimes not then. Call (407) 824-4321 if you want to confirm it's on.

Parade Route and Vantage Points

Magic Kingdom parades circle Town Square, head down Main Street, go around the central hub, and cross the bridge to Liberty Square, where they follow the waterfront, ending in Frontierland. Sometimes they begin in Frontierland, run the route in the opposite direction, and end in Town Square.

Most guests watch from the central hub or from Main Street. One of the best and most popular vantage points is the upper platform of the Walt Disney World Railroad Station at the Town Square end of Main Street. This also is a good place for watching Fantasy in the Sky fireworks. Problem is, you have to stake out your position 30–45 minutes beforehand.

To avoid the largest crowds, watch parades from Liberty Square or Frontierland. Great vantage points are:

1. Sleepy Hollow sandwich shop, on your right as you cross the bridge into Liberty Square.
2. Anywhere along the pathway on the Liberty Square side of the moat from the Sleepy Hollow sandwich shop to Cinderella's Castle.
3. The elevated, covered walkway connecting the Liberty Tree Tavern and Diamond Horseshoe Saloon.
4. Elevated wooden platforms in front of the Frontierland Shootin' Gallery, Frontier Trading Post, and the building labeled "Frontier Merchandise." Be there 10–12 minutes before parade time.
5. Benches along the perimeter of the central hub, between the entrances to Liberty Square and Adventureland. The view is unobstructed, though somewhat removed. What you lose in proximity, however, you make up in comfort.

Assuming it starts on Main Street, the parade takes 16–20 minutes to reach Liberty Square or Frontierland.

Eating and Shopping in the Magic Kingdom

The Magic Kingdom is a wonder and a marvel, but it's almost impossible to get a really good meal there. What's available is the same fare served in every fast-food chain in America. We're sympathetic; it's overwhelming to contemplate serving 130,000 or so meals a day. But understanding doesn't make the food taste better. It isn't awful, mind you, just mediocre in a place that sets the standard for quality in tourism and entertainment. Only the variety suggests that somebody once had the right idea.

Most of our suggestions bypass the Kingdom's full-service restaurants.

• Alternatives and Suggestions •
for Eating in the Magic Kingdom

1. Eat a good breakfast before arriving at the Magic Kingdom. Restaurants outside Disney World offer outstanding breakfast specials.

2. If your schedule is tight, save time by buying snacks from vendors stationed throughout the park.

3. Here's where our researchers eat in the Kingdom:

   Adventureland
   El Pirata y El Perico. Frequently overlooked. Nothing fancy. We usually have tacos.

   Frontierland
   Aunt Polly's Landing. Located on Tom Sawyer Island, this is our favorite lunch spot. Serves cold fried chicken, ham-and-swiss sandwiches, and

PB&J's. But you have to raft to the island to get there, and dining is outdoors—not air-conditioned.

Liberty Square

Sleepy Hollow. Decent food, and if we eat between 2 and 3 p.m., we take a table along the rail and watch the 3 p.m. parade in comfort.

Liberty Tree Tavern. Our favorite full-service restaurant. Now hosts character meals with a very palatable fixed menu served family style.

Fantasyland

Pinocchio Village Haus. The place for breakfast rolls and muffins.

Resort Hotels

Decent dinner buffets at Chef Mickey's at Contemporary Resort and at 1900 Park Fare at Grand Floridian feature characters, so they're noisy. Commuting is easy by monorail. An adult alternative is lunch or the family-style skillet dinner at Whispering Canyon Cafe in Wilderness Lodge. Access aboard launches from the Magic Kingdom docks.

Favorite Snacks

We love churros, a Mexican pastry sold by vendor wagons. Magic Kingdom popcorn is also good. All theme parks began selling fresh fruit streetside in 1994, a move we applaud.

4. If your schedule is tight and the park closes early, stay until closing and eat outside the World before returning to your hotel. If the Kingdom is open late, eat dinner about 4 p.m. in the eatery of your choice. You'll miss the last lunchers and the start of the dinner crowd.

5. Take the monorail to a resort hotel for lunch. The round trip is short, and because most guests are in the parks, restaurants aren't busy. Food, service, and atmosphere beat those in the park, and beer, wine, and mixed drinks are available.

6. Many places sell cold sandwiches. Buy before 11 a.m. and carry your food until you're hungry. Add beverages from any convenient vendor.

7. Most fast-food eateries have more than one service window. Sometimes an out-of-the-way window will have a shorter line. But some windows might serve only soup and salad, others sandwiches.

8. Disney has a rule against bringing your own food and drink into the park. Not everyone observes it. One woman we met stowed a huge picnic in a diaper bag in a locker at Main Street Station and retrieved it when her family was hungry. Another family carried lunch in a small backpack, including frozen juice boxes to keep meat sandwiches cool.

• The Cost of Fast Food and Snacks • in the Magic Kingdom

Sandwiches, hot dogs, burgers, tacos, and such sell for $3–7. A seafood salad and pop at Cosmic Ray's Starlight Cafe costs about $7.50. Snacks and drinks are available throughout the park at standard prices.

What Will Fast Food Cost?
Snack and drink prices, tax included and rounded to the nickel, include:

Pop, iced tea, and lemonade: small, $1.55; large, $1.85

Coffee: small, $1; large, $1.20	Ice cream: $1.50 and up
Popcorn: $1.75	Churros: $1.55
Potato chips: 80¢	Cookies: $1.25

• Shopping in the Magic Kingdom •

Shops add realism and atmosphere to the theme settings and offer extensive souvenirs, clothing, novelties, and decorator items. Many goods, with the exception of trademark souvenirs, are available elsewhere for less. One-day visitors should bypass the shops. Those with more time should browse in early afternoon when rides are crowded. Main Street shops open earlier and close later than the rest of the park. Stow your purchases in lockers at Main Street Station or have the shop forward your packages to Parcel Pick-up for retrieval when you leave. Purchases by Disney resort guests can be delivered to their rooms.

Most trademark merchandise sold at Disney World is available from Walt Disney Attractions Mail Order Department at (407) 363-6200 or (800) 272-6201.

Magic Kingdom
Touring Plans

Our step-by-step Magic Kingdom touring plans are field-tested for seeing *as much as possible* in one day with a minimum of time in lines. They're designed to avoid crowds and bottlenecks on days of moderate to heavy attendance. But there's more to see in the Magic Kingdom than can be experienced in one day.

On days of lighter attendance, touring plans will still save time but won't be as critical to successful touring. Don't worry that other people will be following the same plan. Fewer than 1 in 500 people in the park will have been exposed to it.

Choosing the Right Touring Plan

We offer four Magic Kingdom touring plans:

- Author's Selective Magic Kingdom One-Day Touring Plan for Adults
- Magic Kingdom One-Day Touring Plan for Parents with Young Children
- Magic Kingdom Dumbo-or-Die-in-a-Day Touring Plan for Parents with Young Children
- Magic Kingdom Two-Day Touring Plan

If you have two days (or even two mornings) at the Magic Kingdom, the Two-Day Touring Plan is *by far* the most relaxed and efficient. This plan takes advantage of early morning, when lines are short and the park hasn't filled. It works well all year and eliminates much of the extra walking required by the one-day plans. No matter when the park closes, our two-day plan guarantees the most efficient touring and the least time in line. It's perfect for guests who wish to sample both the attractions and the atmosphere, including parades and fireworks.

If you only have one day, use the Author's Selective One-Day Touring Plan. It features only the best in the park.

If you have children younger than 8, adopt the One-Day Touring Plan for Adults with Young Children. It's a compromise, integrating preferences of younger children with those of older siblings and adults. The plan includes many children's rides in Fantasyland but omits roller-coaster rides and attractions that are frightening or barred by height requirements. An alternative would be the One-Day Touring Plan for Adults or the Author's Selective One-Day Touring Plan, taking advantage of switching off (see page 58).

The Dumbo-or-Die-in-a-Day Touring Plan for Parents with Young Children is designed for parents who will spare no sacrifice for their children. On Dumbo-or-Die, adults generally stand around, sweat, wipe noses, pay for stuff, and watch the children enjoy themselves.

Two-Day Touring Plans for Families with Young Children

If you have young children and are looking for a two-day itinerary, combine the Magic Kingdom One-Day Touring Plan for Parents with Young Children and the second day of the Magic Kingdom Two-Day Touring Plan.

The Single-Day Touring Conundrum

Touring the Magic Kingdom in a day is complicated by the fact that the premier attractions are at opposite ends of the park: Splash Mountain and Big Thunder Mountain in Frontierland, and Space Mountain and *Alien Encounter* in Tomorrowland. It's

Magic Kingdom Attractions Crowded in Early Morning	
Tomorrowland	Space Mountain *Alien Encounter*
Frontierland	Splash Mountain Big Thunder Mountain Railroad
Fantasyland	Dumbo, the Flying Elephant 20,000 Leagues Under the Sea
Adventureland	Jungle Cruise

virtually impossible to ride all without encountering lines at one or another. It doesn't matter which you ride first.

The only effective way to ride all four without long waits is to tour the park over two days: Ride Space Mountain and see *Alien Encounter* first thing one morning and Splash Mountain and Big Thunder Mountain first thing on the other. If you have only one day and are unwilling to wait 45 minutes to two hours, ride one set when the park opens and the other just before closing.

Or, as we recommend in one-day touring plans, arrive early and rush to *Alien Encounter*. After *Alien Encounter*, ride Space Mountain, then speed to Frontierland and ride Splash Mountain. When you leave Splash Mountain, bear left to the Big Thunder Mountain Railroad. If you're fast, your wait should be less than five minutes at *Alien Encounter*, about 10–20 minutes at Space Mountain, and about 25–35 minutes each at Splash Mountain and Big Thunder Mountain.

This strategy takes advantage of the 30- to 45-minute morning lull when those on hand at opening have been absorbed and new arrivals are few. Lines at the Big Four haven't built up again, and the wait is tolerable. Early entry at the Magic Kingdom eliminates any morning lull.

Guests can enjoy all attractions in Fantasyland except *Legend of the Lion King* (and sometimes 20,000 Leagues Under the Sea), as well as all in Tomorrowland except *Carousel of Progress*. Space Mountain, Tomorrowland Transit Authority, and AstroOrbiter, however, usually open a half hour later than other Tomorrowland attractions.

Combining Early Entry with the Touring Plans

1. Adults touring *without children* should arrive when the turnstiles open and experience *Alien Encounter*, then go directly to Space Mountain, which usually opens a half hour later. If the mountain isn't open when you arrive, wait (10 minutes or less). After riding Space Mountain, quiet your nerves on Peter Pan and Snow White in Fantasyland.

Guests ineligible for early entry generally will be admitted 30 minutes before official opening. When they join the early-entry throng, the park becomes stuffed. If you want to ride Splash Mountain and Big Thunder Mountain Railroad without horrendous waits, position yourself on the border of Fantasyland and Liberty Square and hustle to the mountains the second the rest of the park opens. Pick up your touring plan after you've finished at Big Thunder and Splash Mountain, skipping attractions you experienced during early entry.

2. Adults touring with children   should arrive as early as possible and enjoy attractions in Fantasyland and the Grand Prix Raceway in Tomorrowland. Interrupt your touring 10 minutes before day guests are admitted and position yourself to rush to either Frontierland or Adventureland. When the rest of the park opens, ride Splash Mountain if your kids are at least 44 inches tall. Otherwise, ride the Jungle Cruise in Adventureland. Afterward, return to Fantasyland and see *Legend of the Lion King.* Pick up your touring plan after *Legend of the Lion King,* bypassing attractions you've already seen.

If You Don't Have Early-Entry Privileges

If you aren't eligible for early entry, avoid the Magic Kingdom on early-entry days, regardless of time of year.

Preliminary Instructions for All
Magic Kingdom Touring Plans

On days of moderate to heavy attendance, follow your chosen touring plan exactly, deviating only:

1. *When you aren't interested in an attraction it lists.*
2. *When you encounter a very long line at an attraction it calls for.* It's possible that this is a temporary situation caused by hundreds of people arriving from a recently concluded theater performance. Move to the plan's next step and return to the attraction later.

What to Do If You Get Off Track

If you experience an unexpected interruption that throws the touring plan off, consult the "When to Go" information in the individual attraction profiles.

Before You Go

1. Call (407) 824-4321 a day ahead for the official opening time. Ask where early entry will be in effect.
2. Buy your admission.
3. Review your touring plan and clip out its outline.

Author's Selective Magic Kingdom One-Day Touring Plan for Adults

For: Adults touring without young children
Assumes: Willingness to experience all major rides and shows

This plan includes only those attractions the author thinks are the best in the Kingdom. It requires considerable walking and some backtracking to avoid long lines. You might not complete the tour. How far you get depends on how quickly you move among rides, how many times you rest or eat, how quickly the park fills, and what time the park closes.

1. If you're a Disney hotel guest, use Disney transportation to commute to the park, arriving 90 minutes before official opening *on early-entry days* and 30 minutes before official opening *on non-early-entry days.*

   If you're a day guest, arrive at the parking lot 50 minutes before the Magic Kingdom's stated opening time *on non-early-entry days.* Arrive an hour earlier than official opening if it's a holiday period or you must buy your admission. Take the tram to the Transportation and Ticket Center. At the TTC, transfer to the monorail or ferry to reach the park's entrance. If the line is short, take the monorail; otherwise, catch the ferry.

2. At the park, proceed through the turnstiles and have one person go to City Hall for park guide maps containing the daily entertainment schedule.

3. Regroup and move quickly down Main Street to the central hub. Because the Magic Kingdom uses two opening procedures, you'll probably encounter one of the following:

   a. The entire park will be open. In this case, proceed quickly to *Alien Encounter* in Tomorrowland.

    b. Only Main Street will be open. In this case, turn right at the end of Main Street (before you reach the central hub), pass the Plaza Ice Cream Parlor and the Plaza Restaurant, and stand at the entrance of Plaza Pavilion. When the rope barrier drops, jog through the Plaza Pavilion to *Alien Encounter.* Starting at Plaza Pavilion will give you a 50-yard head start over anyone coming from the central hub. Experience *Alien Encounter.*

4. Exit left from *Alien Encounter* and hurry to Space Mountain. Ride.

5. Leave Tomorrowland via the central hub and enter Liberty Square. Turn left and proceed along the waterfront to Splash Mountain. Ride.

6. Exit left from Splash Mountain and go to Big Thunder Mountain. Ride.

7. Exit Big Thunder Mountain. Keeping the waterfront on your left, proceed to Haunted Mansion.

8. Exit left from Haunted Mansion and enter Fantasyland. Bear right toward the castle and see *Legend of the Lion King.* The line will appear long, but the theater holds 500 people.

9. Retrace your steps to Liberty Square. If you're hungry, eat. Fast-food eateries that are generally less crowded include the Columbia Harbour House in Liberty Square, Aunt Polly's Landing on Tom Sawyer Island in Frontierland, El Pirata y El Perico in Adventureland, and the Crystal Palace at the central hub end of Main Street. As a lunchtime alternative, check your guide map for the next performance of the *Diamond Horseshoe Revue.* If timing is right, eat a sandwich while watching the show.

10. After lunch, enter Adventureland through the passage between the Frontierland Shootin' Gallery and the woodcarving shop. Ride Pirates of the Caribbean.

11. Exit left from Pirates and proceed to the Frontierland railroad station. Catch the train to Mickey's Toontown Fair.

12. Quickly tour the fair, exiting via the walkway to Fantasyland. Turn left at Grand Prix Raceway and continue to Tomorrowland.

13. Ride the Tomorrowland Transit Authority.

14. See *Carousel of Progress.*

15. Proceed toward the central hub entrance to Tomorrowland and experience *The Timekeeper.*

16. Return to Liberty Square via the central hub and see *Hall of Presidents.*

17. Exit right from *Hall of Presidents* and return to Fantasyland. Ride It's a Small World.

18. Check the line at Peter Pan's Flight. If the wait is 15 minutes or less, ride. If the wait is longer, skip to Step 19.

19. Retrace your steps from Fantasyland to Liberty Square and Frontierland. See *Country Bear Jamboree.*

20. Return to Adventureland via the shortcut next to the Frontierland Shootin' Arcade. Visit Swiss Family Treehouse.

21. Take the Jungle Cruise, left of the treehouse.

22. If you have time left before the park closes, backtrack to attractions you may have missed or bypassed. See parades, fireworks, or live performances that interest you. Grab a bite.

23. Browse Main Street after the rest of the park has closed.

Magic Kingdom One-Day Touring Plan for Parents with Young Children

---

For: Parents with children younger than 8
Assumes: Periodic stops for rest, toilets, and refreshment

This plan represents a compromise between the observed tastes of adults and the observed tastes of younger children. It includes rides that children may be able to experience at local fairs and amusement parks. Consider omitting these rides. The following cycle-loading rides often have long lines:

Cinderella's Golden Carrousel

Mad Tea Party

Dumbo, the Flying Elephant

AstroOrbiter

Instead of this touring plan, try either of the one-day plans for adults and take advantage of switching off.

Before entering the park, decide whether you will return to your hotel midday for a rest. You won't see as much if you do, but everyone will be more relaxed.

This plan requires considerable walking and some backtracking to avoid long lines. You may not complete the tour. How far you get depends on how quickly you move among rides, how many times you rest or eat, how quickly the park fills, and what time the park closes.

1. If you're a Disney resort guest, use Disney transportation to commute to the park, arriving 90 minutes before official opening *on early-entry days* and 30 minutes before official opening *on non-early-entry days.*

   If you're a day guest, arrive at the parking lot 50 minutes before the Magic Kingdom's stated opening *on a non-early-entry day.* Arrive an hour earlier than official opening if it's a holiday period or you must buy your admission. Take the tram to the Transportation and Ticket Center. At the TTC, transfer to the monorail or ferry to reach the park's entrance. If the line is short, take the monorail; otherwise, catch the ferry.

2. At the Magic Kingdom, proceed through the turn-stiles and have one person go to City Hall for park guide maps containing the daily entertainment schedule.

3. Rent strollers if necessary.

4. Move quickly to the end of Main Street. If the entire park is open, proceed briskly to Fantasyland. Otherwise, stand by the rope barrier at the central hub. When the barrier drops, go through the main door of the castle and ride Dumbo, the Fly-ing Elephant.

5. Ride Peter Pan's Flight.

6. See *Legend of the Lion King*.

7. Exit left from *Lion King* and go to Liberty Square. Turn right at the waterfront and go to Haunted Mansion.

8. Enter Frontierland. See the *Country Bear Jamboree*.

9. Go to Adventureland via the passageway between the Frontierland Shootin' Gallery and the wood-carving shop. Ride Pirates of the Caribbean.

10. Turn left out of Pirates, then right into Frontier-land. At the Frontierland station, catch a train to Mickey's Toontown Fair. Families with strollers must walk to the fair or leave their stroller at the station, returning by train to retrieve it.

11. At Mickey's Toontown Fair, visit the characters, explore the maze, and enjoy Donald's Boat.

12. Return to Main Street by foot or train and leave the park for lunch and a rest at your hotel. Have your hand stamped for re-entry and keep your parking receipt so you won't have to repay when you return refreshed between 3:30 and 5 p.m. Back in the park, walk or ride the train to Frontierland.

13. Take the raft to Tom Sawyer Island. Set time limits based on the park's closing, your energy level, and how many more attractions you want to experience. If you stayed in the park instead of taking a break, consider having lunch at Aunt Polly's Landing on the island.

14. Return to Fantasyland. Ride It's a Small World.

15. Go to Tomorrowland via the castle and central hub. Ride Dreamflight.

16. Ride the Tomorrowland Transit Authority.

17. Head back toward the central hub entrance to Tomorrowland and see *The Timekeeper*.

18. If time remains before the park closes, check the entertainment schedule for live performances, parades, fireworks, and other special events. Grab a bite, or see attractions you might have missed.

19. Browse Main Street after the rest of the park has closed.

Magic Kingdom Dumbo-or-Die-in-a-Day Touring Plan for Parents with Young Children

For: Adults compelled to devote every waking moment to the pleasure and entertainment of their young children, or rich people paying someone else to take their children to the park.

Prerequisite: This touring plan is designed for days when the Magic Kingdom closes at 9 p.m. or later.

Assumes: Frequent stops for rest, toilets, and refreshments

Note: Name aside, this itinerary is not a joke. It will provide a young child with about as perfect a day as is possible at the Magic Kingdom.

This plan addresses the preferences, needs, and desires of young children to the virtual exclusion of those of adults or older siblings. It's wonderful if you're paying a sitter, nanny, or chauffeur to take your children to the Magic Kingdom.

1. If you're a Disney resort guest, use Disney transportation to commute to the park, arriving 90 minutes before official opening *on early-entry days* and 30 minutes before official opening *on non-early-entry days.*

   If you're a day guest, arrive at the parking lot 50 minutes before the Magic Kingdom's stated opening time *on a non-early-entry day.* Arrive an hour earlier than official opening time if it's a holiday period or you must buy your admission. Take the tram to the Transportation and Ticket Center. At the TTC, transfer to the monorail or ferry to reach the park's entrance. If the line is short, take the monorail; otherwise, catch the ferry.

2. At the Magic Kingdom, proceed through the turnstiles and have one person go to City Hall for park

guide maps containing the daily entertainment schedule.

3. Rent a stroller, if needed.

4. Move quickly to the end of Main Street. If the entire park is open, proceed briskly to Fantasyland. Otherwise, stand by the rope barrier at the central hub. When the barrier drops, go through the main door of the castle to King Stefan's Banquet Hall.

5. At King Stefan's (on your right as you enter Cinderella Castle), make dinner reservations for 7 p.m. This will give your kids a chance to see the inside of the castle and meet Cinderella.

6. Ride Dumbo, the Flying Elephant.

7. If your child wants, ride again. To avoid two waits in line, one adult should ride with the child while the other lines up behind another two dozen riders.

8. Ride Mr. Toad's Wild Ride, near Dumbo.

9. Ride Peter Pan's Flight.

10. Ride Cinderella's Golden Carrousel.

11. See *Legend of the Lion King.*

12. Exit left and ride Skyway to Tomorrowland. If you have a stroller, walk to Tomorrowland.

13. Ride Grand Prix Raceway. Let your child "steer" (cars are on guide rails) while you work the gas pedal.

14. Ride the AstroOrbiter. For safety, seat your children before you get in.

15. Ride Dreamflight, near the AstroOrbiter.

16. Return to Main Street via the central hub. Leave the park for a rest break at your hotel. Have your hand stamped for re-entry and keep your parking receipt so you won't have to repay when you return refreshed about 4 or 4:30 p.m.

   If you stay in the park, skip to Step 18.

17. Back from break, take the train to Frontierland.

18. Go by raft to Tom Sawyer Island. Stay as long as the kids want. If you're hungry, eat at Aunt Polly's Landing.

19. Leave the island and see the *Country Bear Jamboree* in Frontierland.

20. Take the train from Frontierland Station to Mickey's Toontown Fair. If you have a stroller, park it temporarily at Frontierland Station.

21. Walk through Mickey's Country House and Minnie's Country House and play on Donald's Boat. Meet the characters and pose for photos.

22. Check your watch. You should be within an hour of your dinner reservations at King Stefan's. If you left your stroller in Frontierland, return by train to retrieve it, then head to Fantasyland. If you don't have a stroller, take the direct path from Mickey's Toontown Fair to Fantasyland. If you have 20 minutes or more before your King Stefan seating, ride It's a Small World.

Note: Main dishes at King Stefan's are average at best, unappetizing at worst, and expensive regardless. Try to get by with a salad for adults and a hot dog and alphabet fries for the kids. Or order dessert only. If you plan to quit early, feed the kids while you have coffee. Back at your hotel, order pizza.

23. Leave Fantasyland and go to Liberty Square. If your children want, see Haunted Mansion. If not, skip to Step 24.

24. Evening parades are excellent. If you're interested, adjust the remaining touring plan to allow you to take a viewing position about 10 minutes before the early parade starts (about 8 or 9 p.m.). If you aren't interested, enjoy attractions in Adventureland during the parade.

25. Go to Adventureland by way of Liberty Square, Frontierland, or the central hub. Take the Jungle Cruise if lines are reasonable. If they're long, see *Tropical Serenade (Enchanted Tiki Birds)* and/or Swiss Family Treehouse. If your children can stand a few skeletons, see Pirates of the Caribbean.

26. If time remains before the park closes, repeat attractions the kids especially liked or try ones you might have missed.

Magic Kingdom Two-Day Touring Plan

For: Parties wishing to spread their Magic Kingdom
visit over two days

Assumes: Willingness to experience all major rides and shows

Timing: This plan takes advantage of early-morning touring.
Each day, you should complete the plan's structured part by
about 4 p.m. This leaves time to enjoy live entertainment.
If the park is open late (after 8 p.m.), consider returning
to your hotel for a midday break. Eat dinner early outside
Disney World and return refreshed to enjoy the
Kingdom at night.

Day One

1. If you're a Disney resort guest, use Disney transportation to commute to the park, arriving 90
   minutes before official opening *on early-entry days*
   and 30 minutes before official opening *on non-
   early-entry days.*

   If you're a day guest, arrive at the parking lot 50
   minutes before the Magic Kingdom's stated opening time *on a non-early-entry day.* Arrive an hour
   earlier than official opening if it's a holiday period
   or you must buy your admission. Take the tram to
   the Transportation and Ticket Center. At the TTC,
   transfer to the monorail or ferry to reach the park's
   entrance. If the line is short, take the monorail;
   otherwise, catch the ferry.

2. At the Magic Kingdom, proceed through the turnstiles and have one person go to City Hall for park
   guide maps containing the daily entertainment
   schedule.

3. Move quickly down Main Street to the central hub.
   Because the Magic Kingdom uses two procedures
   for opening, you'll encounter one of the following:

a. The entire park will be open. In this case, hurry to *Alien Encounter* in Tomorrowland.

b. Only Main Street will be open. In this case, turn right at the end of Main Street (before you reach the central hub), pass the Plaza Ice Cream Parlor and Plaza Restaurant, and stand at the entrance of Plaza Pavilion. When the rope barrier drops, jog through Plaza Pavilion to *Alien Encounter*. Starting at Plaza Pavilion will give you a 50-yard head start over anyone coming from the central hub. Experience *Alien Encounter*.

4. Exit left from *Alien Encounter* and move briskly to Space Mountain. Ride.

5. Exit Space Mountain, bear right past Grand Prix Raceway, and go to Fantasyland. Ride 20,000 Leagues Under the Sea.

6. Exit right from 20,000 Leagues and go through the castle's courtyard. Ride Peter Pan's Flight.

7. Exit right from Peter Pan and turn the corner. See *Legend of the Lion King*.

8. Exit left from Lion King, cross the courtyard, and ride It's a Small World.

9. Exit right from Small World and proceed to Liberty Square. Experience Haunted Mansion.

10. If you're hungry, eat. Fast-food places that are generally less crowded include Columbia Harbour House in Liberty Square, Aunt Polly's Landing on Tom Sawyer Island in Frontierland, El Pirata y El Perico in Adventureland, and Crystal Palace at the central hub end of Main Street. As a lunchtime option, check your guide map for the next performance of the *Diamond Horseshoe Revue*. If timing is right, eat a sandwich while watching the show.

11. After lunch, experience *Hall of Presidents* and Liberty Square Riverboat. Start with the one that has the shorter line.

Note: Check your daily entertainment schedule to see if there are any parades or live performances that interest you.

Plan accordingly. Since you already have seen the attractions that have big lines, an interruption of the touring plan won't cause problems. Simply pick up where you left off before the parade or show.

12. In Frontierland, raft to Tom Sawyer Island. Explore.
13. Returning from Tom Sawyer Island, see *Country Bear Jamboree.*
14. This concludes the day's touring. Enjoy the shops, see live entertainment, or revisit your favorite attractions until you're ready to leave.

Day Two

1. Follow Day One arrival procedure.
2. At the Magic Kingdom, check at City Hall for updates of the daily entertainment schedule.

Note: If you're a Disney resort guest and enter on an early-entry day, revisit your favorite Fantasyland and Tomorrow-land attractions. Just before the park opens to the public, stand at the boundary of Fantasyland and Liberty Square. When the other lands open, head for the Liberty Square waterfront and, from there, for Splash Mountain. Ride. Afterward, ride Big Thunder Mountain Railroad (Step 4), skipping steps that direct you to attractions you experienced during early entry.

3. Proceed to the end of Main Street. If the entire park is open, head immediately for Frontierland and Splash Mountain. Otherwise, turn left past Refreshment Corner and stand in front of Crystal Palace facing the walkway bridge to Adventureland. When the rope barrier drops, cross the bridge and turn left into Adventureland. Cut through Adventureland into Frontierland. Ride Splash Mountain.
4. Ride Big Thunder Mountain Railroad, next door.
5. Return to Adventureland. Ride the Jungle Cruise.
6. Across the street, see *Tropical Serenade (Enchanted Tiki Birds).*
7. Explore Swiss Family Treehouse.
8. Exit left and see Pirates of the Caribbean.

Note: Check your daily entertainment schedule for parades or performances that interest you. Plan accordingly. Since you have already seen all attractions that cause bottlenecks, an interruption of the plan here won't cause problems. Simply pick up where you left off before the parade or show.

9. If you're hungry, eat. Fast-food places that are generally less crowded include Columbia Harbour House in Liberty Square, Aunt Polly's Landing on Tom Sawyer Island in Frontierland, El Pirata y El Perico in Adventureland, and Crystal Palace at the central hub end of Main Street.

10. Go to Frontierland Station. Ride the train to Mickey's Toontown Fair.

11. Tour the fair and meet the characters.

12. Go to Tomorrowland via the path to Fantasyland, turning left at Grand Prix Raceway.

13. If you haven't eaten, try Cosmic Ray's Starlight Cafe (acceptable) or Plaza Pavilion (better).

14. Ride the Tomorrowland Transit Authority.

15. See *Carousel of Progress.*

16. Ride Dreamflight.

17. Proceed toward the central hub entrance of Tomorrowland and experience *The Timekeeper.*

18. This concludes the touring plan. Shop, see live entertainment, or revisit favorite attractions until you're ready to leave.

EPCOT

Not to Be Missed at EPCOT	
World Showcase	*The American Adventure*
	IllumiNations
Future World	Spaceship Earth
	Living With the Land
	Honey, I Shrunk the Audience
	Test Track
	Body Wars
	Cranium Command
	Horizons

• Overview •

Fantasy isn't the focus at EPCOT; education and inspiration are. The park has only two theme areas: Future World and World Showcase. Still, it's more than twice as big as the Magic Kingdom or Disney-MGM Studios and requires considerably more walking among the sights. Lines are equally long.

EPCOT's size means you can't see it in a day without skipping attractions or giving some areas a cursory glance. Fortunately, some attractions can be savored slowly or skimmed, depending on personal interests. For example, the first section of the World of Motion pavilion is a thrill ride, the second a collection of educational exhibits and mini-theaters. Nearly everyone takes the ride, but many people bypass the exhibits.

EPCOT is more an adult place than the Magic Kingdom is. What it gains in taking a futuristic and technological look at the world, it loses in warmth, happiness, and charm.

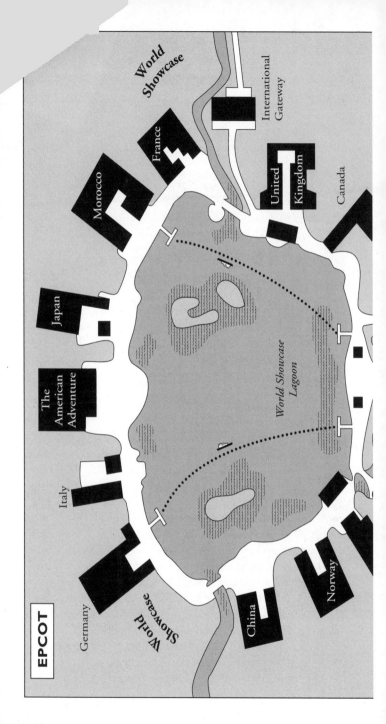

EPCOT

World Showcase

International Gateway

France

Morocco

Japan

The American Adventure

Italy

Germany

World Showcase

United Kingdom

Canada

World Showcase Lagoon

China

Norway

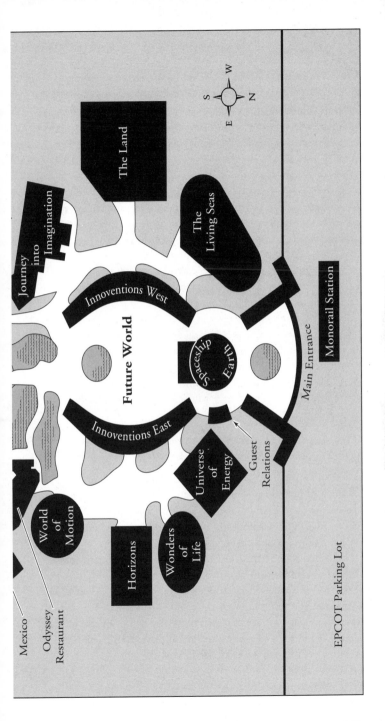

• Operating Hours •

Future World always opens before the World Showcase in the morning and usually closes before World Showcase in the evening. Most of the year, World Showcase opens two hours later than Future World. For exact times, call (407) 824-4321.

• Arriving •

Disney hotel and campground guests are invited to enter EPCOT one hour early two days each week, usually Tuesday and Friday. If you have early-entry privileges, arrive about an hour and a half before official opening.

Those lodging outside Disney World should avoid EPCOT on early-entry days, which pack the park. Regardless, arrive 40 to 50 minutes before official opening.

To verify early-entry days, call (407) 824-4321.

EPCOT has its own parking lot, and there's no need to take a monorail or ferry to reach the entrance. Trams serve the lot, or you can walk to the front gate. Monorail service connects EPCOT with the Transportation and Ticket Center, Magic Kingdom (transfer required), and Magic Kingdom resorts (transfer required).

• Getting Oriented •

EPCOT's theme sections are distinctly different. Future World combines Disney creativity and corporations' technological resources to examine where mankind has come from and is going. World Showcase features landmarks, cuisine, and culture of 11 nations and is a sort of permanent world's fair.

Navigating the park is fairly simple. Its focal point, Spaceship Earth, is visible from almost everywhere in EPCOT. But the 180-foot geosphere is in a busy location, making it a poor meeting place. It's better to regroup at any national pavilion, but be specific. Each pavilion is a mini-town with buildings, monuments, gardens, and plazas. In Japan, for example, pinpoint a spot such as the sidewalk side of the pagoda.

• The New EPCOT •

Disney updated EPCOT in 1994. The Land pavilion and its attractions were renovated. CommuniCore, at the heart of Future World, was replaced by Innoventions, featuring products and technologies of the near future. Spaceship Earth, the attraction inside the huge dome, was partially redesigned, and a new 3-D movie premiered at Journey Into Imagination. Additional street vendors and entertainers were introduced into World Showcase, and two new shows joined the live entertainment.

• Ratings •

In the descriptions of attractions which follow, we give ratings based on a scale of zero to five stars. Five stars is the best rating.

Future World

Gleaming, futuristic structures define this theme area at EPCOT's main entrance. Broad thoroughfares are punctuated with billowing fountains—all reflected in space-age facades. Everything is sparkling clean and seems bigger than life. Pavilions dedicated to mankind's past, present, and future technological accomplishments form the perimeter of Future World. Central is Spaceship Earth, flanked by Innoventions East and West.

Most services are concentrated in Future World's Entrance Plaza, near the main gate. Guest Relations, left of the sphere, is the park headquarters and information center. Staffed information booths and WorldKey information terminals are outside.

Touring Tips Make priority seating/reservations for sit-down restaurants through a WorldKey attendant instead of going to the restaurant itself.

Future World Services	
Wheelchair & Stroller Rental	To the left inside the main entrance toward the rear of the Entrance Plaza
Banking Services	An ATM is outside the main entrance near the kennels.
Currency Exchange	Limited services are available at the American Express Travel Service, outside the entrance and right.
Storage Lockers	Right at Spaceship Earth (lockers cleaned out every night)

Future World Services *(continued)*

Lost & Found	Outside the main entrance, to the right
Live Entertainment Information	Guest Relations, left of Spaceship Earth
Lost Persons	At Guest Relations and at Baby Center on the World Showcase side of Odyssey Restaurant
Dining Reservations	Guest Relations
Walt Disney World & Local Attraction Information	Guest Relations
First Aid	Next to the Baby Center on the World Showcase side of Odyssey Restaurant
Baby Center/ Baby Care Needs	On the World Showcase side of Odyssey Restaurant

Spaceship Earth

What It Is: Educational dark ride through past, present, and future

Scope & Scale: Headliner

When to Go: Before 10 a.m. or after 4 p.m.

Special Comments: If lines are long, try again after 4 p.m.

Author's Rating: One of EPCOT's best. Not to be missed;
★★★★

Overall Appeal by Age Group:

Pre-school	Grade School	Teens	Young Adults	Over 30	Senior Citizens
★★★★	★★★★½	★★★★½	★★★★½	★★★★½	★★★★½

Duration of Ride: About 16 minutes

Avg. Wait in Line per 100 People Ahead of You: 3 minutes

Assumes: Normal operation

Loading Speed: Fast

Description and Comments   This Bell System ride spirals through the 17-story interior of EPCOT's premier landmark, taking visitors past audio-animatronic scenes depicting mankind's developments in communications. The ride is compelling and well done.

Touring Tips   Because it's near EPCOT's main entrance, Spaceship Earth is packed all morning. If you're among the first guests in the park, ride. Otherwise, wait until after 4 p.m.

As you face the entrance to Spaceship Earth, look to see whether the two queuing areas between the direct walkway are in use. If so, bypass Spaceship Earth temporarily. If the line runs only along the right side of the sphere, you'll board in less than 15 minutes.

• Innoventions •

What It Is: Static and hands-on exhibits relating to products and technologies of the near future

Scope & Scale: Major diversion

When to Go: Second day at EPCOT or after you've seen all major attractions

Special Comments: Most exhibits demand time and participation; not much gained here by a quick walk-through.

Author's Rating: Vastly improved; ★★★½

Overall Appeal by Age Group:

Pre-school	Grade School	Teens	Young Adults	Over 30	Senior Citizens
★½	★★★½	★★★★	★★★½	★★★	★★★

Description and Comments   Innoventions consists of two huge, crescent-shaped, glass-walled structures separated by a central plaza. Formerly called CommuniCore, the complex was designed to be EPCOT's communications and community hub. But during EPCOT's first 12 years, it was a staid museum of science and industry.

The changes of 1994 aimed to return it to its original concept. The result is a busy collection of industry-sponsored walk-through and hands-on exhibits. Dynamic, interactive, and forward-looking, Innoventions previews consumer and industrial goods of the near future. Electronics, communications, and entertainment technology are prominent. Exhibits, many changed each year, emphasize the product's or technology's effect on daily life. The most popular attraction is an arcade of video and simulator games. Frequently overlooked is the well-done tour of a Disney Imagineering studio. Innoventions also houses restaurants, shops, and EPCOT Discovery Center.

Touring Tips   Innoventions can be crowded. Readers tell us that young children may not be able to get near some attractions and that noise is awesome. A few complain about exhibits' commercialism. Nonetheless, some exhibits are intriguing. Spend time on your second day at EPCOT. If you have only one day, visit during evening, but be aware that many exhibits are technical and can't be enjoyed or understood if you're too weary.

• The Living Seas •

What It Is: Ride beneath a huge saltwater aquarium, plus exhibits on oceanography, ocean ecology, and sea life

Scope & Scale: Major attraction

When to Go: Before 10 a.m. or after 3 p.m.

Special Comments: The ride is only a small component of this attraction.

Author's Rating: An excellent marine exhibit; ★★★½

Overall Appeal by Age Group:

Pre-school	Grade School	Teens	Young Adults	Over 30	Senior Citizens
★★★	★★★½	★★★½	★★★★	★★★★	★★★★

Duration of Ride: 3 minutes

Avg. Wait in Line per 100 People Ahead of You: 3½ minutes

Assumes: All elevators in operation

Loading Speed: Fast

Description and Comments   This is among Future World's most ambitious attractions. Scientists and divers conduct actual marine experiments in a 200-foot-diameter, 27-foot-deep main tank containing fish, mammals, and crustaceans in a simulation of an ocean ecosystem. Visitors view the activity through 8-inch-thick windows below the surface (including windows in Coral Reef restaurant) and aboard an adventure ride consisting of a movie dramatizing the link between the ocean and human survival, a simulated descent to the bottom of the tank, and a 3-minute gondola voyage through an underwater viewing tunnel.

The underwater ride is over almost before you're settled in the gondola. No matter; the strength of this attraction lies in exhibits afterward. Visitors can view fish-breeding experiments, watch films about sea life, and more.

Living Seas is a high-quality marine/aquarium exhibit, but it's no substitute for visiting Sea World, an outstanding marine theme park at Orlando.

Touring Tips   Exhibits at the ride's end are the best part of Living Seas. In the morning, these are often bypassed by guests trying to stay ahead of the crowd. Linger at Living Seas when you aren't hurried. We recommend visiting in late afternoon or evening or on your second day at EPCOT.

• The Land Pavilion •

Description and Comments   The Land pavilion, sponsored by Nestlé, contains three attractions and several restaurants. Its original emphasis was farming, but changes in 1994 refocused it on environmental concerns.

Touring Tips   The Land is a good place for a fast-food lunch; if you want to see the attractions, don't go during mealtimes.

Living With the Land

What It Is: An indoor boat-ride adventure through the past, present, and future of U.S. farming and agriculture

Scope & Scale: Major attraction

When to Go: Before 10:30 a.m. or after 7:30 p.m.

Special Comments: Ride in early morning, but save other Land attractions for later. Located on the lower level of The Land.

Author's Rating: Interesting and fun. Not to be missed; ★★★★

Overall Appeal by Age Group:

Pre-school	Grade School	Teens	Young Adults	Over 30	Senior Citizens
★★★	★★★	★★★½	★★★★	★★★★★	★★★★★

Duration of Ride: About 12 minutes

Avg. Wait in Line per 100 People Ahead of You: 3 minutes

Assumes: 15 boats operating

Loading Speed: Moderate

Description and Comments Boat ride takes visitors through swamps, past inhospitable environments man has faced as a farmer, and through a futuristic greenhouse where real crops are being grown using the latest agricultural technologies. Inspiring and educational, with excellent effects and a good narrative.

Touring Tips See this attraction before the lunch crowd hits or in the evening.

If you really enjoy this ride or have a special interest in the agriculture demonstrated, take the Backstage Tour. At $6 for adults and $4 for children ages 3–9, this 45-minute guided excursion goes behind the scenes for an in-depth examination of growing methods. Reservations are accepted, space available, at the tour waiting area (far right of restaurants on lower level).

Food Rocks

What It Is: Audio-animatronic theater show about food and nutrition

Scope & Scale: Minor attraction

When to Go: Before 11 a.m. or after 2 p.m.

Special Comments: On lower level of The Land

Author's Rating: Sugarcoated nutrition lesson; ★★½

Overall Appeal by Age Group:

Pre-school	Grade School	Teens	Young Adults	Over 30	Senior Citizens
★★★½	★★★½	★★★	★★★	★★★	★★★

Duration of Presentation: Approximately 13 minutes

Preshow Entertainment: None

Probable Waiting Time: Less than 10 minutes

Description and Comments Audio-animatronic foods and cooking utensils perform in a marginally educational rock concert. Featured artists include the Peach Boys, Chubby Cheddar, Neil Moussaka, and Pita Gabriel. Little Richard is the voice of a singing pineapple. Fast-paced and imaginative, *Food Rocks* is better entertainment than its predecessor, *Kitchen Kaberet,* and delivers the message about as well.

Touring Tips   One of EPCOT's few light entertainment offerings. Though the theater isn't large, we've never waited long, even during mealtimes.

Harvest Theater

What It Is: Film exploring mankind's relationship with the environment

Scope & Scale: Minor attraction

When to Go: Before 11 a.m. and after 2 p.m.

Author's Rating: Highly interesting and enlightening.
Not to be missed; ★★★½

Overall Appeal by Age Group:

Pre-school	Grade School	Teens	Young Adults	Over 30	Senior Citizens
★★★½	★★★★	★★★½	★★★½	★★★★	★★★½

Duration of Presentation: Approximately 12½ minutes

Preshow Entertainment: None

Probable Waiting Time: 10–15 minutes

Description and Comments   The featured attraction is *The Circle of Life,* starring Simba, Timon, and Pumbaa from Disney's *The Lion King.* This superb film spotlights the environmental interdependency of all creatures on Earth. It's sobering, but not too heavy-handed.

Touring Tips   Crowds are least in late afternoon. Lines are long at mealtimes.

• Journey Into Imagination Pavilion •

Description and Comments   Multi-attraction pavilion on the west side of Innoventions West, down the walk from The Land. Outside is an "upside-down waterfall" and one of our favorite Future World landmarks, the "jumping water," a fountain that leapfrogs passersby.

Touring Tips   Go in early morning or late evening.

Journey Into Imagination

What It Is: Fantasy adventure dark ride

Scope & Scale: Major attraction

When to Go: Before 10:30 a.m. or after 6 p.m.

Author's Rating: Colorful but boring; ★★

Overall Appeal by Age Group:

Pre-school	Grade School	Teens	Young Adults	Over 30	Senior Citizens
★★★★	★★★★	★★★	★★★	★★★	★★★

Duration of Ride: Approximately 13 minutes

Avg. Wait in Line per 100 People Ahead of You: 3 minutes

Assumes: 20 trains operating

Loading Speed: Moderate to fast

Description and Comments   This ride stars Figment, an impish purple dragon, and Dreamfinder, a red-bearded adventurer who pilots a contraption designed to search out and capture ideas. The ride, with its happy, humorous orientation, is one of EPCOT's lighter and more fanciful offerings. It's the favorite ride of some; others find it vacuous.

Touring Tips   This ride, combined with the 3-D movie in the same building, draws large crowds, beginning about 10:45 a.m.

The Image Works

What It Is: Hands-on creative playground employing color, music, touch-sensation, and electronic devices

Scope & Scale: Diversion

When to Go: Anytime

Special Comments: You don't have to wait in the ride line to enter Image Works. Go through the door just left of where riders are entering.

Author's Rating: A fun change of pace; be sure to see Dreamfinder's School of Drama; ★★½

Overall Appeal by Age Group:

Pre-school	Grade School	Teens	Young Adults	Over 30	Senior Citizens
★★★	★★★½	★★★	★★★	★★★	★★★

Probable Waiting Time: No waiting

Description and Comments   This is a playground for the imagination. Especially fun is Electronic Philharmonic, at which visitors conduct the brass, woodwind, percussion, and string sections of an orchestra by hand movements. (The secret is raising and lowering your hands over the discs on the console. Don't press them. Raise a hand away from the disc labeled brass, for example, and you get louder brass.)

Dreamfinder's School of Drama is the best of Image Works offerings. Children volunteer to act in a short play augmented by video effects. It's easy and delightful; just don't wear blue, which is invisible against the background screen.

Touring Tips   There are many interesting activities here. Visit on your second day at EPCOT or in late afternoon or evening.

Magic Eye Theater: *Honey, I Shrunk the Audience*

What It Is: 3-D film with special effects

Scope & Scale: Headliner

When to Go: Before 10 a.m. or just before Future World closes

Special Comments: Loud, intense show with tactile effects frightens some young children. Adults shouldn't be put off by the sci-fi theme.

Author's Rating: An absolute hoot! Not to be missed; ★★★★½

Overall Appeal by Age Group:

Pre-school	Grade School	Teens	Young Adults	Over 30	Senior Citizens
★★★½	★★★★½	★★★★½	★★★★	★★★★	★★★½

Duration of Presentation: Approximately 17 minutes

Preshow Entertainment: 8 minutes

Probable Waiting Time: 12 minutes (at suggested times)

Description and Comments   *Honey, I Shrunk the Audience* is a 3-D offshoot of Disney's feature film *Honey, I Shrunk the Kids.* Rich special effects include simulated explosions, smoke, fiber optics, lights, water spray, and moving seats—all played for laughs.

Touring Tips   The sound is earsplitting, frightening some children and discomforting many adults.

Though launched with little fanfare in 1994, *Honey, I Shrunk the Audience* has become the park's most popular attraction. It isn't necessary to ride Journey Into Imagination to enter; the theater is left of the ride. Avoid seats in the first several rows. If you're too close to the screen, 3-D images don't focus properly.

• World of Motion Pavilion •

Description and Comments　World of Motion, presented by General Motors, contains the ride Test Track and TransCenter, an assembly of exhibits and mini-theater productions on the transportation theme. The pavilion is left of Spaceship Earth, toward World Showcase from the Universe of Energy pavilion.

Many readers say World of Motion is one big GM commercial. We recognize the heavy hype, but we consider World of Motion one of the most creatively conceived and executed attractions in Disney World.

Test Track (Opens summer 1997)

What It Is:　Racetrack simulator ride

Scope & Scale:　Super headliner

When to Go:　Before noon and after 4 p.m.

Author's Rating:　Not open at press time

Overall Appeal by Age Group:　Not open at press time

Duration of Ride:　Approximately 5 minutes

Avg. Wait in Line per 100 People Ahead of You:　4 minutes

Assumes:　Normal operation

Loading Speed:　Moderate to fast

Description and Comments　Test Track combines roller-coaster and simulator technologies. Visitors test a future model car at high speeds through hairpin turns, up and down steep hills, and over rough terrain. The track, simulated on film, surrounds you. The six-guest vehicle is a motion simulator that rocks and pitches. Unlike simulators at Star Tours, Body Wars, and Back to the Future, the Test Track model is affixed to a track and actually travels. It accelerates to 45 mph, making it one of the fastest attractions developed.

Touring Tips   Some great technology is at work here. If the ride lives up to expectations, it will be EPCOT's "not-to-be-missed," premier thrill ride. Regardless, it will be popular because it's new. Expect crowds most of the day; try to ride before 10 a.m. or the hour before Future World closes.

• Horizons •

What It Is: A look at mankind's evolving perception of the future

Scope & Scale: Major attraction

When to Go: Before 11 a.m. or after 3:30 p.m.

Author's Rating: Retro-future meets future-future. Not to be missed; ★★★½

Overall Appeal by Age Group:

Pre-school	Grade School	Teens	Young Adults	Over 30	Senior Citizens
★★★★	★★★★	★★★★	★★★★½	★★★★½	★★★★½

Duration of Ride: Approximately 15 minutes

Avg. Wait in Line per 100 People Ahead of You: 4 minutes

Assumes: Normal operation

Loading Speed: Fast

Description and Comments   Horizons looks back at yesterday's visions of the future, including Jules Verne's concept of a moon rocket and a 1930s preview of a neon city. Elsewhere, guests visit FuturePort and ride through a family habitat of the next century.

Horizons closed in 1994 when its corporate sponsor withdrew but reopened when nearby World of Motion closed for construction of Test Track. While the long-term future of Horizons is unclear, it probably will remain open until summer 1997.

Touring Tips   The pavilion is devoted to a single, continuously loading, high-capacity ride. If it's open, don't miss it. Hesitate only when up to 580 patrons exit a Universe of Energy show and queue up at Horizons en masse. Return in 15 minutes, and you'll walk right in.

• **Wonders of Life Pavilion** •

Description and Comments   This newest addition to Future World deals with the human body, health, and medicine. Housed in a 100,000-square-foot, gold-domed structure and presented by Metropolitan Life Insurance Co., Wonders of Life focuses on the capabilities of the human body and the importance of keeping fit.

Body Wars

What It Is: Flight-simulator ride through the human body

Scope & Scale: Headliner

When to Go: As soon as possible after the park opens

Special Comments: Not recommended for pregnant women or those prone to motion sickness

Author's Rating: Absolutely mind-blowing. Not to be missed;
★★★★

Overall Appeal by Age Group:

Pre-school	Grade School	Teens	Young Adults	Over 30	Senior Citizens
★★★	★★★★½	★★★★★	★★★★	★★★★	★★★

Duration of Ride: 5 minutes

Avg. Wait in Line per 100 People Ahead of You: 4 minutes

Assumes: All simulators operating

Loading Speed: Moderate to fast

Description and Comments   This thrill ride through the human body was developed along the lines of the Star Tours space-simulation ride. The story is that you're a passenger in a miniature capsule injected into a body to retrieve a scientist who has been inspecting a splinter in the patient's finger. The scientist, however, is sucked into the circulatory system, and you chase throughout the body to rescue her. The simulator creates a visually graphic experience as it seems to hurtle at fantastic speeds through human organs.

Touring Tips   Body Wars is popular with people of all ages, but it makes a lot of riders motion sick. It isn't unusual for a simulator to be taken off line to clean up a previous rider's mess. If you're at all susceptible to motion sickness, reconsider riding. If you're on the ride and become nauseated, look away from the screen (at the ceiling or side and back walls, for example). Without the visual effects, the ride isn't rough enough to disturb most guests. If you get queasy, rest rooms are nearby as you exit. (*Note:* Star Tours at Disney-MGM Studios is just as wild but makes very few people sick. Successfully riding Star Tours doesn't mean you'll tolerate Body Wars. Conversely, if Body Wars made you ill, don't assume Star Tours will, too.)

Motion sickness aside, Body Wars is too intense (even terrifying) for some, especially preschoolers and seniors.

Cranium Command

What It Is: Audio-animatronic theater show about the brain

Scope & Scale: Major attraction

When to Go: Before 11 a.m. or after 3 p.m.

Author's Rating: Funny, outrageous, and educational.
   Not to be missed; ★★★★★

Overall Appeal by Age Group:

Pre- school	Grade School	Teens	Young Adults	Over 30	Senior Citizens
★★★	★★★★★	★★★★★	★★★★★	★★★★★	★★★★★

Duration of Presentation: About 20 minutes

Preshow Entertainment: Explanatory lead-in to feature presentation

Probable Waiting Time: Less than 10 minutes at times suggested

Description and Comments   *Cranium Command* is EPCOT's great sleeper. Stuck on the backside of Wonders of Life and far less promoted than Body Wars, this most humorous attraction is bypassed by many people. Characters called "brain pilots" are trained to operate human brains. The show consists of a day in the life of one of these Cranium Commanders as he tries to pilot the brain of an adolescent boy. EPCOT and Disney World could use a lot more of this type of humor.

Touring Tips   To understand the program, you need to see the preshow cartoon in the waiting area. Most preschoolers enjoy *Cranium Command,* but many don't really understand it.

The Making of Me

What It Is: Humorous movie about human conception and birth

Scope & Scale: Minor attraction

When to Go: Early in the morning or after 4:30 p.m.

Author's Rating: Sanitized sex education; ★★★

Overall Appeal by Age Group:

Pre-school	Grade School	Teens	Young Adults	Over 30	Senior Citizens
★★★	★★★	★★★½	★★★½	★★★	★★★

Duration of Presentation: 14 minutes

Preshow Entertainment: None

Probable Waiting Time: About 25 minutes (or more), unless you go at recommended times

Description and Comments   This lighthearted and very sensitive movie about human conception, gestation, and birth was originally considered controversial, but most viewers agree that the material is tasteful and creative. The plot's main character goes back in time to watch his parents date, fall in love, marry and, yes, conceive and give birth to him. Look for the biological error in the film. If you spot it, write us.

Sexual material is well handled, with emphasis on loving relationships, not plumbing. Parents say the sexual information went over the heads of children younger than 7. In older children, however, the film precipitates questions.

Touring Tips   The Making of Me is excellent and should be moved from its tiny space to a larger theater. Until (and if) it is, expect long lines unless you go at recommended times.

Fitness Fairgrounds

Description and Comments   Participatory exhibits allow guests to test their senses in a funhouse, get computer-generated health analyses, work out on sophisticated equipment, and watch a video called *Goofy about Health* (starring, who else?).

Touring Tips   Save Fitness Fairgrounds for your second day or the end of your first day at EPCOT.

• Universe of Energy Pavilion •

What It Is: Combination ride/theater presentation about energy

Scope & Scale: Major attraction

When to Go: Before 10:30 a.m. or after 4:30 p.m.

Special Comments: Don't be dismayed by lines; 580 people enter the pavilion each time the theater empties.

Author's Rating: A creative combination of theater and ride. Not to be missed; ★★★

Overall Appeal by Age Group:

Pre-school	Grade School	Teens	Young Adults	Over 30	Senior Citizens
★★★	★★★	★★★½	★★★½	★★★½	★★★½

Duration of Presentation: Approximately 26½ minutes

Preshow Entertainment: 8 minutes

Probable Waiting Time: 20–40 minutes

Description and Comments Audio-animatronic dinosaurs and the unique traveling theater make this Exxon pavilion one of Future World's most popular. Visitors are seated in what appears to be an ordinary theater to watch an animated film on fossil fuels. Then the theater seats divide into six 97-passenger traveling cars, which glide among swamps and reptiles of a prehistoric forest. Special effects include warm, moist air from the swamp, the smell of sulphur from an erupting volcano, and the sight of lava hissing and bubbling toward passengers. Nifty cinematic techniques bring you back to the leading edge of energy research and development.

Universe of Energy is a toss-up for kids. The dinosaurs sometimes frighten preschoolers, and almost all kids (and many adults) are bored by the educational segments.

Touring Tips Universe of Energy can operate more than one show at a time, so lines generally are tolerable. If you bypass the show, try to see the great dinosaur topiaries at the pavilion.

• The "Mom, I Can't Believe It's Disney!" Fountain •

What It Is: Combination fountain and shower

When to Go: When it's hot

Scope & Scale: Diversion

Special Comments: Secretly installed by Martians during
   IllumiNations

Author's Rating: Yes!! ★★★★

Overall Appeal by Age Group:

Pre-school	Grade School	Teens	Young Adults	Over 30	Senior Citizens
★★★★★	★★★★★	★★★★	★★★★	★★★★	★★★★★

Duration of Experience: Indefinite

Probable Waiting Time: None

Description and Comments   This fountain on the walkway link-
ing Future World and World Showcase doesn't look like much,
but it offers the only truly spontaneous experience in Walt Disney World.

Spouts of water erupt randomly from the sidewalk. You can
swim in the water or let it cascade down on you or blow up your
britches. On a broiling Florida day, people fling themselves into
the fountain, dancing, skipping, singing, and splashing. Kids
throw off their clothes. It's hard to imagine so much personal
freedom in carefully controlled Disney World, but here it is.
Hurrah!

Touring Tips   Your kids will be in the middle of this before your
brain sounds the alert. Our advice: Pack dry shorts and turn
them loose.

World Showcase

World Showcase, EPCOT's second theme area, is an ongoing world's fair set on a picturesque lagoon. Architecture, culture, cuisine, and history of 11 nations is permanently displayed at pavilions replicating familiar landmarks. Representative street scenes from host countries are spaced along a 1.2-mile promenade circling the 40-acre lagoon.

Most adults enjoy World Showcase, but many children find it boring. To help this, the Camera Center in Future World sells a Passport Kit (about $9). Each contains a blank passport and stamps for each Showcase nation. As kids visit a country, they tear out the appropriate stamp and stick it in the passport. The kit also contains basic information on the countries. Parents say the kit helps children tour World Showcase with minimal impatience.

Double-decker buses carry visitors around the promenade, and boats ferry guests across the lagoon. Lines at bus stops can be pushy, however, and it's almost always quicker to walk than to ride buses or boats. Moving clockwise around the promenade, nations represented are:

• Mexico Pavilion •

Description and Comments Pre-Columbian pyramids dominate the architecture. One forms the pavilion's facade; the other overlooks the restaurant and plaza beside the boat ride, El Rio del Tiempo.

Touring Tips Romantic and exciting testimony to Mexico's charms, this pavilion also contains authentic and valuable artifacts and art. The village scene is beautiful and exquisitely detailed. See this pavilion before 11 a.m. or after 6 p.m.

El Rio del Tiempo

What It Is: Indoor scenic boat ride

Scope & Scale: Minor attraction

When to Go: Before 11 a.m. or after 3 p.m.

Author's Rating: Light and relaxing; ★★½

Overall Appeal by Age Group:

Pre-school	Grade School	Teens	Young Adults	Over 30	Senior Citizens
★★★	★★★	★★★	★★★	★★★	★★★

Duration of Ride: Approximately 7 minutes (plus 1½-minute wait to disembark)

Avg. Wait in Line per 100 People Ahead of You: 4½ minutes

Assumes: 16 boats in operation

Loading Speed: Moderate

Description and Comments   El Rio del Tiempo (River of Time) winds among audio-animatronic and cinematic scenes depicting Mexico's history. Special effects include simulated fireworks.

Pleasant and relaxing, but not particularly interesting, El Rio del Tiempo isn't worth a long wait.

Touring Tips   The ride is crowded in early afternoon.

• Norway Pavilion •

Description and Comments   The Norwegian pavilion is complex, beautiful, and architecturally diverse. Surrounding a courtyard are traditional Scandinavian buildings, including a replica of the 14th-century Akershus Castle, a wooden stave church, red-tiled cottages, and replicas of historic buildings. The pavilion also offers an adventure boat ride, a movie and, in the stave church, an art gallery. Located between China and Mexico, Norway houses the sit-down Restaurant Akershus (reservations required) serving koldtboard (cold buffet) and hot Norwegian fare. An outdoor cafe and a bakery cater to the hurried. Shoppers find native handicrafts.

Maelstrom

What It Is: Adventure indoor boat ride

Scope & Scale: Major attraction

When to Go: Before noon or after 4:30 p.m.

Author's Rating: Too short, but has its moments; ★★★

Overall Appeal by Age Group:

Pre-school	Grade School	Teens	Young Adults	Over 30	Senior Citizens
★★★★	★★★★	★★★★	★★★★	★★★★	★★★★

Duration of Ride: 4½ minutes, followed by a 5-minute film with a short wait in between; about 14 minutes total

Avg. Wait in Line per 100 People Ahead of You: 4 minutes

Assumes: 12–13 boats operating

Loading Speed: Fast

Description and Comments   In one of Disney's shorter boat rides, guests board dragon-headed ships for an adventure voyage through waters of Viking history and legend. They encounter trolls, gorges, waterfalls, and a storm at sea. Impressive special effects combine visual, tactile, and auditory stimuli. After this fast-paced and often humorous odyssey, guests see a 5-minute film on Norway. A vocal minority of readers considers the ride too brief and resents the "travelogue."

Touring Tips   Return later if several hundred guests from a recently concluded performance of *Wonders of China* have arrived en masse.

• People's Republic of China Pavilion •

Description and Comments   A half-sized replica of the Temple of Heaven in Beijing identifies this pavilion. Gardens and reflecting ponds simulate those in Suzhou, and an art gallery features a "Lotus Blossom" gate and saddle roofline.

Pass through the Hall of Prayer for Good Harvest to see the Circle-Vision 360° movie, *Wonders of China*. Warm and appealing, the film is a brilliant introduction to the nation. A fast-food eatery and a lovely, full-service establishment are available.

Touring Tips A beautiful, serene pavilion, yet exciting. The audience stands for the movie, but lines usually are short. If you're touring World Showcase counterclockwise and plan to go next to Norway and ride Maelstrom, stand on the far left of the theater (as you face the podium). After the show, be one of the first to exit, and beat the horde.

Wonders of China

What It Is: Film about Chinese people and country

Scope & Scale: Major attraction

When to Go: Anytime

Special Comments: Audience stands.

Author's Rating: Well produced, though film glosses over
   political unrest and recent events in Tibet; ★★★

Overall Appeal by Age Group:

Pre-school	Grade School	Teens	Young Adults	Over 30	Senior Citizens
★★★	★★★½	★★★½	★★★★½	★★★★½	★★★★

Duration of Presentation: Approximately 19 minutes

Preshow Entertainment: None

Probable Waiting Time: 10 minutes

• Germany Pavilion •

Description and Comments A clock tower rises above the Platz (plaza) marking the German pavilion. Dominated by a fountain depicting St. George and the dragon, the Platz is encircled by buildings in traditional architecture. The Biergarten, a full-service (reservations) restaurant, features German food and beer, yodeling, folk dancing, and oompah music.

Touring Tips Pleasant and festive, Germany is recommended anytime.

• Italy Pavilion •

Description and Comments The entrance to Italy is marked by a 105-foot bell tower mirroring that of Venice's St. Mark's

Square. To the left is a replica of the 14th-century Doge's Palace, another Venetian landmark. Other buildings are composites of Italian architecture. The pavilion has a waterfront on the lagoon with gondolas tied to striped moorings.

Touring Tips   Streets and courtyards in the pavilion are among the most realistic in World Showcase. Since there is no film or ride at Italy, touring is recommended anytime.

• The American Adventure •

What It Is: Patriotic mixed-media and audio-animatronic theater presentation on U.S. history

Scope & Scale: Headliner

When to Go: Anytime

Author's Rating: Disney's best historic/patriotic attraction. Not to be missed; ★★★★½

Overall Appeal by Age Group:

Pre-school	Grade School	Teens	Young Adults	Over 30	Senior Citizens
★★★	★★★★	★★★★	★★★★½	★★★★★	★★★★★

Duration of Presentation: Approximately 29 minutes

Preshow Entertainment: Voices of Liberty choral singing

Probable Waiting Time: 16 minutes

Description and Comments   The United States pavilion, generally referred to as *American Adventure,* encompasses a fast-food restaurant and a patriotic audio-animatronic show. *American Adventure* is a composite of everything Disney does best. Presented in an imposing brick structure reminiscent of colonial Philadelphia, the production is a stirring 29-minute rendition of American history narrated by Mark Twain and Ben Franklin. Behind a stage almost half the size of a football field is a 28-by-155-foot rear-projection screen (the largest ever used) on which images are interwoven with the action onstage.

Touring Tips   *American Adventure* isn't as interesting externally as most other pavilions, but the show is the best historic attraction in the Disney repertoire. It usually plays to capacity audiences from noon to 3:30 p.m., but it isn't hard to get into because the theater is large. Even during busy times, the wait averages 25 to 40 minutes. Because of its patriotic theme, *American Adventure* is decidedly less compelling to non-Americans.

The adjacent Liberty Inn restaurant serves a quick, non-ethnic meal.

• Japan Pavilion •

Description and Comments   A 5-story, blue-roofed pagoda inspired by a 7th-century shrine in Nara sets this pavilion apart. A hill garden behind blends waterfalls, rocks, flowers, lanterns, paths, and bridges. The building on the right of the entrance echoes the coronation hall of the Imperial Palace at Kyoto. This one, however, contains restaurants and a retail store.

Touring Tips   Tasteful and elaborate, Japan can be toured anytime.

• Morocco Pavilion •

Description and Comments   The bustling market, winding streets, lofty minarets, and stuccoed archways re-create the intrigue of Tangiers and Casablanca. Attention to detail makes Morocco one of the most exciting World Showcase pavilions. It also has a museum of Moorish art and Restaurant Marrakesh, which serves North African specialties.

Touring Tips   Morocco has neither ride nor theater; tour anytime.

• France Pavilion •

Description and Comments   Predictably, a replica of the Eiffel Tower is this pavilion's centerpiece. Beyond it, streets recall La Belle Epoque, the "beautiful time" between 1870 and 1910. The sidewalk cafe and the restaurant are very popular, as is the pastry shop (for its croissants).

Impressions de France is an 18-minute movie projected over 200° onto 5 screens. The audience sits to view this well-made introduction to the people, cities, and natural wonders of France.

Touring Tips Detail enriches the atmosphere of this pavilion, but the small streets become congested when lines form for the film. Waits can be long.

Impressions de France

What It Is: Film essay on the French people and country
Scope & Scale: Major attraction
When to Go: Before noon and after 4 p.m.
Author's Rating: Exceedingly beautiful film. Not to be missed;
   ★★★½

Overall Appeal by Age Group:

Pre-school	Grade School	Teens	Young Adults	Over 30	Senior Citizens
★★½	★★★½	★★★½	★★★★½	★★★★½	★★★★½

Duration of Presentation: Approximately 18 minutes
Preshow Entertainment: None
Probable Waiting Time: 12 minutes (at suggested times)

• United Kingdom Pavilion •

Description and Comments A variety of architectural styles are used to capture Britain's city, town, and rural atmospheres. The pavilion is mostly shops. The Rose & Crown Pub and Dining Room is World Showcase's only full-service restaurant with dining on the promenade's water side.

Touring Tips There are no attractions to create congestion; tour anytime. Reservations aren't required for the Rose & Crown's pub; stop for a beer in midafternoon.

• Canada Pavilion •

Description and Comments Thirty-foot totem poles embellish an Indian village at the foot of a château-style hotel in this large pavilion. Near the hotel is a rugged stone building modeled after a landmark near Niagara Falls. A fine film, *O Canada!,* demonstrates the immense pride Canadians have in their beautiful country. Visitors leave the theater through Victoria Gardens, inspired by British Columbia's famed Butchart Gardens.

Touring Tips Because Canada is the first pavilion as one travels counterclockwise around the lagoon, *O Canada!* is crowded in late morning. View the stand-up movie in late afternoon or early evening. Le Cellier, a cafeteria on the pavilion's lower level, is the only restaurant in World Showcase not requiring reservations.

O Canada!

What It Is: Film essay on the Canadian people and country

Scope & Scale: Major attraction

When to Go: Anytime

Special Comments: Audience stands.

Author's Rating: Makes you want to catch the first plane to Canada!; ★★★½

Overall Appeal by Age Group:

Pre-school	Grade School	Teens	Young Adults	Over 30	Senior Citizens
★★½	★★★	★★★½	★★★★	★★★★½	★★★★½

Duration of Presentation: Approximately 18 minutes

Preshow Entertainment: None

Probable Waiting Time: 10 minutes

Live Entertainment in EPCOT

Live entertainment in the World Showcase reflects the nations represented. Future World spotlights new and experimental performances. Obtain specifics on either at Guest Relations.

Here are performers you're apt to encounter.

Future World Brass Roving brass band marches and plays near Spaceship Earth and elsewhere in Future World.

Disney Characters Disney characters once were considered inconsistent with the image of EPCOT. That's changed. They now appear for meals at the Garden Grill Restaurant at The Land pavilion and in shows on American Gardens Stage and at Showcase Plaza between Mexico and Canada. Times are listed in the free guide map from Guest Relations.

American Gardens Stage Top talent worldwide plays American Gardens Stage near American Adventure, facing World Showcase Lagoon. Many shows highlight the performer's home country.

IllumiNations A not-to-be-missed multimedia program performed after dark on World Showcase Lagoon when the park is open late.

Around World Showcase Impromptu performances occur in and near World Showcase pavilions. They include strolling mariachis in Mexico, street actors in Italy, and a fife-and-drum corps or singing group (The Voices of Liberty) at *American Adventure.* Street entertainment occurs at pavilions about every half hour (though not necessarily on the hour or half hour).

Dinner & Lunch Shows World Showcase restaurants offer floor shows during mealtimes. Find singing waiters in Italy and belly dancers in Morocco, for example. Entertainment is at dinner only in Italy and Germany, but at both lunch and dinner in Morocco.

IllumiNations

IllumiNations integrates fireworks, laser lights, neon, and music in a stirring nightly tribute to nations represented at World Showcase. Presented on the lagoon, it's EPCOT's great outdoor spectacle.

Getting Out of EPCOT after IllumiNations

Pick your viewing spot after you decide how quickly you want to leave the park after the show. IllumiNations ends the day at EPCOT. Afterward, only a few shops remain open. With nothing to do, the crowd exits en masse, jamming Package Pick-up, the monorail station, and the Disney bus stop. Parking lot trams are at capacity.

If you're staying at an EPCOT resort (Swan and Dolphin hotels, Yacht and Beach Club resorts, and Boardwalk Inn and Villas), watch IllumiNations from the southern *(American Adventure)* half of the lagoon, then exit through International Gateway and walk or take a boat back to your hotel. If you have a car and are visiting EPCOT for dinner and IllumiNations, park at the Yacht or Beach Club. After the show, duck through International Gateway and be on the road in 15 minutes. If you're staying at any other Disney World hotel and don't have a car, join the exodus through the main gate and catch a bus or monorail.

More groups get separated, and more children lost, after IllumiNations than at any other time. In summer, the audience numbers up to 30,000 people. Anticipate this congestion and designate a spot in the EPCOT entrance area where you'll reassemble if you're separated. We recommend the fountain just inside the main entrance. No one in your party should exit the turnstiles until the whole group is together.

The main problem with having a car is getting to it. If you know where it is, skip the tram and walk. But hang on tightly to your children. The parking lot is extremely busy at this time.

Good Locations for Viewing IllumiNations and Other World Showcase Lagoon Performances

A seat on the lakeside veranda of Cantina de San Angel in Mexico is the best place to watch any show on World Showcase Lagoon. Come early (at least 90 minutes for IllumiNations) and relax with a cold drink while waiting for the show. The Rose & Crown Pub in the United Kingdom also has lagoonside seating, but a small wall downgrades the view.

If you want to combine dinner on the Rose & Crown's veranda with IllumiNations, make a reservation for about an hour and 15 minutes before showtime. Report a few minutes early for your seating and ask the host for a table outside where you can view IllumiNations. Our experience is that the Rose & Crown folks will bend over backward to accommodate you. If you can't get a table outside, eat inside and linger until show-time. When lights dim for IllumiNations, you'll be allowed onto the terrace.

Because most guests run for the exits after a presentation, and because islands in the southern half of the lagoon block the view from some places, the most popular spectator positions are along the northern waterfront from Norway and Mexico to Canada and the United Kingdom. The view is excellent; the trade-off is that you have to claim a spot 35–60 minutes before Illumi-Nations. For anyone who doesn't want to stand by a rail for 45 minutes, there are good viewing spots along the southern perime-ter (counterclockwise from United Kingdom to Germany) that often go unnoticed until 10–20 minutes before show time:

1. *The Once-Secret Park.* There's a wonderful waterside park that's known to only a few. To reach it, walk toward France from the Rose & Crown Pub in the United Kingdom. As you near the end of the pub, stay on the sidewalk and bear left. You'll find yourself in an almost private park, complete with benches and a perfect view of IllumiNations. En route is a roped-off back entrance to the pub's terrace. This is another good viewing spot; duck under the rope. Don't expect the park to be empty when you arrive—this guide gets around. Also, the park is frequently closed for private parties.

2. *International Gateway Island.* The pedestrian bridge across the canal near International Gateway spans an island that offers

great viewing spots. It normally fills 30 minutes or more before show time.

3. *Second-Floor (Restaurant-Level) Deck of the Mitsukoshi Building in Japan.* An oriental arch slightly blocks your sightline, but this covered deck offers shelter if it rains. Only Cantina de San Angel is more protected.

4. *Gondola Landing at Italy.* The elaborate waterfront promenade is excellent, but you must claim a spot at least 30 minutes before show time.

5. *The Boat Dock Opposite Germany.* The dock generally fills 30 minutes before show time.

6. *Waterfront Promenade by Germany.* Views are good from the 90-foot lagoonside walkway between Germany and China.

None of these viewpoints is reserved for *Unofficial Guide* readers, and on busier nights, many are claimed early. But we still won't hold down a slab of concrete for two hours before IllumiNations, as some people do. Most nights, you can find an acceptable spot 15–30 minutes before show time. And you needn't be right on the rail or have an unobstructed view of the water. Most of the action is significantly above ground. It's important, however, not to stand under a tree, awning, or anything that would block your overhead perspective.

Eating in EPCOT

EPCOT boasts 13 full-service restaurants: 2 in Future World and 11 in World Showcase. With a couple of exceptions, they rank among the best at Disney World.

Eating In EPCOT	
Future World Full-Service Restaurants	
Coral Reef	The Living Seas
The Garden Grill Restaurant	The Land
World Showcase Full-Service Restaurants	
Biergarten	Germany
Bistro de Paris	France
Chefs de France	France
L'Originale Alfredo di Roma Ristorante	Italy
Restaurant Akershus	Norway
Restaurant Marrakesh	Morocco
Tempura Kiku	Japan
Teppanyaki Dining Room	Japan
Nine Dragons Restaurant	China
Rose & Crown Dining Room	United Kingdom
San Angel Inn Restaurante	Mexico

For ratings of these full-service restaurants, refer to Dining in and Around Walt Disney World, pages 85–95.

Fifteen Years and Counting

We've been reviewing EPCOT's food service since the park opened in 1982 and we can report that it has improved. Choices are many for people too hurried for a sit-down meal, and the fast food is better here than in the Magic Kingdom or Disney-MGM Studios. Full-service ethnic restaurants now offer sampler platters and are bolder about serving authentic dishes.

Many EPCOT restaurants are overpriced, most conspicuously Nine Dragons (China) and Coral Reef (The Living Seas pavilion). Chefs de France and Bistro de Paris (France), Restaurant Akershus (Norway), Biergarten (Germany), and Restaurant Marrakesh (Morocco) offer relatively good value through well-prepared food and nice ambiance. If expense is an issue, have your main meal at lunch when entrees are similar but prices lower than at dinner.

Making dining reservations/priority seating requires standing in line at Guest Relations or going to the restaurant itself, but the restaurants are such an integral part of EPCOT that it would be a mistake not to eat at one.

Getting a Priority Seating/Reservation at an EPCOT Full-Service Restaurant

Disney resort guests may dial 55 or 56 from their rooms to arrange priority seating/reservations one to three days in advance.

Officially, persons lodging outside the World must book on the day of the meal. Since 1995, however, reservationists have accepted reservations from these guests. Thus, for all guests, we recommend reserving at (407) 939-3463 before you leave home.

For same-day reservations on site during busier seasons, arrive at the entrance turnstiles, ticket in hand, 45 minutes before EPCOT opens. When admitted, hurry to the Guest Relations reservations service. Book lunch and dinner at the same time. Be ready with alternatives if your first choices aren't available.

If you visit during slower seasons, you don't need to be compulsive about booking first thing. Most restaurants have seats available. One notable exception is the small San Angel Inn in Mexico.

If you follow one of our touring plans, you'll be near the U.S. pavilion at lunch. We suggest a reservation for 12:30 or 1 p.m. at nearby Germany. Or, for a lighter meal, try Tempura Kiku in Japan. For dinner, book the San Angel Inn in Mexico or Akershus in Norway. If you plan to eat dinner at the Coral Reef in Future World, wait until after dinner to see the attraction.

If you arrive late or can't plan ahead but still want to eat in a World Showcase restaurant:

1. Go to the chosen restaurant before mealtime and apply at the door for a reservation. Sometimes only lunch bookings are taken at the door, but lunch and dinner menus are comparable. Have your main meal at lunch.
2. Walk in at a restaurant about 11 a.m. or between 3 and 4 p.m.
3. Show up at Restaurant Marrakesh. Seats often go unfilled because Americans don't know the cuisine.

Avoiding the Bum's Rush

Efficient Disney staff processes diners out quickly. To linger over your expensive meal, do not order it all at once. Place drink orders while you study the menu. Next, order appetizers, but tell the waiter you need more time to choose your main course. Order your entree only after appetizers have been served. Dawdle over dessert.

EPCOT Dining for Families with Young Children

EPCOT's restaurants offer an excellent (though expensive) opportunity to introduce children to ethnic food. No matter how formal a restaurant looks or sounds, the staff is accustomed to dealing with children. Waiters keep little ones supplied with crackers and rolls and serve dinner much faster than in comparable restaurants. Children's menus, booster seats, and highchairs are available.

Preschoolers most enjoy Biergarten in Germany, San Angel Inn in Mexico, and Coral Reef in The Living Seas. Biergarten and San Angel offer reasonable value, plus good food. Coral Reef is overpriced but serves palatable food.

Our Favorites for a Meal

Author's Recommendation for Lunch: Regardless of where you're touring at lunchtime, we recommend eating in Mexico or Norway.

Author's Recommendation for Dinner: You can eat your evening meal in any EPCOT restaurant without interrupting the sequence or efficiency of one of our touring plans. We recommend a 7 p.m.

reservation when it gets dark early and an 8 p.m. reservation during late spring, summer, and early fall. Timing is important if you want to see IllumiNations.

For dinner, we suggest the sit-down restaurants in Norway, Mexico, Germany, and Morocco and Bistro de Paris in France. We also like sashimi at Matsu No Ma Lounge in Japan, followed by dinner at Tempura Kiku. If you prefer American cuisine, try the Garden Grill in Future World's Land pavilion.

Alternatives for Guests on the Go or on a Tight Budget

1. For fast food, eat before 11 a.m. or after 2 p.m. Odyssey Restaurant and Liberty Inn at *American Adventure* serve fast. Service is reasonably speedy in The Land, which is a cut above average, as are many counter-service restaurants in World Showcase.

2. If you want ethnic food without sit-down prices, try:

Norway	Kringla Bakeri og Kafé for pastries, open-face sandwiches (not all are bargains), and Ringnes beer (our favorite)
Germany	Sommerfest, for bratwurst and beer
Japan	Matsu No Ma Lounge, for sushi and sashimi
France	Boulangerie Pâtisserie, for French pastries
United Kingdom	Rose & Crown Pub for beers and ales

3. Review "Alternatives and Suggestions for Eating in the Magic Kingdom," pages 141–143. Tips for the Magic Kingdom also apply to EPCOT.

Other Things to Know about EPCOT

• Shopping in EPCOT •

Merchandise available in Future World generally is also sold elsewhere, except for EPCOT and Disney trademark souvenirs.

World Showcase shops add realism and atmosphere to the settings. Much of the merchandise, however, is overpriced and available elsewhere. But some shops really are special. In the United Kingdom, visit Queen's Table (fine china); China, Yong Feng Shangdian (crafts, rugs, carvings, furniture); Japan, Mitsukoshi Department Store (porcelain, bonsai trees, pearls from a live oyster).

Clerks will forward purchases to Package Pick-up. Allow three hours, and retrieve them when you leave the park. Specify whether you'll depart through the main entrance or International Gateway. Disney resort guests can have them sent to their rooms.

• Behind-the-Scenes Tours in EPCOT •

Readers rave about guided walking tours that explore architecture of the international pavilions (Hidden Treasures of World Showcase) and/or Walt Disney World's landscaping (Gardens of the World). Each lasts about four hours and is open to persons age 16 and older. Either costs about $25, plus EPCOT admission. For a discount, charge on an American Express card. For reservations, call (407) 939-8687.

A shorter option is The Land Backstage Tour, which goes behind the scenes at vegetable gardens in The Land. Make same-day reservations on the lower level of The Land (far right of the fast-food windows). Cost of the hour-long tour is $6 for adults and $4 for children ages 3–9.

• Traffic Patterns in EPCOT •

After admiring the traffic flow at the Magic Kingdom, we were amazed by EPCOT, which has no feature such as the Magic Kingdom's Main Street, which funnels visitors to a central hub that distributes them almost equally to the lands.

Spaceship Earth, EPCOT's premier landmark and a headliner attraction, is just inside the main entrance. Arriving visitors head straight for it, and crowds form as soon as the park opens. The congestion, however, does provide opportunities for avoiding lines at other Future World attractions.

Crowds in Future World build between 9 and 11 a.m. Even when World Showcase opens (usually 11 a.m.), more people are entering Future World than leaving it for World Showcase. Throngs continue to grow until between noon and 2 p.m., when guests head for lunch in World Showcase. Exhibits at the far end of World Showcase play to capacity audiences from about noon through 6:30 or 7:30 p.m. Not until evening do crowds equalize in Future World and World Showcase. Attendance throughout EPCOT is lighter then.

Some guests leave EPCOT after dinner, but most stay for IllumiNations and exit en masse. Even so, the crush isn't as intense as it is when the Magic Kingdom closes, primarily because the parking lot is next to the park and guests don't have to use a monorail or boat to reach their cars.

EPCOT Touring Plans

The EPCOT touring plans are field-tested, step-by-step itineraries for seeing all major attractions with minimum waiting. They keep you ahead of the crowds in the morning and place you at less crowded attractions during busier times of day. They assume you'd prefer a *little* extra walking to a lot of standing in line.

Touring EPCOT is much more strenuous than touring the Magic Kingdom. EPCOT is twice as large, and it has no effective transportation system; wherever you want to go, it's always quicker to walk. Touring plans help you avoid bottlenecks on days of moderate to heavy attendance and organize your visit on days of lighter attendance. In either case, they can't shorten the walk.

EPCOT touring plans include:

- Author's Selective EPCOT One-Day Touring Plan
- EPCOT Two-Day Touring Plan

• EPCOT Touring Plans and Young Children •

EPCOT is educationally oriented and more adult than the Magic Kingdom. Most younger children enjoy EPCOT if their visit is seven hours or less in duration and emphasizes Future World. Younger children, especially grade-schoolers, find World Showcase exciting but don't have the patience for much more than a walk-through.

If possible, adults touring with children age 8 and younger should use the Two-Day Touring Plan (pages 210–213) or the Author's Selective One-Day Touring Plan (pages 207–209). The two-day plan is comprehensive but divides the tour into two less arduous visits. The selective one-day plan includes only the best attractions and is shorter and less physically demanding. Adults with young children following the one-day plan should consider bypassing movies in Canada and China, where the audience must stand. Also, review "Disney, Kids, and Scary Stuff" on pages 57–59.

You and your young children will enjoy the day more if you leave the park after lunch to swim and nap. Even families lodging outside Disney World should consider taking a break. If you're following one of our touring plans, simply suspend it after lunch and return to your hotel. Resist the temptation to rest in the park unless your children are small enough to take a long nap in a stroller. When you return refreshed in late afternoon, visit any attractions in Future World that you missed in the morning.

• About the International Gateway •

The International Gateway is a secondary entrance to EPCOT between the United Kingdom and France in World Showcase. It provides easy access by boat or foot to lodgers at Disney's Swan and Dolphin hotels, the Boardwalk Inn and Villas, and Disney's Yacht and Beach Club resorts. Stroller and wheelchair rentals are available. If you enter here in the morning before World Showcase opens (around 10 or 11 a.m.), you'll be taken to Future World on double-decker buses.

Preliminary Instructions for All EPCOT Touring Plans

On days of moderate to heavy attendance, follow the plans exactly. Don't deviate from them except:

1. When you don't want to experience an attraction the plans include. Skip that step and proceed to the next.
2. When you encounter an extremely long line at an attraction called for by the plans. Crowds build and dissipate throughout the day. The plans anticipate recurring crowd patterns but can't predict the unexpected (Spaceship Earth breaking down, for instance). If a line is unduly long, skip that step and go to the next. You can retry the attraction later.

Park Opening Procedures

Your success during your first hour of touring will be affected by the opening procedure at the park that day.

EPCOT almost always opens a half hour before official opening time, using one of two procedures:

1. When attendance is expected to be heavy, all of EPCOT opens at once. In this case, go directly to Guest Relations (left of the sphere) and make dining reservations, if needed. Then begin the touring plan you've chosen.
2. On other days, only Spaceship Earth (in the sphere) and Guest Relations will be open when guests are admitted. In this case, ride Spaceship Earth after making dining reservations, then line up as follows:

   a. If you're going first to Body Wars in the Wonders of Life pavilion, proceed to Innoventions East (left of Earth Station as you exit Spaceship Earth).

When the rest of the park opens, pass through Innoventions East, take the first exit to the left, and proceed directly to Wonders of Life.

b. If you're going first to Living With the Land's boat ride in The Land, proceed to Innoventions West (right of Earth Station as you exit Spaceship Earth). When the rest of the park opens, pass through Innoventions West, take the second exit to the right, and walk directly to The Land.

Early Entry at EPCOT

Two days each week (usually Tuesday and Friday), Disney resort and campground guests are allowed to enter EPCOT 90 minutes before the park opens to the general public. Attractions in The Living Seas, The Land, and Journey Into Imagination pavilions, as well as Spaceship Earth, are usually open for early-entry touring.

In summer and over holiday periods, bigger crowds resulting from the early-entry program create considerable congestion in Future World by 10:30 a.m. Even if you're eligible for early entry, you'll be better off touring a park where early entry isn't in effect. Another strategy, if you're eligible, is to take advantage of early entry for an hour or two in the morning, then head to another park. Early entry works better for resort guests during less busy seasons, adding an hour to an otherwise short touring day. Those ineligible for early entry should avoid EPCOT on days when it's scheduled, regardless of season.

Early entry is less important at EPCOT than at the Magic Kingdom. At EPCOT, only three attractions—Body Wars, *Honey, I Shrunk the Audience,* and Test Track (opens summer 1997)—draw above-average crowds. All three are engineered to accommodate many guests per hour. The need to get a jump on other guests just isn't there.

Combining Early Entry with the Touring Plans

If you wish to combine early entry with one of our touring plans:

1. Arrive when the turnstiles open and experience Spaceship Earth. Go next to the Imagination pavilion and see *Honey, I Shrunk the Audience,* followed

by the Living With the Land boat ride in The Land.

2. After the boat ride, if you're interested in the Body Wars and Test Track thrill rides, position yourself at Innoventions East. When the rest of EPCOT opens, ride Body Wars and Test Track in that order. Afterward, proceed with your touring plan, skipping attractions you've already seen.

Before You Go

1. Call (407) 824-4321 a day ahead to confirm the official opening time.
2. Buy admission.
3. Make dining reservations.
4. Familiarize yourself with park opening procedures and reread the touring plan you've chosen.

Author's Selective EPC
One-Day Touring Plar

For: All parties

Assumes: Willingness to experience major rides and shows

This touring plan includes only what the author believes is the best EPCOT has to offer. The exclusion of an attraction doesn't mean it isn't worthwhile.

1. If you're a Disney resort guest, arrive 90 minutes before official opening *on early-entry days* and 30 minutes before official opening *on non-early-entry days.* If you're a day guest, arrive at the parking lot 45 minutes before EPCOT's stated opening time *on a non-early-entry day.*

2. When admitted to the park, move quickly around the left side of Spaceship Earth to Guest Relations (across the walkway from the sphere) and make dining reservations, if needed. If not, skip ahead to Step 3.

3. **If only Spaceship Earth and Guest Relations are open** when you're admitted, ride Spaceship Earth after making restaurant reservations. Exit left from Spaceship Earth to Innoventions East. When the rest of the park opens, pass through Innoventions East, bear left through the first exit, and go to Wonders of Life and Body Wars.

   If the entire park is open, make restaurant reservations, ride Spaceship Earth, and go to Body Wars by way of Innoventions East.

   If you want to eliminate some backtracking in the touring plan, go straight from making restaurant reservations and riding Spaceship Earth to The Land (Step 5), temporarily skipping Body

Wars. If you aren't keen on Body Wars or don't mind risking a long wait (30–55 minutes) for Body Wars later, bouncing ahead to Step 5 will save about 10 minutes of crisscrossing the park. If Body Wars is important to you, stick with the plan.

4. Ride Body Wars. Remember, it makes some people motion sick. Save the other attractions at the pavilion for later. If you don't want to ride Body Wars, skip to Step 5.

5. Go to The Land and ride Living With the Land. Temporarily bypass other attractions in The Land and go to Step 6.

6. Exit right from The Land to Journey Into Imagination. Enter through doors on the upper left of the building. Follow the corridor to Magic Eye Theater and see *Honey, I Shrunk the Audience.*

7. Take the first path from Journey Into Imagination to Innoventions West. Cut through, cross the plaza, and pass through Innoventions East to World of Motion.

8. Experience Test Track. Don't linger long in the exhibit afterward.

9. Exit left from World of Motion's exhibit area and bear left on the path that leads to Odyssey Restaurant. Cut through the restaurant to World Showcase.

10. Turn left and proceed clockwise around World Showcase. Visit the courtyard at Mexico, but skip the boat ride.

11. Continue left to Norway. Ride Maelstrom.

12. Continue left to China. See *Wonders of China.*

Note: If it's time for your lunch reservation, suspend the touring plan and eat. Afterward, resume. Circle back to Future World to see attractions the plan skipped earlier. Also: If you burn daylight shopping, you may not finish the touring plan.

13. Continue clockwise to Germany and Italy. If you don't have restaurant reservations, consider eating

at Germany's Sommerfest (fast food), which serves tasty bratwurst, soft pretzels, desserts, and beer.

14. Continue clockwise to the U.S. pavilion. See *American Adventure.* If you don't have restaurant reservations, consider eating at the Liberty Inn (fast food; left side of *American Adventure*), which offers hamburgers, hot dogs, and chicken breast sandwiches.

15. Continue to Japan and Morocco.

16. Continue to France. See *Impressions de France.*

17. Go to the United Kingdom.

18. Continue left to Canada. *O Canada!* is quite good, but the audience must stand. Optional.

19. Return to Future World via the central plaza and cut through Innoventions East. Ride Horizons.

20. Exit right from Horizons and return to Wonders of Life. See *Cranium Command.*

Note: Preshow is essential to understanding the attraction.

21. Ride Body Wars if you missed it earlier.

22. Exit right from Wonders of Life to Universe of Energy. Don't be deterred by a long line.

Note: If it's time for your dinner reservation, suspend the touring plan and eat. Afterward, check the entertainment schedule for the time of IllumiNations. Allow at least 30 minutes to find a viewing spot (tips on pages 194–195).

23. Exit Universe of Energy, cross Future World, and pass through Innoventions East and West to The Living Seas. Try to be one of the last to enter the theater from the preshow area. Sit at the end of a middle row. This positions you to be first on the ride that follows. Afterward, enjoy exhibits at Sea Base Alpha.

24. If you have time or energy before IllumiNations, visit attractions you missed or shop. Unless a holiday schedule is in effect, everything at EPCOT closes after IllumiNations except a few shops. See pages 193 for tips on coping with the ensuing exodus.

EPCOT Two-Day Touring Plan

For : All parties

This plan is for people who wish to tour EPCOT comprehensively over two days. Day One takes advantage of early-morning touring opportunities. Day Two begins in late afternoon and continues until the park closes.

Many readers spend part of their Disney World arrival day traveling and checking into their hotels. They head for the theme parks in the afternoon. This plan's second day is ideal for people who enter EPCOT later in the day.

Families with children age 8 and younger should break off Day One no later than 2:30 p.m. to return to their hotel for rest. Add attractions missed on Day One to Day Two.

Day One

1. If you're a Disney resort guest, arrive 90 minutes before official opening *on early-entry days* and 30 minutes before official opening *on non-early-entry days.* If you're a day guest, arrive at the parking lot 45 minutes before EPCOT's stated opening *on a non-early-entry day.*

2. When admitted, move quickly around the left side of Spaceship Earth to Guest Relations (across walkway from the sphere). Make dining reservations, if needed. If not, skip to Step 3.

3. **If only Spaceship Earth and Guest Relations are open** when you're admitted, ride Spaceship Earth after making your reservations. Exit left from Spaceship Earth and proceed to Innoventions East. When the rest of the park opens, pass through Innoventions East, bear left through the first exit, and go to Wonders of Life pavilion and Body Wars.

If the entire park is open, make your dining reservations, ride Spaceship Earth, and go through Innoventions East to Wonders of Life.

If you want to eliminate some backtracking in the touring plan, make your reservations, ride Spaceship Earth, and go to The Land (Step 5), temporarily skipping Body Wars and *The Making of Me* in Wonders of Life. If you aren't keen on Body Wars or don't mind risking longer waits (30–55 minutes) later, bouncing to Step 5 will save about 10 minutes of crisscrossing the park. If Body Wars or *The Making of Me* is important to you, stick with the plan.

4. Ride Body Wars. Remember, it makes some people motion sick. If you don't want to ride, skip to Step 5.
5. Go to The Land, passing through both Innoventions buildings. Ride Living With the Land. Save the pavilion's other attractions for later.
6. Bear right from The Land to the left side of Journey Into Imagination and see *Honey, I Shrunk the Audience.*
7. Exit left and experience Journey Into Imagination.
8. Leave Journey Into Imagination, cut through Innoventions West, cross the plaza, and pass through Innoventions East to World of Motion.
9. Experience Test Track. Don't linger long in the exhibit afterward.
10. Exit left from the exhibit, then bear left on the path to Odyssey Restaurant. Cut through the restaurant to World Showcase.
11. Turn left and proceed clockwise around World Showcase. Experience El Rio del Tiempo boat ride at Mexico. It's in the far left corner of the interior courtyard and isn't well marked.
12. Continue left to Norway. Ride Maelstrom.

Note: If it's time for your lunch reservations, suspend the touring plan and eat. Afterward, resume.

13. Continue left to China. See *Wonders of China.*

14. Visit Germany and Italy. If you don't have a restaurant reservation, consider eating at Germany's Sommerfest (fast food), which serves tasty bratwurst, soft pretzels, desserts, and beer.

15. Continue clockwise to the U.S. pavilion. See *American Adventure.* If you don't have restaurant reservations, consider eating at Liberty Inn (fast food; left side of *American Adventure*), which offers hamburgers, hot dogs, and chicken breast sandwiches.

16. Visit Japan and Morocco.

17. Go left to France. See *Impressions de France.*

18. This concludes the touring plan for Day One. Attractions not included today will be experienced tomorrow. If you wish to continue, start at Step 17 in the EPCOT Selective One-Day Touring Plan. If you've had enough, exit through International Gateway or the main entrance. To reach the main entrance without walking around the lagoon, catch a boat near Morocco.

Day Two

1. Enter EPCOT about 2 p.m. Obtain a park map containing the daily entertainment schedule from Guest Relations.

2. Make dining reservations, if needed. Because it's past the usual time for doing so, you may have to summon a reservationist by using the WorldKey Information Service terminals.

   You can eat your evening meal in any EPCOT restaurant without interrupting the touring plan's efficiency. We recommend a 7 p.m. reservation when it gets dark early, an 8 p.m. reservation during late spring, summer, and early fall. Timing of the reservation is important if you want to see IllumiNations.

   If your preferred restaurants are unavailable, try Morocco or Norway. Ethnic dishes of these countries aren't well-known to most Americans, and it's often possible to get a reservation late in the day.

3. Go to The Living Seas. Try to be one of the last people to enter the theater from the preshow area. Sit close to the end of a middle row. This positions you to be first on the ride that follows. Afterward, enjoy the exhibits of Sea Base Alpha.

4. Exit right from Living Seas and return to The Land. See *Food Rocks* and the film at the Harvest Theater.

5. Cross the park, passing through Innoventions East and West, and see the show at Universe of Energy.

6. Exit left to Wonders of Life. See *Cranium Command.* Be sure to catch the preshow.

7. See *The Making of Me.*

8. Exit left from Wonders of Life. Ride Horizons.

Note: If it's time for your dinner reservation, suspend the touring plan and eat. Afterward, check the daily entertainment schedule for the time of IllumiNations. Allow at least 30 minutes to find a viewing spot (tips on the best viewing spots, pages 194–195).

9. Leave Future World and walk counterclockwise around World Showcase Lagoon to Canada. See *O Canada!*

10. Turn right from Canada and visit the United Kingdom.

11. This concludes the touring plan. Enjoy your dinner and IllumiNations. If you have time, shop or revisit favorite attractions.

12. Unless a holiday schedule is in effect, everything at EPCOT closes after IllumiNations except a few shops. See page 193 for tips on coping with the ensuing exodus.

Disney-MGM Studios and Universal Studios Florida

Disney-MGM Studios

Several years ago, Disney decided to make movies for adults and formed a new production company to handle them. The result has been a complete rejuvenation of Disney movies, with new faces, tremendous creativeness, and amazing resurgence at the box office.

How better to showcase and promote this product than with an all-new motion picture and television entertainment park at Walt Disney World?

• The MGM Connection •

To broaden appeal and lend additional historical impact, Disney obtained rights to the MGM (Metro-Goldwyn-Mayer) name, film library, motion picture and television titles, excerpts, costumes, music, sets, and even Leo, the MGM lion. Probably the two most recognized names in motion pictures, Disney and MGM account for more than 65 years of movie history.

• Comparing Disney-MGM Studios • to the Magic Kingdom and EPCOT

The Magic Kingdom entertains. EPCOT educates. Disney-MGM does both. All rely heavily on special effects and Audio-Animatronics (robotics).

Not to Be Missed at Disney-MGM Studios

Star Tours
Backstage Studio Tour
Animation Tour
Indiana Jones Stunt Spectacular
The Great Movie Ride
MuppetVision 4-D
Voyage of the Little Mermaid
"Twilight Zone" Tower of Terror

The Studios and Magic Kingdom are about the same size, each half as big as EPCOT. Unlike the others, Disney-MGM is a working motion picture and television production facility, meaning that about half is open only to guests on guided tours or observation walkways.

If you're interested in the history and technology of film and TV, Disney-MGM offers plenty. If you just want to be entertained, the Studios provide megadoses of action, suspense, surprise, and fun.

• How Much Time to Allocate •

It's impossible to see all of EPCOT or the Magic Kingdom in one day. Disney-MGM is more manageable. There's less ground to cover by foot. Trams run through much of the back lot and working areas, and attractions in the open-access parts are concentrated in an area about the size of Main Street, Tomorrowland, and Liberty Square combined.

Because it's smaller, Disney-MGM is more affected by large crowds. Our touring plans will keep you a step ahead of the mob and minimize waits in line. Even when the park is heavily attended, however, you can see almost everything in a day.

• Disney-MGM Studios in the Evening •

Because Disney-MGM can be seen in a short day, most guests who arrive in early morning run out of things to do by 3:30 or 4 p.m. and leave. Their departure thins the crowds and

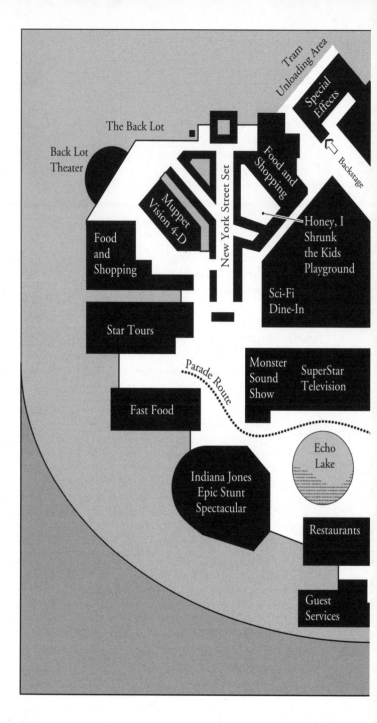

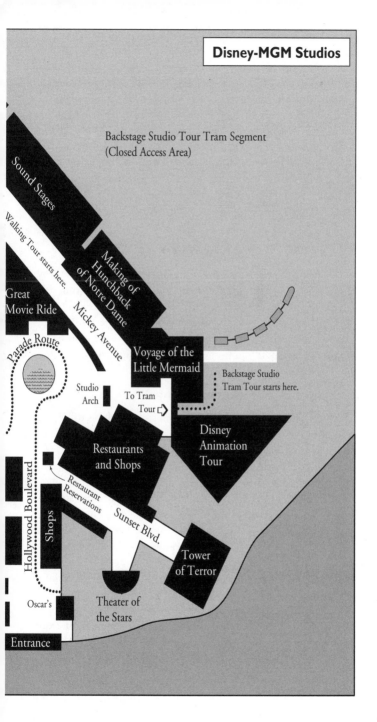

Disney-MGM Studios

Backstage Studio Tour Tram Segment
(Closed Access Area)

Sound Stages

Walking Tour starts here.

Making of
Hunchback
of Notre Dame

Great
Movie Ride

Mickey Avenue

Parade Route

Voyage of the
Little Mermaid

Backstage Studio
Tram Tour starts here.

Studio
Arch

To Tram
Tour

Disney
Animation
Tour

Restaurants
and Shops

Hollywood Boulevard

Restaurant
Reservations

Sunset Blvd.

Shops

Tower
of Terror

Oscar's

Theater of
the Stars

Entrance

makes the park ideal for evening touring. Lines for most attractions are manageable, and the park is cooler. Outdoor theater productions are infinitely more enjoyable after midday's heat. And, finally, there's Sorcery in the Sky, thought by many readers to be Disney World's most spectacular fireworks show. A drawback to evening touring is that activity has waned on sound stages and in the Animation Building. Also, you might get stuck eating dinner here. If you must, try Mama Melrose's or the Hollywood Brown Derby, for full-service dining, or the Hollywood & Vine cafeteria.

• Arriving •

Disney-MGM has its own pay parking lot and is served by the Disney transportation system, shuttling guests from the Magic Kingdom, EPCOT, the resort hotels, and other Disney World destinations. Many larger hotels out of the World offer shuttles to the Studios. If you drive, Disney World's ubiquitous trams will transport you to the ticketing area and entrance gate.

• Getting Oriented •

Guest Services, left of the entrance, is the park headquarters and information center. Check here for a map with schedule of live performances, lost persons, lost objects, emergencies, and general information. Right of the entrance are lockers and stroller and wheelchair rentals.

About half of the Studios is a theme park. The main street is Hollywood Boulevard of the 1920s and '30s. At boulevard's end is a replica of Hollywood's famous Chinese Theater. While not as imposing as the Magic Kingdom's Cinderella Castle or EPCOT's Spaceship Earth, the theater is Disney-MGM's central landmark and is a good meeting place if your group becomes separated.

The Studios' theme-park areas are at the theater end of Hollywood Boulevard, off Sunset Boulevard (branching right from Hollywood Boulevard), and around Echo Lake (left of Hollywood Boulevard as you face the theater). Attractions include rides and shows. The remainder of the complex has working sound stages, technical facilities, wardrobe shops, administrative offices, animation studios, and back lot sets with restricted access.

• **What to See** •

Try everything. Disney rides and shows are always surprising. (In the descriptions of attractions which follow, we give ratings based on a scale of zero to five stars; five stars is the best rating.)

Open-Access
Movie-Theme Park

Hollywood Boulevard

Hollywood Boulevard is a palm-lined re-creation of Hollywood's main drag during the city's golden age. Architecture is streamlined *moderne* with art deco embellishments. Most service facilities are here, interspersed with eateries and shops. Merchandise includes Disney trademark items, Hollywood and movie-related souvenirs, and one-of-a-kind collectibles obtained from studio auctions and estate sales.

Hollywood characters and roving performers entertain on the boulevard, and daily parades pass this way.

Hollywood Boulevard Services	
Most park services are centered on Hollywood Boulevard, including:	
Wheelchair & Stroller Rental Service	Right of the entrance at Oscar's
Banking Services	An automated bank teller is right of the entrance turnstiles (outside the park).
Storage Lockers	Right of the entrance on Hollywood Boulevard, left side of Oscar's
Lost & Found	Guest Services, left of the entrance

Hollywood Boulevard Services *(continued)*	
Live Entertainment/ Parade Information	Listed in the free park guide map available at Guest Services and other locations in the park
Lost Persons	Guest Services
Walt Disney World & Local Attraction Information	Guest Services
First Aid	Guest Services
Baby Center/ Baby Care Needs	Guest Services. Oscar's sells baby food and other necessities.
Film	The Darkroom, right side of Hollywood Boulevard, just beyond Oscar's

Sunset Boulevard

Sunset Boulevard, evoking the 1940s, is a major new addition to Disney-MGM. Intersecting Hollywood Boulevard near the Brown Derby restaurant, it provides another venue for dining, shopping, and street entertainment.

"Twilight Zone" Tower of Terror

What It Is: Sci-fi-theme indoor thrill ride

Scope & Scale: Super headliner

When to Go: Before 10 a.m. and after 5 p.m.

Author's Rating: Not to be missed; ★★★★★

Overall Appeal by Age Group:

Pre-school	Grade School	Teens	Young Adults	Over 30	Senior Citizens
★★★★	★★★★★	★★★★★	★★★★★	★★★★½	★★★★½

Duration of Ride: About 4 minutes plus preshow

Avg. Wait in Line per 100 People Ahead of You: 4 minutes

Assumes: All elevators operating

Loading Speed: Moderate

Description and Comments   Tower of Terror is a new species of thrill ride, though it borrows elements of the Magic Kingdom's Haunted Mansion. The idea is that you're touring the ruins of a once-famous Hollywood hotel. The queuing area draws guests into the adventure, taking them through the hotel's once-opulent public rooms. From the lobby, they enter the hotel's library, where Rod Serling, speaking on a black-and-white television, greets them and introduces the plot.

Tower of Terror is a whopper, 13-plus-stories tall. You can see the entire park from the top, but you have to look quickly.

The ride vehicle, one of the hotel's elevators, takes guests on a tour of the haunted hostelry. It begins innocuously, but by the fifth floor things get weird. You have just entered the Twilight Zone. Guests are subjected to special effects as they encounter unexpected horrors and illusions. The climax occurs when the elevator reaches the top floor (thirteenth, of course) and the cable snaps.

Though the final plunge is calculated to thrill, the soul of the attraction is its extraordinary visual and audio effects. There's enough richness and subtlety to keep the ride stimulating through many repetitions.

The Tower has great potential for terrifying children and rattling adults.

Touring Tips   This ride is worth your admission to Disney-MGM. Because of its height, it's a beacon luring the curious. Because of its popularity with teens and young adults, count on a footrace to the attraction when the park opens. It's mobbed most of the day.

To save time, when you enter the library waiting area, stand in the far back corner at the opposite end of the long wall from the television set. When loading doors open, you'll be among the first admitted. If you have children or anyone else apprehensive about this attraction, ask the attendant about switching off.

The Great Movie Ride

What It Is: Movie history indoor adventure ride
Scope & Scale: Headliner
When to Go: Before 10 a.m. and after 5 p.m.

Special Comments: Elaborate, with several surprises

Author's Rating: Not to be missed; ★★★½

Overall Appeal by Age Group:

Pre-school	Grade School	Teens	Young Adults	Over 30	Senior Citizens
★★★★	★★★★	★★★★	★★★★½	★★★★½	★★★★½

Duration of Ride: About 19 minutes

Avg. Wait in Line per 100 People Ahead of You: 2 minutes

Assumes: All trains operating

Loading Speed: Fast

Description and Comments   Entering through a re-creation of Hollywood's Chinese Theater, guests board vehicles for a fast-paced tour through sets from classic films, including *Casablanca, The Wizard of Oz, Aliens,* and *Raiders of the Lost Ark.* Each is populated with new-generation audio-animatronic robots and an occasional human, all assisted by dazzling special effects. Disney's largest and most ambitious ride-through attraction, Great Movie Ride encompasses 95,000 square feet and showcases some of the most famous scenes in filmmaking.

Touring Tips   The ride draws large crowds from the moment the park opens. Its high capacity keeps lines moving, but even so, waits can exceed an hour after midmorning.

SuperStar Television

What It Is: Audience participation television production

Scope & Scale: Major attraction

When to Go: After 10 a.m.

Author's Rating: Well-conceived; ★★★

Overall Appeal by Age Group:

Pre-school	Grade School	Teens	Young Adults	Over 30	Senior Citizens
★★★½	★★★★★	★★★★★	★★★★½	★★★★½	★★★★½

Duration of Presentation: 30 minutes

Preshow Entertainment: Participants selected from guests in the preshow area

Probable Waiting Time: 10–20 minutes

Description and Comments   Volunteers participate in a television production using special effects to integrate the amateurs' actions with footage of stars of past and current TV shows. The result is broadcast on large-screen monitors above the set. The outcome, always rated in laughs, depends on how the volunteers respond in their debut.

Touring Tips   The theater seats 1,000, so it's usually easy to get in. If you want to be in the production, however, it's essential that you enter the preshow holding area at least 15 minutes before the next performance. Participants for the show are drafted from both genders and all age groups. Those who stand near the casting director and those who are outlandishly attired seem to be selected most often. One reader screamed "Honeymooners!" and was picked.

Star Tours

What It Is: Space-flight simulation indoor ride

Scope & Scale: Headliner

When to Go: First hour and a half the park is open

Special Comments: Pregnant women or anyone prone to motion sickness are advised against riding. The ride is too intense for many children under age 8.

Author's Rating: Not to be missed; ★★★★½

Overall Appeal by Age Group:

Pre-school	Grade School	Teens	Young Adults	Over 30	Senior Citizens
★★★★	★★★★★	★★★★★	★★★★★	★★★★★	★★★★

Duration of Ride: Approximately 7 minutes

Avg. Wait in Line per 100 People Ahead of You: 5 minutes

Assumes: All simulators operating

Loading Speed: Moderate to fast

Description and Comments   Guests ride in a flight simulator modeled after those used in training pilots and astronauts. Pilot is a droid on his first flight with real passengers. Mayhem ensues, scenery flashes by, and the simulator bucks and pitches. After several minutes, the droid manages to land the spacecraft.

Touring Tips   Star Tours hasn't been as popular at Disney-MGM as at Disneyland in California. Except on unusually busy days, waits rarely exceed 30 to 40 minutes. If you have children who are apprehensive about this attraction, ask the attendant about switching off.

Monster Sound Show

What It Is: Audience-participation show demonstrating sound effects

Scope & Scale: Minor attraction

When to Go: Before 11 a.m. or after 5 p.m.

Author's Rating: Funny and informative; ★★★

Overall Appeal by Age Group:

Pre-school	Grade School	Teens	Young Adults	Over 30	Senior Citizens
★★★½	★★★★½	★★★★½	★★★★½	★★★★½	★★★★½

Duration of Presentation: 12 minutes

Preshow Entertainment: David Letterman and Jimmy McDonald video

Probable Waiting Time: 15–30 minutes, except during the first half hour the park is open

Description and Comments   Selected guests go onstage for a crash course in sound effects. If participants are duds, the show suffers. First a short film demonstrates what the sound effects should be, then guests try to provide them. The results are played back at show's end.

Touring Tips   Because the theater is small, long waits (partly in sun) are common. *Monster Sound Show* is inundated periodically by throngs from just-concluded performances of SuperStar Television or the *Indiana Jones Stunt Spectacular.* Don't line up with them; come back in 20 minutes.

One reader took in *Sound Show* just before the afternoon parade, exiting just in time to see the marchers. If the parade starts on Hollywood Boulevard, it takes about 15 to 18 minutes to reach *Sound Show.*

Being chosen for participation in *Monster Sound Show* is pretty much luck.

Indiana Jones Stunt Spectacular

What It Is: Movie stunt demonstration and action show
Scope & Scale: Headliner
When to Go: First three morning shows or last evening show
Special Comments: Performance times are posted
    at the theater entrance.
Author's Rating: Done on a grand scale; ★★★★
Overall Appeal by Age Group:

Pre-school	Grade School	Teens	Young Adults	Over 30	Senior Citizens
★★★★½	★★★★★	★★★★★	★★★★½	★★★★½	★★★★½

Duration of Presentation: 30 minutes
Preshow Entertainment: Selection of "extras" from audience
Probable Waiting Time: None

Description and Comments   Coherent and educational, though somewhat unevenly paced, this popular production showcases professionals who demonstrate dangerous stunts. Sets, props, and special effects are elaborate.

Touring Tips   Stunt Theater holds 2,000; capacity audiences are common. On busy days, you can walk into the first performance, even if you arrive five minutes late. For the second performance, go 15–25 minutes early. For the third and subsequent shows, arrive 30–45 minutes ahead. If you tour in late afternoon and evening, attend the last performance. If you want to beat the crowd out of the stadium, sit near the top on the far right (as you face the stage).

To be chosen as an "extra" in the stunt show, arrive early, sit in front, and display boundless enthusiasm.

Theater of the Stars

What It Is: Live Hollywood-style musical, usually featuring
    Disney characters; performed in open-air theater
Scope & Scale: Major attraction
When to Go: In the evening
Special Comments: Performance times are listed in the daily
    entertainment schedule.

Author's Rating: Excellent; ★★★★

Overall Appeal by Age Group:

Pre-school	Grade School	Teens	Young Adults	Over 30	Senior Citizens
★★★★½	★★★★	★★★	★★★★	★★★★	★★★½

Duration of Presentation: 25 minutes

Preshow Entertainment: None

Probable Waiting Time: 20–30 minutes

Description and Comments Theater of the Stars combines Disney characters with singers and dancers in upbeat and humorous Hollywood musical productions. *Beauty and the Beast,* in particular, is outstanding. The theater, on Sunset Boulevard, offers a clear view from almost every seat. Best of all, a canopy protects the audience.

Touring Tips Unless you visit during cooler months, see this show in the evening. Show up 20–50 minutes early at any time.

Voyage of the Little Mermaid

What It Is: Musical stage show featuring characters from the Disney movie *The Little Mermaid*

Scope & Scale: Major attraction

When to Go: Before 9:30 a.m., or just before closing

Author's Rating: Romantic, lovable, and humorous in the best Disney tradition. Not to be missed; ★★★★

Overall Appeal by Age Group:

Pre-school	Grade School	Teens	Young Adults	Over 30	Senior Citizens
★★★★	★★★★	★★★½	★★★★	★★★★	★★★★

Duration of Presentation: 15 minutes

Preshow Entertainment: Taped ramblings about the holding area's decor

Probable Waiting Time: Before 9:30 a.m., 10–30 minutes; after 9:30 a.m., 50–90 minutes

Description and Comments *Voyage of the Little Mermaid* is a winner, appealing to every age. Cute without being saccharine, and infinitely lovable, *Little Mermaid* is the most tender and romantic entertainment in Disney World. The story is simple and engaging, the special effects are impressive, and the characters are memorable.

Touring Tips   Because it's excellent and located at a busy pedestrian intersection, the show plays to capacity crowds all day. Unless you make the first or second show, you'll probably have to wait an hour or more.

When you enter the preshow lobby, stand near the theater doors. When you enter, pick a row and let about 6 to 10 people enter ahead of you. The strategy is to get a good seat and be near the exit doors.

The Making of The Hunchback of Notre Dame

What It Is: Documentary about the making of Disney's latest animated feature

Scope & Scale: Minor attraction

When to Go: Anytime

Author's Rating: Educational and fun; ★★★

Overall Appeal by Age Group:

Pre-school	Grade School	Teens	Young Adults	Over 30	Senior Citizens
★★½	★★★	★★★½	★★★½	★★★½	★★★½

Duration of Presentation: 17 minutes

Preshow Entertainment: Tour of post-production facilities

Probable Waiting Time: 20 minutes

Description and Comments   A short documentary follows a tour of Disney-MGM post-production studios, where sound and film animation is explained.

Touring Tips   Because the focus is more on production technology than story or characters, children are sometimes disappointed. Adults, however, gain better understanding and appreciation of Disney animation. The presentation is usually uncrowded; see it anytime.

Jim Henson's *MuppetVision 4-D*

What It Is: 4-D movie starring the Muppets

Scope & Scale: Major attraction

When to Go: Before 11 a.m. and after 4 p.m.

Author's Rating: Uproarious. Not to be missed; ★★★★½

Overall Appeal by Age Group:

Pre-school	Grade School	Teens	Young Adults	Over 30	Senior Citizens
★★★★½	★★★★★	★★★★½	★★★★½	★★★★½	★★★★½

Duration of Presentation: 17 minutes

Preshow Entertainment: Muppets on television

Probable Waiting Time: 12 minutes

Description and Comments   *MuppetVision 4-D* provides a total sensory experience, with wild 3-D action augmented by auditory, visual, and tactile special effects. If you're tired and hot, this zany presentation will make you feel brand new.

Touring Tips   Before noon, waits are about 20 minutes. During midday, until about 4 p.m., expect long lines. Also, watch out for crowds arriving from just-concluded performances of *Indiana Jones Stunt Spectacular.* Don't line up with them; return later.

Honey, I Shrunk the Kids
Movie Set Adventure Playground

What It Is: Small but elaborate playground

Scope & Scale: Diversion

When to Go: Before 10 a.m. or after dark

Author's Rating: Great for young children, expendable for adults; ★★½

Overall Appeal by Age Group:

Pre-school	Grade School	Teens	Young Adults	Over 30	Senior Citizens
★★★★½	★★★★	★★	★★½	★★★	★★½

Duration of Presentation: Varies

Avg. Wait in Line per 100 People Ahead of You: 20 minutes

Description and Comments   This elaborate playground especially appeals to kids age 11 and younger. The idea is that you've been "miniaturized" and have to make your way through a yard full of 20-foot-tall grass blades, giant ants, lawn sprinklers, and other oversized features.

Touring Tips   This imaginative playground has tunnels, slides, rope ladders, and oversized props. All surfaces are padded, and Disney personnel help control children. Only 240 people are allowed "on the set" at once, not nearly the number who'd like to play. By 10:30 or 11 a.m., the area is full, with dozens waiting (some impatiently).

There's no provision for getting people to leave. Kids play as long as parents allow. This creates uneven traffic flow and unpredictable waits. If this attraction weren't poorly ventilated and hot as a swamp, there's no telling when anyone would leave.

One reader accessed the playground through Backstage Plaza fast-food and retail area and bought snacks and beverages while the kids were playing. When the youngsters emerged, refreshments were waiting.

Studio Tours

Disney-MGM Studios Animation Tour

What It Is: Walking tour of the Disney Animation Studio

Scope & Scale: Major attraction

When to Go: Before 11 a.m. and after 5 p.m.

Author's Rating: A masterpiece. Not to be missed; ★★★★½

Overall Appeal by Age Group:

Pre-school	Grade School	Teens	Young Adults	Over 30	Senior Citizens
★★★★	★★★★	★★★★	★★★★★	★★★★★	★★★★★

Duration of Presentation: 36 minutes

Preshow Entertainment: Gallery of animation art in waiting area

Avg. Wait in Line per 100 People Ahead of You: 7 minutes

Description and Comments The public, for the first time, sees Disney artists at work.

The Animation Tour exceeds expectations. It's dynamic, fast-paced, educational, and fun. After entering the Animation Building, guests wait in a gallery of Disney animation art. From there, they enter a theater for an 8-minute film about animation narrated by Walter Cronkite and Robin Williams.

After the film, guests enter the studio and watch artists and technicians through large windows. Each work station and task is explained by Cronkite and Williams via video monitors. Next, guests gather to see a multimonitor video in which animators share their perspectives on the creative process. It entertains but is warm, endearing, and worthwhile in its own right. Finally, the group enters a theater for a film that melds all elements of animation production. Clips from Disney animation classics are featured.

The tour depends on video and film narration and only secondarily on the work of animators in the studio. Though animation is well-explained, you may be disappointed if you thought you'd see lots of animators working.

Touring Tips   Some days, Animation Tour doesn't open until 11 a.m.; check the daily entertainment schedule and try to go before noon. Lines begin to build on busy days by mid- to late morning.

After the introductory film, stay as long as you like in the studio. The narrative repeats at each work station every 2 to 3 minutes. Let most of your 160-person tour group pass you at the first station. Then take your time watching artists. You'll likely catch up with your group. If not, move with the next group.

Backstage Studio Tour

What It Is: Tram and walking tour of modern film and video production

Scope & Scale: Headliner

When to Go: Anytime

Author's Rating: One of Disney's better efforts; efficient, compelling, informative, fun. Not to be missed; ★★★★

Overall Appeal by Age Group:

Pre-school	Grade School	Teens	Young Adults	Over 30	Senior Citizens
★★★★½	★★★★½	★★★★	★★★★½	★★★★	★★★★

Duration of Presentation: About 1 hour overall; 15 minutes for the tram segment and 40 minutes for the walking segment called *Inside the Magic*

Special Comments: You can leave the tour after the tram segment.

Preshow Entertainment: A video in the tram boarding area

Avg. Wait in Line per 100 People Ahead of You: 2 minutes

Assumes: 16 tour departures per hour

Loading Speed: Fast

Description and Comments   A working film and television facility occupies about two-thirds of Disney-MGM. Actors, artists, and technicians work there year-round. This tour takes visitors behind the scenes to learn about methods and technologies of motion picture and TV production.

Visitors enter the limited-access area through an ornate studio gate at the end of Hollywood Boulevard, right of the Chinese Theater. Lines form in the interior plaza on the left for the Backstage Studio Tour and on the right for the Animation Tour.

The Tram Segment

The Backstage Studio Tour is the anchor (though not most popular) attraction at Disney-MGM. Fast-paced, informative, and well-designed, it begins aboard trams that wind among production and shop buildings to elaborate back lot sets.

The tour stops first at the wardrobe and crafts shops. Guests watch craftsmen through large picture windows in the shops.

The tour proceeds to the back lot, where desert canyons and New York City brownstones exist beside suburban residential streets. The highlight for many guests is going through Catastrophe Canyon, a special-effects adventure that includes thunderstorm, earthquake, oil-field fire, and flash flood.

The tram part of the tour ends at Backstage Plaza, where guests can use rest rooms (recommended), eat, or shop before commencing the tour's walking segment. Follow the large, pink rabbit footprints out of the tram unloading area to start the walking segment.

The Walking Segment: *Inside the Magic*

Guests walk or stand throughout the half-hour walking segment. It begins at a special-effects water tank, where technicians demonstrate rain effects, a naval battle, and a storm at sea. Miniature naval vessels used in filming famous war movies are displayed in the waiting area.

Next is the special-effects workshop, where enlargement, miniaturization, and stop-frame photographic animation are explained.

Guests proceed to the sound stages, where soundproofed platforms let them watch production. A video explores technical and artistic aspects of the work.

The Lottery, a four-minute movie starring Bette Midler and produced entirely at Disney-MGM, is played before guests are taken to inspect the sets and props used in its filming.

Touring Tips   Don't be deterred if the tram line appears long. Trams depart every 4 minutes on busy days and carry up to 200 guests. During warm months, the most comfortable time to ride is evening. A drawback is that most workers have gone home. Their absence, however, affects only a small part of the tour.

You'll almost never have to wait longer than 15 minutes to join the walking segment.

Live Entertainment at Disney-MGM Studios

The afternoon parade, elaborate productions at Theater of the Stars, and Sorcery in the Sky fireworks put Disney-MGM's live entertainment on an equal footing with that in the other theme parks.

Afternoon Parade Staged one or more times a day, the parade features floats and characters from Disney animated features. One route begins near the park's entrance, continues down Hollywood Boulevard, circles in front of The Great Movie Ride, passes SuperStar Television and *Monster Sound Show,* and ends at Star Tours. The alternate route begins at the far end of Sunset Boulevard and turns right onto Hollywood Boulevard.

The parade is colorful, creative, and upbeat, but it brings pedestrian traffic to a standstill along its route and complicates movement within the park. If you're on the route when the parade begins, stay put and enjoy. There are no unusually good or frequently overlooked vantage points.

Theater of the Stars This covered amphitheater on Sunset Boulevard showcases a variety of revues, usually featuring music from Disney movies and starring Disney characters. Performance times are posted at the theater and listed in the entertainment schedule in the park's guide map.

Backlot Theater This stage offers musical productions featuring Disney characters and/or films. To find it, follow New York Street toward the back of the park and turn left at the end of the street.

Disney Characters See them at Theater of the Stars, Backlot Theater, parades, Studio Courtyard on New York Street (usually in front of the Animation Building), in Backstage Plaza, or along Mickey Avenue (next to the sound stages). Mickey appears regularly on Sunset Boulevard at times listed in the daily entertainment schedule. A character breakfast is offered most mornings at Soundstage Restaurant.

Sorcery in the Sky An excellent fireworks show based on Mickey Fireworks Mouse's exploits as the sorcerer's apprentice in *Fantasia*. Held daily at closing time when the park stays open after dark. Watch anywhere along Hollywood Boulevard.

Eating and Shopping
at Disney-MGM Studios

• Eating at Disney-MGM Studios •

The park has four reservations-recommended restaurants: Hollywood Brown Derby, '50s Prime Time Cafe, Sci-Fi Dine-In Theater Restaurant, and Mama Melrose's Ristorante Italiano (ratings on pages 92–95). Readers generally praise the atmosphere and pan the food.

Reservations Make reservations at the restaurant, at the Restaurant Reservations Desk on the corner of Hollywood and Sunset boulevards or, for Disney resort guests, by dialing 55 or 56 at least one day in advance. If you want to patronize a restaurant but don't have reservations, try about 11 a.m. or from 3 to 4 p.m. To make reservations before leaving home, call (407) 939-3463.

Other Disney-MGM Studios Restaurants

A cut below headliner restaurants is Hollywood and Vine, featuring baby-back ribs, steaks, prime rib, rotisserie chicken, and salads. Lunch entrees run $7–12; dinners, $8–16. Beer and wine are available.

The 560-seat Soundstage Restaurant, the 600-seat Backlot Express, and several small sandwich and pastry vendors range from down-home cooking to California *nouvelle cuisine.* Soundstage Restaurant and Backlot Express sell beer and wine.

• Shopping at Disney-MGM Studios •

Movie-oriented merchandise and Disney trademark souvenirs star in shops throughout the park. Most are on Hollywood Boulevard.

Animation Gallery, in the Animation Building, sells reproductions of "cels" from animated features and other animation art. Sid Cahuenga's near the park entrance sells vintage movie posters and celebrity autographs. Find Disney collectibles at Once Upon a Time on Sunset Boulevard. Mickey's of Hollywood on Hollywood Boulevard is the place to buy trademark items.

Disney-MGM Studios One-Day Touring Plan, for Visitors of All Ages

For: Adults and children of any age
Assumes: Willingness to experience all major rides and shows

Because it offers fewer attractions, Disney-MGM isn't as complicated to tour as the Magic Kingdom or EPCOT.

Crowds are more concentrated among the fewer attractions. If a line seems unusually long, ask an attendant what the wait is. If it exceeds your tolerance, try again while *Indiana Jones,* a parade, or a special event is in progress.

Star Tours, The Great Movie Ride, the Tower of Terror, and the Catastrophe Canyon segment of the Backstage Studios Tour may frighten young children. Star Tours may cause motion sickness.

When following the touring plan, skip any attraction you don't wish to experience.

Early Entry at Disney-MGM Studios

Two days each week (usually Wednesday and Sunday), Disney resort guests are invited to enter Disney-MGM Studios 90 minutes before official opening. During the early-entry hour, guests usually can enjoy The Great Movie Ride, *MuppetVision 4-D,* Star Tours, and the "Twilight Zone" Tower of Terror.

Early entry at Disney-MGM offers some real advantages. Attractions open early are those not to be missed that draw huge crowds. If you experience these early, the rest of your touring will be a cinch. If you participate in early entry, be at the turnstiles 90 minutes before official opening. Once in the park, hurry to Tower of Terror, then The Great Movie Ride and Star

Tours. If you use our touring plan, skip steps that call for seeing these attractions.

If you aren't eligible for early entry, arrive 40 minutes before official opening on a day when early entry isn't in effect.

Before You Go

1. Call (407) 824-4321 to learn park hours and which days early entry is in effect.
2. Buy your admission.
3. Make dining reservations at (407) 939-3463. Disney resort guests can dial 55 or 56 from their rooms.

At the Disney-MGM Studios

1. Arrive at the park an hour and 40 minutes before official opening if you're a Disney resort guest taking advantage of early entry. *On non-early-entry days,* arrive 40 minutes before official opening. Persons ineligible for early entry should avoid the park on those days.
2. When you're admitted, go to Guest Services and get a free guide map with the daily entertainment schedule. Proceed down Hollywood Boulevard, turn right at Sunset Boulevard, and ride the Tower of Terror. If you have children or adults who don't wish to ride, switch off.
3. After the Tower are four more attractions that draw big crowds. Two—The Great Movie Ride and Star Tours—are rides. The others—*Voyage of the Little Mermaid* and *Indiana Jones Stunt Spectacular*—are theater presentations.

    Check your entertainment schedule for the first performance of *Voyage of the Little Mermaid* and *Indiana Jones.* See the first of each show, working the rides in as you can. You need to know:

    a. *Before 10 a.m.,* it usually takes about 30 minutes to experience The Great Movie Ride and about 15–20 minutes to ride Star Tours. These estimates include your time in line and riding *but not* the time to walk between the attractions.

b. *Voyage of the Little Mermaid* lasts about 20 minutes; *Indiana Jones Stunt Spectacular,* about 35. Their first performances usually don't play to capacity audiences. To see the first performance of *Little Mermaid,* arrive about five minutes before show time. At *Indiana Jones,* guests are usually admitted up to 3–5 minutes *after* the first show has begun (you miss nothing crucial).

Here's how one family applied this information:

Pete and Marie and their 12-year-old twins visited on a non-early-entry day when the official opening was 9 a.m. The park opened at 8:30 a.m. They entered at 8:35 a.m. and were at the Tower of Terror by 8:40 a.m. They'd finished at the Tower at 9 a.m. They noted that the first *Little Mermaid* was at 9:15 a.m. and the first *Indiana Jones* at 10 a.m.

There wasn't enough time to catch one of the rides, so the family went straight to *Little Mermaid* and saw the first show. They exited the theater at 9:35 a.m. There wasn't enough time to experience The Great Movie Ride (takes 30 minutes) and make the 10 a.m. *Indiana Jones,* so they hurried to Star Tours, arriving at 9:40. They completed the ride and reached *Indiana Jones* just before show time. After *Indiana Jones,* they went to The Great Movie Ride, arriving about 10:40. The ride had a fairly long line, and the family waited 30 minutes. When they completed the ride at 11:30, however, the family had experienced all attractions in the park that require lengthy waits.

Some what-ifs:

- What if you miss the first performance of one of the shows? If you're too late for the first show, ask an attendant at *Little Mermaid* when you'll be admitted to the next if you line up then. If the wait is 30 minutes or less, that's probably the best you can expect all day unless you try during a parade. *Indiana Jones* is easier to get into after the first show. Arrive 20–30 minutes before the second show; you shouldn't have trouble getting in. Before you queue up, however, check timing with an attendant.

- What if the first shows of *Little Mermaid* and *Indiana Jones* are at the same time? See *Little Mermaid* and catch the second showing of *Indiana Jones.*

- What if you're a Disney resort guest on early entry? Arrive an hour and 40 minutes before official opening. When you're admitted, experience Tower of Terror, Great Movie Ride, and Star Tours, in that order. After Star Tours, check the schedule for the first performance of *Little Mermaid.* If the show is within 35 minutes, line up at *Little Mermaid.* If you have more than 35 minutes, try to squeeze in *MuppetVision 4-D.* Go to *MuppetVision* and ask when the next show begins. If it starts in less than 10 minutes, see the show, then hurry to *Little Mermaid.* If you don't want to see *Little Mermaid,* proceed directly from Star Tours to *MuppetVision.*

4. After completing Star Tours, Great Movie Ride, *Little Mermaid,* and *Indiana Jones,* see *Muppet-Vision 4-D.*

5. Backtrack through the arch (past *Little Mermaid)* and continue across the square to the Animation Building, on the far right. Take the Animation Tour.

6. If you're hungry, eat lunch.

7. Proceed through the archway left of the Animation Building to the tram loading area of Backstage Studio Tour. Board; the tram segment takes about 15 minutes.

8. Leave the tram, pause for the rest room, lunch, or a snack, then follow the pink rabbit footprints to

the tour's walking segment. The segment takes about 30 minutes.

9. See *The Making of The Hunchback of Notre Dame* on Mickey Avenue between the sound stages and *Little Mermaid.*

10. Check the entertainment schedule for parades, live shows, or special events that interest you. Work them into your itinerary.

11. By now, you've seen all major attractions except SuperStar Television and *Monster Sound Show.* Check the entertainment schedule for SuperStar Television times. If a show is within 20 to 30 minutes, see it. Otherwise, see *Monster Sound Show* first. If the line at *Monster Sound Show* has ballooned with throngs leaving *Indiana Jones,* try again later.

12. After *Monster Sound Show* and SuperStar Television, bear right and explore the New York Street set.

13. Tour Hollywood and Sunset boulevards. Consult the entertainment schedule for parades, special events, and theater performances. Musicals at Theater of the Stars and Backlot Theater are particularly worthwhile.

14. This concludes the touring plan. Eat, shop, enjoy live entertainment, or revisit your favorite attraction as desired. When you leave, walk (the parking lot isn't excessive), or take a tram to your car.

Although people with fewer than five days in the Orlando area probably won't have time to see more than Walt Disney World, here's information on one other top destination.

Universal Studios Florida

Universal Studios Florida and its sister facility in California are alike, but very different. They share the TV/movies theme, and both are spacious, beautifully landscaped, meticulously clean, and varied in their entertainment. But Florida has no efficient tram tour by reservation that covers all major attractions. Guests must walk among shows and rides and wait in line for all, including educational presentations.

• Arriving and Getting Oriented •

Universal Studios Florida is on Kirkman Road, accessible from I-4 via exits 29 or 30B. The parking lot holds about 7,000 cars and is filled each day starting with areas closest to the gate. Parking costs $5 for cars, $7 for RVs and trailers. A tram carries guests to the ticket booths and entrance. One- and two-day tickets are available (including tax) at about $37 and $55, respectively, for adults; $30 and $44 for children (ages three to nine). Universal frequently offers such specials as "2nd Day Free."

The park is laid out in an upside-down L. Beyond the entrance, a wide boulevard stretches past rides and shows to a New York City back lot set. Branching right from this pedestrian thoroughfare are five streets accessing other areas and ultimately intersecting a promenade circling a large lake.

The park is divided into six sections: Front Lot, Production Central, New York, Hollywood, San Francisco/Amity, and Expo Center. The area open to visitors is about equal to EPCOT.

Almost all guest services, including stroller rental and lockers, are in Front Lot, just inside the entrance.

Universal Studios information is (407) 363-8000; guest services, (407) 354-6339.

• Universal Studios Florida Attractions •

Terminator 2 3-D

What It Is: 3-D thriller mixed-media presentation
Scope & Scale: Headliner
When to Go: First thing after experiencing the rides
Special Comments: Very intense for some preschoolers
    and grade schoolers
Author's Rating: Furiously paced high-tech. Not to be missed;
    ★★★★★
Overall Appeal by Age Group:

Pre-school	Grade School	Teens	Young Adults	Over 30	Senior Citizens
★★★	★★★★½	★★★★★	★★★★	★★★★	★★★★

Duration of Presentation: 10 minutes, plus 5-minute preshow
Probable Waiting Time: 20–40 minutes

Description and Comments   The Terminator cop from the *Termi-nator 2* movie "morphs" to life and battles Arnold Schwarzeneg-ger's T-800 cyborg character. If you missed the Terminator flicks, don't worry. The attraction is all action; you don't need to understand much. What's interesting in this version is that it uses 3-D film and sophisticated technology to integrate the real with the imaginary. Remove your 3-D glasses momentarily, and the motorcyle is actually onstage.

Touring Tips   The theater holds 700 and changes audiences about every 12 minutes. Even so, expect to wait 20–40 minutes. Make *Terminator 2 3-D* your first show after you've experienced all rides. Note to families: Violence characteristic of *Terminator* movies is largely absent here. There's suspense and action, but not much blood.

The Funtastic World of Hanna-Barbera

What It Is: Flight-simulation ride
Scope & Scale: Major attraction
When to Go: Before 11 a.m.
Special Comments: Very intense for some preschoolers

Universal Studios Florida

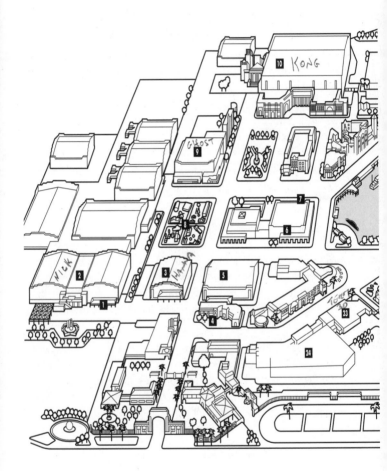

1. Production Tram Tour
2. Nickelodeon Studios
3. The Funtastic World of Hanna Barbera
4. Lucy, A Tribute
5. "Alfred Hitchcock: The Art of Making Movies"
6. "Murder, She Wrote" Mystery Theater
7. The Adventures of Rocky and Bullwinkle
8. The Boneyard
9. *Ghostbusters*
10. Kongfrontation
11. *Bettlejuice's Graveyard Revue*

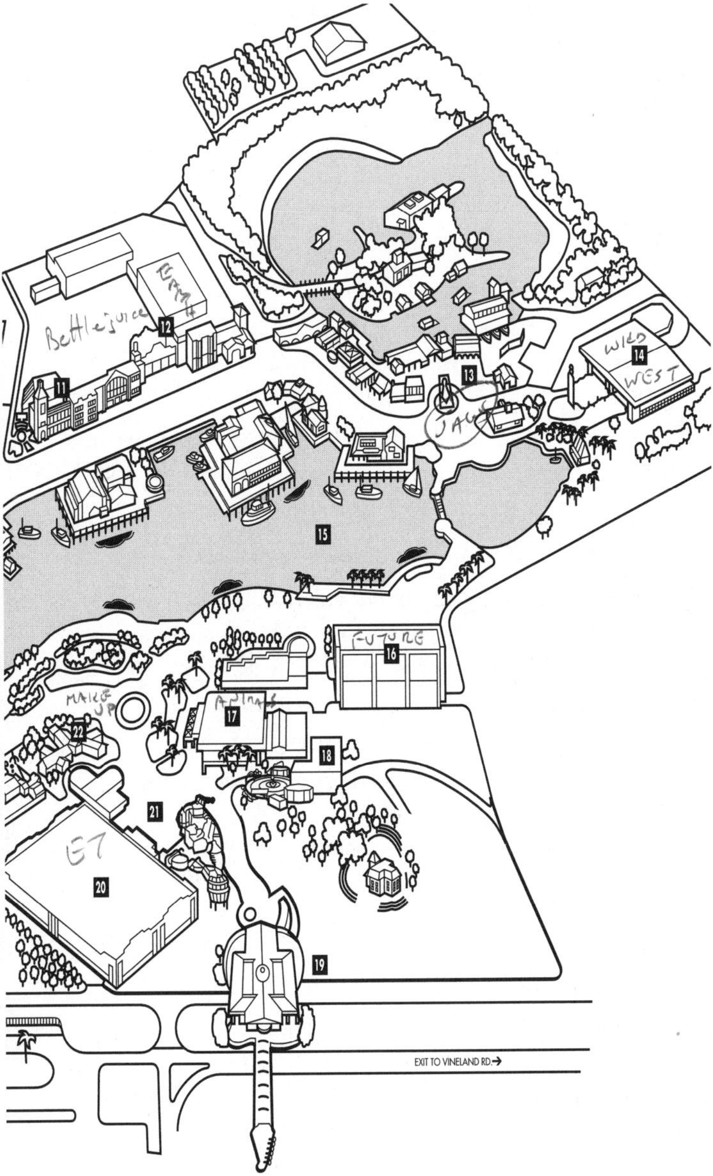

12. Earthquake—The Big One
13. Jaws
14. *The Wild, Wild, Wild West Stunt Show*
15. *Dynamite Nights Stunt Spectacular*
16. Back to the Future—The Ride
17. *Animal Actors Stage*
18. *A Day in the Park with Barney*
19. Hard Rock Cafe
20. The E.T. Adventure
21. Fievel's Playland
22. *The Gory, Gruesome & Grotesque Horror Make-Up Show*
23. *Terminator 2 3-D*

Author's Rating: A delight for all ages; ★★★½
Overall Appeal by Age Group:

Pre-school	Grade School	Teens	Young Adults	Over 30	Senior Citizens
★★★★	★★★★½	★★★★	★★★★	★★★★	★★★★

Duration of Ride: 4½ minutes, with a 3½-minute preshow
Loading Speed: Moderate to slow

Description and Comments Flight-simulation ride in the same family as Disney's Body Wars, but all visuals are cartoons. Guests accompany Yogi Bear in a chase to rescue a kidnapped child.

Touring Tips Large lines build early at this slow-loading ride and move glacially. Ride during the first two hours the park is open.

"Alfred Hitchcock: The Art of Making Movies"

What It Is: Mini-course on filming action sequences and a testimonial to Alfred Hitchcock
Scope & Scale: Major attraction
When to Go: After you've experienced all rides
Special Comments: May frighten young children.
Author's Rating: A little slow-moving, but well done; ★★★½
Overall Appeal by Age Group:

Pre-school	Grade School	Teens	Young Adults	Over 30	Senior Citizens
★★½	★★★	★★★½	★★★½	★★★½	★★★½

Duration of Presentation: 40 minutes
Probable Waiting Time: 22 minutes

Description and Comments Guests view a collage of famous scenes from Hitchcock films (including some unreleased 3-D footage), then exit to a sound stage where the stabbing scene from *Psycho* is re-created with audience volunteers. In a third area, technology of filming action scenes is explained. The Hitchcock "greatest hits" film is disjointed and confusing unless you recall the movies. The stabbing re-enactment is informative and entertaining, as are sets and techniques shown in the third area.

Touring Tips Lines are long but usually disappear quickly. Nevertheless, see this attraction just before you leave in the evening.

Nickelodeon Studios Walking Tour

What It Is: Behind-the-scenes guided tour

Scope & Scale: Minor attraction

When to Go: When Nickelodeon shows are in production (usually weekdays)

Author's Rating: ★★★

Overall Appeal by Age Group:

Pre-school	Grade School	Teens	Young Adults	Over 30	Senior Citizens
★★½	★★★	★★★	★★★	★★★	★★★

Duration of Tour: 36 minutes

Probable Waiting Time: 30–45 minutes

Description and Comments Walking tour of the Nickelodeon studio examines set construction, sound stages, wardrobe, props, lighting, video production, and special effects. While much of the same information is presented more creatively in "Alfred Hitchcock," Murder, She Wrote, and *Horror Makeup Show,* the Nickelodeon Tour is specifically geared to kids.

Touring Tips While grade-schoolers, in particular, enjoy this tour, it's expendable for everyone else. Go on a second day at Universal. If Nickelodeon isn't in production, forget it.

Production Tram Tour

What It Is: Guided tram tour of outdoor sets

Scope & Scale: Minor attraction

When to Go: Late afternoon

Special Comments: Not comparable to the Disney-MGM Studios tram tour

Author's Rating: Interesting; ★★

Overall Appeal by Age Group:

Pre-school	Grade School	Teens	Young Adults	Over 30	Senior Citizens
★★	★★	★★	★★½	★★½	★★½

Duration of Tour: 20 minutes

Probable Waiting Time: Varies widely, but usually less than 12 minutes

Description and Comments   The tour offers an informative, effortless way to view back lot sets. You see essentially the same sights when you tour on foot, but the background provided by the guide enhances your understanding.

Touring Tips   Ride if the wait is short. The tour offers a good orientation to Universal but isn't the best way to use your morning. Try it in late afternoon if you're interested in learning more about the sets.

Ghostbusters

What It Is: Theater presentation featuring characters and special effects from *Ghostbusters*

Scope & Scale: Major attraction

When to Go: Should be your first show after experiencing all rides and *Terminator 2 3-D*

Special Comments: A limited potential for frightening young children

Author's Rating: Upbeat and fun, with great special effects; ★★★½

Overall Appeal by Age Group:

Pre-school	Grade School	Teens	Young Adults	Over 30	Senior Citizens
★★★★	★★★★½	★★★★½	★★★★½	★★★★	★★★★

Duration of Presentation: 15 minutes

Probable Waiting Time: 26 minutes

Description and Comments   An elaborate set from *Ghostbusters* is used to demonstrate incredible special effects. Fast-paced, with lots of humor, Ghostbusters has a new story line and excellent preshow.

Touring Tips   This fun show draws big crowds. Go in the morning after you've experienced the rides. The entrance to Ghostbusters isn't well marked. Find the Ghostbusters sign hanging over the sidewalk, then duck into the first open door to its right.

Kongfrontation

What It Is: Indoor adventure ride featuring King Kong

Scope & Scale: Major attraction

When to Go: Before 11 a.m.

Special Comments: May frighten young children.

Author's Rating: Not to be missed; ★★★★

Overall Appeal by Age Group:

Pre-school	Grade School	Teens	Young Adults	Over 30	Senior Citizens
★★★½	★★★★★	★★★★★	★★★★	★★★★	★★★★

Duration of Ride: 4½ minutes

Loading Speed: Moderate

Description and Comments   Guests board an aerial tram to ride from Manhattan to Roosevelt Island. En route, they hear that the giant ape has escaped. The tram passes evidence of Kong's rampage and encounters the monster, who hurls your tram to the ground.

Touring Tips   Truly amazing. Ride in the morning after Back to the Future, E.T. Adventure, and Jaws.

The Gory Gruesome & Grotesque Horror Makeup Show

What It Is: Theater presentation on the art of makeup

Scope & Scale: Major attraction

When to Go: After you've experienced all rides

Special Comments: May frighten young children.

Author's Rating: A gory knee-slapper; ★★★½

Overall Appeal by Age Group:

Pre-school	Grade School	Teens	Young Adults	Over 30	Senior Citizens
★★★	★★★★	★★★★	★★★½	★★★½	★★★½

Duration of Presentation: 25 minutes

Probable Waiting Time: 20 minutes

Description and Comments   A lively, well-paced look at how makeup artists create film monsters, realistic wounds, severed limbs, and other unmentionables. Excellent and enlightening, if somewhat gory, introduction to cinema monster-making.

Touring Tips   *Horror Makeup Show* exceeds most guests' expectations and is Universal's "sleeper" attraction. Humor transcends the gruesome effects, and even preschoolers take the blood and guts in stride. It usually isn't hard to get into.

Murder, She Wrote Mystery Theater

What It Is: A multisequence mini-course on post-production techniques of sound effects, editing, background music, and dubbing

Scope & Scale: Major attraction

When to Go: After you've experienced all rides

Special Comments: Air-conditioned break during hottest part of the day

Author's Rating: Well-presented; ★★★½

Overall Appeal by Age Group:

Pre-school	Grade School	Teens	Young Adults	Over 30	Senior Citizens
★★	★★½	★★★	★★★½	★★★★	★★★½

Duration of Presentation: 40 minutes

Probable Waiting Time: 20 minutes

Description and Comments   Guests move among theaters to learn about post-production technology. The presentation consists of editing, dubbing, and adding sound effects to a climactic scene from *Murder, She Wrote*. Audience members assist with sound effects and voice-overs.

Touring Tips   Informative and often hilarious, it makes technical information understandable. In spite of the name, nothing here will intimidate children.

Earthquake—The Big One

What It Is: Combination theater presentation and adventure ride

Scope & Scale: Major attraction

When to Go: In the morning, after Kongfrontation

Special Comments: May frighten young children.

Author's Rating: Not to be missed; ★★★★

Overall Appeal by Age Group:

Pre-school	Grade School	Teens	Young Adults	Over 30	Senior Citizens
★★★	★★★★★	★★★★★	★★★★½	★★★★½	★★★★½

Duration of Presentation: 20 minutes
Loading Speed: Moderate

Description and Comments   Guests view a film on how miniatures are used to create special effects in earthquake movies, followed by a demonstration starring audience volunteers. They then board a subway and experience an earthquake. Special effects range from fires and runaway trains to exploding tanker trucks and tidal waves.

Touring Tips   One of Universal's more compelling rides. Go in the morning, after Back to the Future, E.T., Jaws, and Kongfrontation.

Jaws

What It Is: Adventure boat ride
Scope & Scale: Headliner
When to Go: Before 11 a.m.
Special Comments: Will frighten young children.
Author's Rating: Not to be missed; ★★★★½
Overall Appeal by Age Group:

Pre-school	Grade School	Teens	Young Adults	Over 30	Senior Citizens
★★★★	★★★★★	★★★★★	★★★★★	★★★★★	★★★★½

Duration of Ride: 5 minutes
Loading Speed: Fast

Description and Comments   Unlike its predecessor, this version of the ride is mechanically reliable—usually. It delivers five minutes of nonstop action, with the huge shark attacking repeatedly. The story line is predictable, but the shark is quite realistic. Jaws builds an amazing degree of suspense and anticipation using inventive sets and powerful special effects. It's first-rate.

A variable is the enthusiasm and acting ability of your boat guide. The guide sets the tone, reveals the plot, pilots the boat, and fights the shark—every eight minutes. Most guides are quite good.

Touring Tips   Jaws handles crowds well; waits aren't long if all boats are operating. People on the boat's left side get splashed more. Skip Jaws if your children frighten easily, or switch off (see page 58).

Back to the Future

What It Is: Flight-simulator thrill ride

Scope & Scale: Super headliner

When to Go: First thing in the morning

Special Comments: Very rough ride; may induce motion sickness. Must be 3' 4" tall to ride.

Author's Rating: Not to be missed, if you have a strong stomach; ★★★★★

Overall Appeal by Age Group:

Pre-school	Grade School	Teens	Young Adults	Over 30	Senior Citizens
†	★★★★★	★★★★★	★★★★★	★★★★	★★½

† Sample size too small for accurate rating

Duration of Ride: 4½ minutes

Loading Speed: Moderate

Description and Comments   This is Universal's most popular thrill ride. Guests in Doc Brown's lab join a high-speed chase spanning a million years. Extremely intense, Back to the Future is similar to Star Tours and Body Wars at Disney World but is much rougher. The story line makes little sense, but visual effects are wild and powerful. The vehicles (Delorean time machines) are much smaller than those of Star Tours and Body Wars, so the ride feels more personal.

Because the height requirement has been lowered from 46 inches to 40 inches, younger children are riding. Many benefit from some preparation. One reader suggested reassuring children that (1) it's only a movie and (2) the car doesn't go anywhere, it just shakes. Switching off is available.

Touring Tips   When the park opens, there's a stampede to Back to the Future. Be in it. If you don't ride before 10 a.m., you'll encounter long lines. Sitting in the car's rear seat makes the ride more realistic.

E.T. Adventure

What It Is: Indoor adventure ride based on the movie *E.T.*

Scope & Scale: Major attraction

When to Go: Before 10 a.m.

Special Comments: Renovated and greatly improved in 1992.

Author's Rating: ★★★★

Overall Appeal by Age Group:

Pre-school	Grade School	Teens	Young Adults	Over 30	Senior Citizens
★★★★½	★★★★½	★★★★	★★★★	★★★★	★★★★

Duration of Ride: 4½ minutes

Loading Speed: Moderate

Description and Comments   Guests board a bicycle-like conveyance to escape with E.T. from earthly law enforcement officers, then journey to E.T.'s planet. Wilder and more elaborate than Disney World's Peter Pan's Flight. Guests who balk at sitting on the bicycle can ride in a gondola.

Touring Tips   Most preschoolers and grade-school children love E.T. We thought it worth a 20–30 minute wait, but nothing longer. Lines build quickly, and waits on busy days can be two hours. The wait to enter the building may be short, the wait inside much longer. Ride in the morning, right after Back to the Future.

Animal Actors Stage

What It Is: Trained animals stadium performance

Scope & Scale: Major attraction

When to Go: After you've experienced all rides

Author's Rating: Warm and delightful; ★★★½

Overall Appeal by Age Group:

Pre-school	Grade School	Teens	Young Adults	Over 30	Senior Citizens
★★★★	★★★★	★★★★	★★★★	★★★★	★★★★

Duration of Presentation: 20 minutes

Probable Waiting Time: 25 minutes

Description and Comments   Humorous demonstration of how animals are trained for film work. Well-paced and informative, the show stars cats, dogs, monkeys, birds, and others. Animals sometimes don't behave as expected, but that's half the fun.

Touring Tips   We wish guests were allowed to enter the theater at their leisure. Instead, they must wait in line to be admitted. The show is presented 6 to 10 times daily; check the daily entertainment guide for times. Go at your convenience; line up about 15 minutes before show time.

Dynamite Nights Stunt Spectacular

What It Is: Simulated stunt-scene filming

Scope & Scale: Major attraction

When to Go: In evening according to the daily entertainment schedule

Author's Rating: Well done; ★★★★

Overall Appeal by Age Group:

Pre-school	Grade School	Teens	Young Adults	Over 30	Senior Citizens
★★★	★★★★½	★★★★½	★★★★½	★★★★	★★★★

Duration of Presentation: 20 minutes

Probable Waiting Time: None

Description and Comments   Nightly on the lagoon, professionals demonstrate spectacular stunts and special effects. The plot involves lawmen trying to apprehend drug smugglers. The lagoon is so large that it's somewhat difficult to follow the action.

Touring Tips   The audience members take positions along the lagoon's encircling rail. Stake yours out about 25 minutes before show time. The best are along the docks at Lombard's Landing and adjacent areas on the Embarcadero waterfront, across the street from Earthquake. The park map identifies primo viewing spots with a "PV" icon.

Wild, Wild, Wild West Stunt Show

What It Is: Stunt show with western theme

Scope & Scale: Major attraction

When to Go: After you've experienced all rides, go at your convenience.

Author's Rating: Solid and exciting; ★★★½

Overall Appeal by Age Group:

Pre-school	Grade School	Teens	Young Adults	Over 30	Senior Citizens
★★★★½	★★★★★	★★★★½	★★★★	★★★★	★★★★

Duration of Presentation: 16 minutes

Probable Waiting Time: None

Description and Comments A Wild West stunt show with shootouts, fistfights, horse tricks, and high falls. Staged about 10 times daily in a 2,000-seat covered stadium. Quick-paced, exciting, and well-executed. Unlike the stunt show on the lagoon, action is easy to follow.

Touring Tips The daily entertainment guide lists show times. In summer, the stadium is more comfortable after dusk.

Fievel's Playland

What It Is: Children's play area with water slide

Scope & Scale: Minor attraction

When to Go: Anytime

Author's Rating: A much-needed attraction for preschoolers; ★★★★

Overall Appeal by Age Group:

Pre-school	Grade School	Teens	Young Adults	Over 30	Senior Citizens
★★★★	★★★★	★★★	★★★	★★★	★★★

Probable Waiting Time: 20–30 minutes for the water slide; otherwise, no waiting

Description and Comments Imaginative playground where ordinary household items are reproduced on a giant scale, as a mouse would experience them. Kids climb nets and a cow skull, walk through a big boot, splash in a sardine-can fountain, and seesaw on huge spoons. Though most of Fievel's Playland is reserved for preschoolers, a water slide/raft ride is open to everyone.

Touring Tips Younger children love the oversized items, and there's enough to keep teens and adults busy while little ones frolic. Stay as long as you want. The water slide is extremely slow-loading and accommodates only 300 riders per hour. Waits average 20–30 minutes for the 16-second ride. It isn't worth it. Plus, you'll probably get soaked. A major shortcoming of this attraction is lack of shade. Don't visit at midday.

Beetlejuice's Rock 'N Roll Graveyard Revue

What It Is: Rock-and-roll stage show
Scope & Scale: Minor attraction
When to Go: At your convenience
Author's Rating: Outrageous; ★★★½
Overall Appeal by Age Group:

Pre-school	Grade School	Teens	Young Adults	Over 30	Senior Citizens
★★★★	★★★★½	★★★★½	★★★★	★★★★	★★★½

Duration of Presentation: 16 minutes
Probable Waiting Time: None

Description and Comments   *Graveyard Revue* is a high-powered rock-and-roll stage show starring Beetlejuice, Frankenstein, the Bride of Frankenstein, Wolfman, Dracula, and the Phantom of the Opera. In addition to fine vintage rock, the show features exuberant choreography. Sets and special effects are impressive.

Touring Tips   Mercifully, this attraction has been moved under cover.

A Day in the Park with Barney

What It Is: Live character stage show
Scope & Scale: Major attraction
When to Go: Anytime
Author's Rating: A hit with preschoolers; ★★★★
Overall Appeal by Age Group:

Pre-school	Grade School	Teens	Young Adults	Over 30	Senior Citizens
★★★★	★★★	★★	★★½	★★★	★★★

Duration of Presentation: 12 minutes plus character greeting
Probable Waiting Time: 15 minutes

Description and Comments   Barney, the purple dinosaur of public television fame, and his sidekicks Baby Bop and BJ lead a sing-along augmented by effects that include wind, falling leaves, snow, and clouds and stars in a simulated sky. Afterward, Barney greets children, hugging each and posing for photos.

Touring Tips   If your kids like Barney, this show is a must. It's happy and upbeat, and the character greeting afterward is the best-organized we've seen: no lines and no fighting for attention. Relax by the rail and await your hug.

Lucy, a Tribute

What It Is: Walk-through tribute to Lucille Ball
Scope & Scale: Diversion
When to Go: Anytime
Author's Rating: A touching remembrance; ★★★
Overall Appeal by Age Group:

Pre-school	Grade School	Teens	Young Adults	Over 30	Senior Citizens
★	★	★★	★★★	★★★	★★★

Probable Waiting Time: None

Description and Comments   Exhibit traces the life and career of comedian Lucille Ball of TV's *I Love Lucy.* Well-designed and informative, the attraction succeeds admirably in honoring the beloved redhead.

Touring Tips   Go during midafternoon heat or on your way out of the park. Adults could spend 15–30 minutes here; children get restless sooner.

Disney-MGM Studios vs. Universal Studios Florida

Nearly half of Disney-MGM Studios is off limits except by guided tour, while virtually all of Universal Studios Florida is accessible.

Universal emphasizes that it's a working motion picture and television studio first, and only incidentally a tourist attraction. It's true that guests are more likely to see movie or television production in progress at Universal than at Disney-MGM.

Universal is large, eliminating most of the congestion familiar at Disney-MGM. Attractions at both parks are excellent, though Disney-MGM attractions move people more efficiently. This disadvantage is somewhat offset by Universal's having more rides and shows. Although Universal has pioneered innovative rides, its attractions break down more often than Disney-MGM's. Jaws and Kongfrontation, in particular, are notorious for breakdowns. Each park offers a distinct product mix, so a person can visit both with little or no redundancy. Both offer good exposure to the cinematic arts, though Disney's presentations are crisper, better integrated, and more coherent.

Disney's stunt shows win for drama and intensity. Universal gets the call for variety.

Try one park. If you enjoy it, you'll probably enjoy the other. If you have to choose between them, consider:

1. *Touring Time.* It takes about 8 hours to see Disney-MGM (includes lunch break). Because Universal Studios Florida is larger and has more attractions, touring requires 9 to 11 hours (includes one meal). Readers complain that much of the time is spent in lines.

2. *Convenience.* If you're lodging on International Drive, I-4's northeast corridor, the Orange Blossom Trail (US 441) or in Orlando, Universal is closer. If you're on US 27, on FL 192, or in Disney World or Kissimmee, Disney-MGM is more convenient.

3. *Endurance.* Universal is larger and requires more walking, but it's less congested. Wheelchairs and handicapped access are available at both parks.

4. *Cost.* Both cost about the same for one-day admission, food, and incidentals. If you go for two days, Universal's 2nd Day Free promotion (if available) is a bargain.

5. *Best Days to Go.* In order, Tuesdays, Mondays, Thursdays, and Wednesdays are best for Universal. Saturdays, Fridays, and Mondays are best for Disney-MGM during busy seasons. During off-season, visit Disney-MGM on Fridays, Tuesdays, Mondays, and Thursdays.

6. *Young Children.* Both parks offer relatively adult entertainment. By our reckoning, half the rides and shows at Disney-MGM and about two-thirds at Universal have significant potential for frightening young children.

7. *Food.* Food is much better at Universal.

One-Day Touring Plan for Universal Studios Florida

This plan is for all visitors. Skip rides or shows that don't interest you and go to the plan's next step. Move briskly among attractions and stop for lunch after Step 10.

Buying Admission to Universal Studios Florida

Universal Studios never opens enough ticket windows in the morning to accommodate the crowd. Buy your admission before you arrive. Passes are sold by mail through TicketMaster (phone (800) 745-5000) and at hotels' concierge desk or box office. Guest Services at Radisson Twin Towers (phone (407) 351-1000), across from Universal's entrance at the intersection of Major Boulevard and Kirkman Avenue, also sells them.

Many hotels selling admissions issue vouchers that are redeemed at the park. Fortunately, the voucher window is separate from ticket sales. Redemption is quick.

Touring Plan

1. Call (407) 363-8000 the day before your visit for the official opening time.
2. Eat breakfast before you arrive 50 minutes before opening with your admission pass or voucher in hand. Redeem your voucher.
3. Obtain a map and daily entertainment schedule at the front gate. Ask an attendant what rides or shows are closed that day. Adjust the touring plan accordingly.
4. When you're admitted, go right on Hollywood Boulevard, pass Mel's Diner (on your left), and

keep the lagoon on your left. Arrive at Back to the Future. Ride.

5. Exit left and pass the International Food Bazaar. Bear left past the Animal Actors Stage to E.T. Adventure. Ride.

6. Retrace your steps toward Back to the Future. Keeping the lagoon on your left, cross the bridge to Amity. Ride Jaws.

7. Exit left down the Embarcadero to Kongfrontation in the New York set. Go ape.

8. Ride Earthquake in San Francisco.

9. Head toward the main entrance and ride Funtastic World of Hanna-Barbera. Expect to wait 25–40 minutes. If you've had enough simulator rides for the moment, skip to Step 10.

10. Return to Hollywood Boulevard and see *Terminator 2 3-D.*

11. Return to New York for Ghostbusters.

12. This is a good time for lunch. Cafe La Bamba in Hollywood serves tacos and burgers, and Mel's Diner nearby has good milkshakes. The International Food Bazaar adjacent to Back to the Future has gyros, bratwurst, pizza, and other ethnic foods. Good but often overlooked is Studio Stars Restaurant across from the prop Boneyard and down a block from "Alfred Hitchcock." It alternates California and Italian cuisines and has a buffet. Louie's Italian Restaurant in New York serves pizza, calzone, and salads. Sandwiches and pastries are specialties of Beverly Hills Boulangerie near the park entrance. Upscale and relaxed Lombard's Landing on the waterfront, across from Earthquake, offers prime rib, creative seafood entrees, and an exceptional hamburger at a fair price.

The Hard Rock Cafe is fun if you enjoy rock and roll. Food is good and service usually efficient. It's considered outside the park; have your hand stamped for re-entry. Be prepared to wait at any time, more than an hour in the evening.

13. You have seven major attractions left to see:

 1. *The Gory Gruesome & Grotesque Horror Makeup Show*
 2. "Murder, She Wrote" Mystery Theater
 3. *Animal Actors Stage*
 4. *Dynamite Nights Stunt Spectacular*
 5. *Wild, Wild, Wild West Stunt Show*
 6. "Alfred Hitchcock: The Art of Making Movies"
 7. *Beetlejuice's Rock 'N Roll Graveyard Revue*

 Animal Actors Stage, the *Beetlejuice* show, and stunt shows are performed several times daily. Check the entertainment schedule, and plan the remainder of your itinerary according to their show times. The *Horror Makeup Show* and "Murder, She Wrote" Mystery Theater (on opposite sides of Mel's Diner) run continuously. Work them in as time permits. Save "Alfred Hitchcock" for last.

 We haven't included Nickelodeon Studios Tour, Production Tram Tour, or *A Day in the Park with Barney.* If you have schoolchildren, consider experiencing Nickelodeon in late afternoon or on a second day at the park. If you're touring with preschoolers, see *Barney* after you ride E.T. The tram tour covers territory you've already seen; skip it.

14. This concludes the touring plan. Spend the remainder of your day revisiting favorite attractions or inspecting sets and street scenes you may have missed. Also, check the schedule for live performances.

12

Water Theme Parks, Discovery Island, and the Disney Institute

---

The Water Theme Parks

Short-timers are unlikely to spend their hours at Walt Disney World's three swimming theme parks or the Orlando area's two independent water parks, but they should know what they are. Making up Disney's trio are River Country, the oldest and smallest; Typhoon Lagoon, the most diversified; and Blizzard Beach, which has the most slides and most unusual theme. Outside the World are Wet 'n Wild and Water Mania. (The full-sized *Unofficial Guide to Walt Disney World* has expanded descriptions. For Disney details, call (407) 824-4321.)

● Blizzard Beach ●

Blizzard Beach conjures a ski resort in Florida. Alas for the make-believe entrepreneur, the ice of savage storms is melting, palms have grown back, and the Alpine lodge and ski lifts survive among dripping icicles. Ski slopes and bobsled runs have become water slides, and a great lagoon is fed by gushing mountain streams.

This wild story has spawned a wave pool, 17 slides (two long), a children's swimming area, and a tranquil stream for tubing. Picnic areas and sunbathing beaches dot the park. Summit

Plummet, the world's longest speed slide, begins with a steep 120-foot descent. Teamboat Springs is 1,200 feet long.

Each Disney water park rents water gear (even towels) and lockers and sells food, swimming gear, and footwear. Picnics are welcome (no alcoholic beverages or glass containers allowed). Admission to Blizzard Beach and Typhoon Lagoon is about $26 per day for adults, $19 for children ages three to nine, and free for kids under age three. The smaller River Country charges $16 and $13.

In busy seasons, Blizzard Beach and Typhoon Lagoon fill early, and gates close by 11 a.m. The parks are widely scattered: Blizzard Beach is near All-Star Resorts, Typhoon Beach east of EPCOT, and River Country near Fort Wilderness Campground. Disney transportation reaches all, but it's a time-gobbling commute for River Country. Each has a parking lot.

Thunderstorms, common in afternoon, may close the parks. Lines for water slides can seem endless; ride early or return to an uncrowded park when it reopens after a storm.

• Typhoon Lagoon •

Typhoon Lagoon evokes the "aftermath of a typhoon." Landmark is a boat beached atop the 100-foot Mount Mayday. Caves, dinosaur "fossils," a ramshackle tropical town, geysers, and a misty rain forest add to the adventure. The park is about the size of Blizzard Beach and four times as big as River Country. It has nine water slides and streams, activity pools, and tube rapids. Two attractions—the surf pool and Shark Reef—are unique.

Shark Reef

At Shark Reef, snorkelers (equipped and instructed for free) swim with tropical fish, small rays, and a few harmless sharks. It's fun in early morning before lines become intolerable and attendants must enforce the direct route 60 feet across the crowded pool.

An underwater viewing chamber is available for nonswimmers.

Surf Pool

The world's largest inland surf facility, this pool is swept by 5- to 6-foot waves about every 90 seconds. They're perfectly formed, ideal for riding and larger than most folks encounter in the ocean. Each breaks in almost the same place. Unlike ocean waves, they don't slam you down. Still, watch other riders' technique before you try it.

• River Country •

For pure and simple swimming and splashing, River Country gets high marks. Rocky canyons and waterfalls blend with white sand beaches in this beautifully landscaped park. It has only two slides, and lines become long. Sunbathing and tubing are more relaxed. A breeze blowing from Bay Lake cools the lakefront.

Access to River Country by car is a hassle. You must bus from the parking lot, and the long ride can be crowded. Solution: Catch the bus to Pioneer Hall (loads in River Country parking lot) and walk from the hall to River Country.

• Disney vs. Wet 'n Wild • and Water Mania Theme Parks

Wet 'n Wild, on International Drive in Orlando, is open until 11 p.m. during summer. (Disney parks and Water Mania close between 5 and 8 p.m.) Live music is featured evenings on Wave Pool Stage.

Water Mania, on US 192 south of I-4, is the only water park that offers a *surfing wave*. The facility is less crowded than its competitors.

Wet 'n Wild costs about the same as Typhoon Lagoon and Blizzard Beach. Tickets are 50 percent off after 5 p.m. when the park is open late. Water Mania costs about the same as River Country. Look for discount coupons in visitor magazines at hotels and tourist facilities.

For slides, Wet 'n Wild is on par with Blizzard Beach and beats Typhoon Lagoon, River Country, and Water Mania. Headliners are the Black Hole, the Surge, and the Fuji Flyer. At Black Hole, guests descend on a two-person tube down a totally enclosed corkscrew slide, a sort of wet version of Space Mountain—only much darker. The Surge launches groups of five down a twisting, 580-foot course. The Fuji Flyer is a 450-foot water toboggan course.

The independents can't compete with Disney's attention to detail, variety, adventure, and impact. Water Mania is nicely landscaped but themeless. Wet 'n Wild, though attractive and clean, is cluttered and not very appealing to the eye.

Typhoon Lagoon's surf pool wins hands down, with Wet 'n Wild in second. Each park has an area for young children, and all except River Country feature unique attractions.

• When to Go •

The best way to avoid lines is to visit the water parks when they're less crowded. Weekends (except Sunday morning) are tough because they're popular with locals. Go Monday or Tuesday, when most other tourists will be in the Magic Kingdom, EPCOT, or Disney-MGM Studios. Locals will be at work. Friday is also good because people traveling by car routinely start home then. Be at the gates a half hour before opening.

Discovery Island and the Disney Institute

• Discovery Island •

Situated in Bay Lake close to the Magic Kingdom, Discovery Island is a small, tropically landscaped zoological park featuring birds. Intimate trails wind through exotic foliage. Plants and trees are labeled for identification, and there's an enormous walk-through aviary.

Discovery Island offers three shows: *Feathered Friends* (cockatoos and macaws), *Birds of Prey* (most "stars" are disabled raptors convalescing at the island), and *Reptile Relations* (alligators and snakes). All are interesting and well-presented, but their outdoor seating can be miserable at midday, when the shows are scheduled.

Access is by boat from the main Bay Lake docks. Vessels run every 15 to 20 minutes. Admission is about $12 for adults, $7 for children.

Some people are bored here. Others savor the tranquillity, boating from the Magic Kingdom for a peaceful, uncrowded lunch.

• The Disney Institute •

Launched in 1996, the Disney Institute offers a variety of educational and life-enriching courses and programs on its own campus in the Villas section of Disney World. Participants enroll by the day, choosing among four dozen subjects ranging from the arts to sports. Courses have no prerequisite. Evenings offer concerts, cinema, lectures, and storytelling. For information, call (800) 496-6337.

13

Night Life
Inside and Outside
Walt Disney World

Walt Disney World at Night

Anybody still standing after touring the theme parks all day will find a lot to do in the evening at Walt Disney World.

In the Parks

At EPCOT, the major after-dark event is IllumiNations, a laser and fireworks show on World Showcase Lagoon. Show time is listed in the daily entertainment schedule.

In the Magic Kingdom are evening parade(s) and Fantasy in the Sky fireworks. See the schedule for times.

Disney-MGM Studios offers Sorcery in the Sky, a laser and fireworks spectacular, nightly when the park is open late. Check the schedule for show time.

At the Hotels

The Floating Electrical Pageant is a parade of barges in Seven Seas Lagoon. One of our favorite Disney productions, the short show of light and music starts at 9 nightly off the Polynesian Resort docks. It circles, then repeats at 9:15 p.m. at the Grand Floridian. Afterward, it goes to Fort Wilderness, Wilderness Lodge, and Contemporary Resort.

Many Disney Village hotels have lively bars with rock bands and other entertainment.

At Fort Wilderness Campground

The free, nightly campfire program is open only to Disney resort guests. It begins with a sing-along led by Disney characters and progresses to a Disney feature movie.

• Walt Disney World Dinner Theaters •

Several dinner theater shows are staged each night at Disney World. Call (407) 824-8000 for same-day reservations. Disney resort guests can book at their lodging or up to 60 days in advance by calling (407) 939-3463. Getting seats at the *Polynesian Revue* isn't too tough. Not so the *Hoop-Dee-Doo Musical Revue.*

The Polynesian Revue (Luau)

Presented nightly at the Polynesian Resort, the evening consists of a "Polynesian-style" all-you-can-eat meal followed by South Sea native dancing. The dancing is interesting and largely authentic, but we consider the evening average. Cost is about $34 for adults, $18 for children ages 3 to 11. Sea World presents a similar dinner show each evening.

At the Polynesian Resort's Luau Cove is *Mickey's Tropical Revue,* which features Disney characters. This show starts at 4:30 p.m.—too early to be hungry and too hot to be outdoors. Cost is about $30 for adults, $14 for children ages 3 to 11.

Hoop-Dee-Doo Musical Revue

Presented nightly at Pioneer Hall at Fort Wilderness Campgrounds, this is the most popular Disney dinner show. The meal includes barbecued ribs, fried chicken, corn on the cob, and baked beans. Most dishes are satisfactory.

Western dance-hall song, dance, and humor are presented by a talented, energetic, and memorable cast. Cost of the delightful evening is about $36 for adults, $18 for children ages 3 to 11. Show times are 5, 7:15, and 9:30 p.m.

Unfortunately for last-minute guests, *Hoop-Dee-Doo Revue* is sold out months in advance to lodgers at Disney properties who booked it when they booked their room. Nonetheless, try (407) 824-2748 at 9 a.m. each morning while you're at Disney World for same-day reservations. Generally, 3 to 24 people are admitted.

Pleasure Island

Pleasure Island, Disney World's nighttime entertainment complex, offers seven nightclubs for one admission price (about $18). Located on a man-made island in Walt Disney World Village, it's accessible by shuttle bus from the theme parks and the Transportation and Ticket Center.

The six-acre playground also has a ten-theater movie complex, restaurants, and shops. Some restaurants and shops are open in daytime, but Pleasure Island doesn't come alive until after 7 p.m., when the nightclubs open. Guests younger than 18 must be accompanied by a parent after 7 p.m.

Have It All It's possible to visit all of the island's clubs in one night. Nightclub shows outside Disney World are an hour or more long; Pleasure Island's (except Comedy Warehouse) are shorter and more frequent. Guests can circulate without missing much.

The music clubs (Rock & Roll Beach Club, 8TRAX, Neon Armadillo, Baton Rouge Lounge, Mannequins, and Jazz Company) go nonstop. Adventurers Club and Comedy Warehouse offer scheduled shows.

In a nutshell, here's a one-night touring plan Arrive at 6 p.m. if you want to eat on the island, 8 p.m. if you don't. Catch the first or second performance at the tough-ticket Comedy Warehouse. See the library show at Adventurers Club. Scoot a boot at Neon Armadillo Music Saloon (country and western). Grab the '70s beat at 8TRAX. Backtrack to techno-pop Mannequins Dance Palace. Step out at Pleasure Island Jazz Company, then move to Rock & Roll Beach Club for oldies. Stop by the jumping West End Stage.

Alcoholic Beverages All Pleasure Island nightclubs serve alcohol. Guests not obviously older than 21 must provide proof of age if they wish to buy alcoholic beverages. To avoid repeated checking, color-coded eligibility wristbands are issued.

Dress Code   Casual is in. Shirts and shoes are required.

Good News for the Early-to-Bed Crowd   All bands, dancers, comedians, and showmen come on like gangbusters from the very beginning of the evening.

Invited Guests Only   Occasionally before 9 p.m., selected clubs will be closed for private parties.

Parking Hassle   Pleasure Island has its own parking lot, but it's convoluted, poorly marked, and often full. Study landmarks near your space so you'll be able to relocate it.

Advice   Park adjacent to the movie theaters and enter via the bridge connecting the movie complex to Pleasure Island. An admissions booth is on the bridge; you don't have to go to the main gate.

Restaurants   Though noisy, crowded, and expensive, restaurants serve a variety of well-prepared dishes. It isn't necessary to buy club admission to eat at one. Most are open during the day.

The new headliner is Fulton's Crab House on the *Empress Lily* riverboat. Adjacent is Portobello Yacht Club, serving seafood, pasta, and pizza. Fireworks Factory specializes in barbecue, with several types of ribs, delicious slaw, and cornbread; skip the appetizers. Food at Planet Hollywood, near the movie theaters, is pretty good, but waits are long unless you eat at odd hours. The decor of Hollywood memorabilia is the draw.

Sandwiches and snacks are served in clubs.

Shopping   Pleasure Island has some shops that are attractions in themselves. At Cover Story, guests dress up to be photographed for the mock cover of a major magazine. Superstar Studio lets you star in your own music video. At either, it's almost as much fun just to watch.

There's no admission fee for daytime shoppers. At night, however, the island (except restaurants) is gated.

INDEX